Steam

LOCOMOTIVES THAT GALVANISED THE NATION

AUSTRALIA

Steam

LOCOMOTIVES THAT GALVANISED THE NATION

AUSTRALIA

Tim Fischer

NLA Publishing

This book is dedicated to all who used steam over the decades in Australia, especially those who travelled to and from the First World War and to and from all other conflicts by steam-hauled trains.

Contents

FOREWORD

—◆—

Steam locomotives were the workhorses of Australia's railways for over 100 years. While the popular anecdote is that Australia rode to wealth on the sheep's back, we should consider instead changing the analogy, as Australia rode to wealth behind the locomotives of our railways. Without the railways, the locomotives that operated on them and the men and women who worked them, moving all manner of goods and produce to markets, none of that wealth and prosperity could have been created.

The first steam locomotives of the colonies railways were imported from England and assembled in fledgling railway workshops. Later, as demand grew and knowledge, experience and capability developed, those railway workshops grew to be major industrial facilities employing thousands, turning out and maintaining hundreds of steam locomotives in a single year. Each state had a major railway workshop facility, designing, building and repairing steam locomotives to operate the railways. These workshops were invariably the engineering showpiece of each state, demonstrating the best in railway technology and innovation and included Eveleigh in New South Wales, Newport in Victoria, Ipswich in Queensland, Islington in South Australia, Inveresk in Tasmania and Midland in Western Australia.

Today, these workshops no longer function as major industrial facilities, but continue to be significant as a focus for those whose hearts and minds are devoted to sharing the wonders of our railways, and their significant role in Australia's social and economic history. Many of the people who worked in them—designing, building, maintaining and operating these giants of steam—have passed their stories to us. They have recorded amazing stories of what it was like to work in the railways and to operate and maintain these locomotives. Each locomotive had its own particular nuances, a 'personality' and specific traits that earned them evocative nicknames from the drivers and firemen who drove them.

Sadly, as the steam era drew to a close in the 1950s and 1960s, many of these locomotives were no longer deemed relevant, however a few were saved by dedicated people who recognised their role and importance. Today, a number of these locomotives rest in the museums, big and small throughout the country, attesting to their role in building a nation. The major rail museums across the country—NSW Rail Museum, Thirlmere; National Railway Museum, Adelaide; The Workshops Rail Museum, Ipswich, Queensland; and Railway Museum, Bassendean, Perth—hold impressive collections of steam locomotives and have a vibrant range of activities and programs designed to engage visitors of all ages and fire their passion for steam.

A small number of these locomotives have been painstakingly restored and are maintained in operating condition by volunteers and staff in the nation's preserved, or heritage, railway movement. The challenges of keeping the knowledge and skills alive to maintain these machines cannot be underestimated. At sites and locations such as Puffing Billy in Victoria, the NSW Rail Museum Thirlmere, Pichi Richi in South Australia, The Workshops Rail Museum in Queensland and numerous others, the work continues to maintain these locomotives so that you cannot only read about a steam experience, but enjoy the thrill and excitement of seeing or riding behind one of these steam locomotives in operation.

Once commonplace, today it is a rarity to see these magnificent machines in operation. There is something about a steam locomotive that captures people's imagination. Is it the sound, the smell, the wonder at how it moves, the romance of a bygone era, the oddity of seeing a steam engine from the 1880s juxtaposed against the sleek lines of a twenty-first-century high-speed train? Whether it is a large or small locomotive, in the city or the country, it is a magical sight and one that always draws a crowd of onlookers and participants both young and old. There is just something about a steam locomotive in operation!

Steam Australia: Locomotives that Galvanised the Nation is an insightful contribution to the fascinating story of the development of Australia's railways, the locomotives that operated on them, the way they impacted on our social history and development. It reminds us all of the contributions of the men and women working in the railways to build Australia.

To steam!

Andrew Moritz
CHIEF EXECUTIVE OFFICER OF TRANSPORT HERITAGE NSW

INTRODUCTION

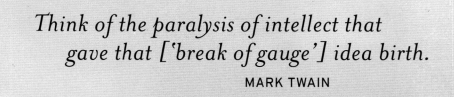

Think of the paralysis of intellect that gave that ['break of gauge'] idea birth.
MARK TWAIN

FROM SMALL STEAM LOCOMOTIVES
TO GIANT WORKHORSES

<< Every angle is different with steam in action: crossing a bascule bridge at Tempe, NSW, in the 1930s.

It appeared as a tiny speck, way off to the east, coming over a big hill on the horizon. Gradually, minute by minute, it grew in size until it could be made out as a hard-working steam locomotive, hauling the South West Mail passenger train into Narrandera from Sydney via Junee Junction.

The sun shone brightly that morning, and the train was a sight to behold, with smoke and steam billowing as it clickety-clacked along this key regional standard-gauge line of the New South Wales Government Railways (NSWGR). It was a shining example of steam locomotion, even if then in its twilight after 100 years of doing so much to open up the vast continent of Australia.

It was 1956, and school holidays. I was 10 years old and doing some trainspotting – standing on the Newell Highway overbridge, near Narrandera

Railway Station, craning my neck to observe all the colour, action and movement. From my vantage point, I could look down directly onto the footplate where the fireman was hanging up his shovel, the hard work done now as the driver was applying the brakes.

The South West Mail glided to a halt. It comprised five carriages, including 'sleepers' (with their quaint centre doors), a freight or parcel louvre van and a guard's van; it had left Sydney about 12 hours earlier and undergone one or two changes of locomotives. The passengers stepped out, many to change to rail motors, one heading to Hay and the other to Tocumwal, with an onward connection to Melbourne by Irish broad-gauge steam train.

Yet again steam had done its job, connecting the Riverina with Sydney, Canberra and Melbourne, which had been the nation's capital for its first 27 years. Steam dominated the country's transportation grid for nearly a century before the arrival of small, medium and large diesel-electric locomotives. Steam had provided vital haulage for freight trains, mixed goods and overnight mail trains through the rapid expansion of the diverse Australian economy, especially between 1850 and 1901. Coal-fired steam locomotives clearly deserve an elevated place in the sun, and in our modern history texts.

My thoughts that morning were fully engaged by the brilliant colour, action and movement of the big black steam locomotive hauling some rust red carriages with gold trimmings. This experience was not often repeated, as I lived on a farm 40 minutes south of Narrandera in the Riverina. Closer to home was my local railway station of Boree Creek on the original branch line from The Rock to Oaklands. On Monday nights, around 7 pm, I would go with my father to meet the CPH rail motor ('Arr 6.52 pm Dep 6.55 pm', according to the 1968 *NSW Government Railways Timetable*).

Why did we bother? It was not just to observe a handful of passengers step off the train, but it was to buy the Sydney Sunday morning newspapers, some 36 hours after their publication. For the sheer excitement: what joy as the rail motor with its big searching headlight came sweeping around the corner in winter; a quick whistle stop, and then off it would hurtle into the night. What agony when somebody forgot to transfer the Sunday papers from the Riverina express at The Rock! Nowadays, I get upset if I cannot download, in 36 seconds, newspapers from around the world, London and Rome included, on my farm near Albury–Wodonga.

So much has changed on the communication front during the lifetime of the so-called 'baby boomers'; telegrams and party line telephones have given way to the worldwide web and instantaneous skype calls. However, the change from horse — or camel or elephant — haulage to steam haulage was perhaps an even greater advance. It gave countries with huge productive inland areas, and hinterlands that swept hundreds of kilometres inland from key port cities, a big

« The South West Mail at Cootamundra in 1939. This is still a busy rail hub with an operational large triangle, north of these platforms, for trains going to Griffith and Parkes.

3

≫ It was the golden
harvests of the 1880s
that generated so much
freight and revenue
for rail.

uplift in so many ways. Australia was not suited to the big canal developments that dominated Britain and the north-eastern United States in the nineteenth century. Here it was steam haulage that had the greatest impact.

Steam Australia: Locomotives That Galvanised the Nation tells the fascinating and important story of steam transportation in Australia. The book is a joint project with the National Library of Australia that draws on the superb John Buckland collection of photography, one of the largest collections on Australian railways in public ownership. The National Library of Australia was established by act of parliament in 1960, emerging from the federal Parliamentary Library, which dates back to Federation in 1901. Today the National Library has a huge and diverse set of 'Australiana' collections, not only key national documents and manuscripts but also old photography ranging from glass-plate photography brilliantly executed by John Flynn of the Inland to the comprehensive set of Buckland photographs.

For my part, while I was never a trainspotter in the classic British sense, for over seven decades I have been totally committed to understanding and promoting rail transport, and to examining the essential role both passenger trains and rail freight have played in our modern economy. Growing up in the Riverina, I had occasional encounters with trains, mainly freight trains, as I helped to load sheep at Boree Creek, to collect heavy bags of superphosphate, and at harvest time to deliver grain to the big silos at Boree Creek and nearby stations.

Then it was off to Melbourne to boarding school and further education, travelling of course by train. Sometimes this would be from Springhurst to Melbourne, sometimes from Morundah to Tocumwal by rail motor before changing to a steam train through Shepparton to Melbourne. More often than not, it was at the big 'break of gauge' station at Albury where I boarded — or more happily where I returned to — after a long term away from my family in 'the big smoke'. For eight decades, Albury was where everyone travelling between Sydney and Melbourne had to change trains. It was there that the Stephenson standard gauge 4 ft 8½ in (1,435 mm) used by the NSWGR network gave way to the Irish broad gauge 5 ft 3 in (1,600 mm) of the Victorian network. Also commonly found in Australia was the narrow gauge (Anglo Cape 3 ft 6 in [1,067 mm]), used extensively in Western Australia, Queensland and Tasmania. From now on, these gauges will simply be referred to as *standard*, *broad* and *narrow*.

In 1895 the famous American humourist Mark Twain was forced to change trains at Albury around dawn, and wrote, 'Think of the paralysis of intellect that gave that idea birth.' He strongly objected to being routed out of bed by lantern light to make the change across the platform. Even to this day, I often recall the many VIPs who have had to change trains there over the years: people such as prime ministers Edmund Barton, Billy Hughes, Robert Menzies and Ben Chifley (a former steam train driver); Dame Enid Lyons, the first female federal MP and cabinet minister; Sister Mary MacKillop, Australia's first Roman Catholic saint; General Sir John Monash and US General Douglas MacArthur (who hated flying); and other notables such as Rudyard Kipling (the famous writer who was a friend of Monash), artist Russell Drysdale (who famously painted a tired Second World War soldier waiting on the platform) and cricketing legend Sir Donald Bradman. In 1931 hundreds stood on the platform to pay their respects as Dame

⌄ Photographer Frank Hurley at his best in this shot of steam locomotive No. 7 on the move in Newcastle.

Nellie Melba's coffin made the trip from Sydney to Melbourne; in her life, the great opera singer had been a frequent traveller on the line. And the body of Sir William Bridges passed though after he was sniped on Gallipoli in 1915. Phar Lap, the legendary Melbourne Cup winner, also changed trains here. Menzies was the last prime minister to make regular use of trains before aviation came to dominate politicians' travel.

Between 1883 and 1962 Albury may even have been the world's most used railway station by the bold and the beautiful, the famous and the great. While many famous people used rail in Europe and the United States during that period, typically the big capital cities all had multiple stations for long-distance trains. For example, then (and now) London had seven grand terminals, which meant that VIPs were dispersed among a variety of stations. But for its part Albury handled all rail passenger traffic between the two largest cities of Australia.

I think I can claim to be the last MP to regularly use trains from Albury Station. I recall one foggy night when around midnight I boarded the sleeper carriage which was then detached at Goulburn and shunted around to a connecting Canberra train. (For many years, steam was used on the short haul to Canberra.) There was much banging as the buffers, air hoses and couplings were disconnected and then re-engaged. The main advantage was that I awoke to disembark at Canberra platform around breakfast time.

Eventually, in 1962, a standard-gauge link was built from Albury to Melbourne, thus eliminating this 'break of gauge'; but, given the fact that Australia had developed 22 different gauges over some 16 decades of rail operation, 'break of gauge' still existed elsewhere for many years and critically affected economic growth, creating artificial choke points in places.

So the good, the bad and the ugly of rail travel was firmly implanted on my mind as I entered the Australian Army in 1966 and served for a period as Transport Officer, 1st Battalion, Royal Australian Regiment, both in Australia

≫ The magisterial main station building at Albury, c. 1890. It is still in use, with many freight trains and 10 passenger trains using the station each day.

ALBURY'S 'BREAK OF GAUGE' PLATFORM

Albury Railway Station opened in 1881 with the arrival of the main line from Sydney. Two years later, the Victorian Irish broad gauge was built across the Murray River, and at last a rail connection was made between Australia's largest two cities. From 1883 until 1962, all through rail passengers between Sydney and Melbourne had to change at Albury, across the long platform. New South Wales trains operated on the eastern side and Victorian trains, including the *Spirit of Progress*, on the western side.

Nothing can match the list of VIPs and others who changed trains at Albury, not even at the key stations between France and Spain or between Poland and Russia. Europe is largely Stephenson standard gauge, but with a 'break of gauge' at the Spanish and Russian borders. Canada, the United States and Mexico all employ standard gauge.

⌃ Royalty always prompted extra effort, starting with Queen Victoria on the LNER in the nineteenth century, and continuing into the twentieth with the NSWGR. Here the Duke of Cornwall visits Albury Railway Station, c.1905.

25 Great Albury Train-changers
*At various times over many decades.

Edmund Barton*	Walter Burley Griffin*	Dame Nellie Melba (1931)
William Bridges (1915)	WM Hughes*	RG Menzies*
Ben Chifley*	Isaac Isaacs (1933)	Thomas Mitchell*
Agatha Christie (1920)	DH Lawrence (1922)	John Monash (1891)
The Duke of Cornwall (later King George V) (1901)	Dame Enid Lyons*	Robert Louis Stevenson (1890)
Arthur Conan Doyle (1920)	Rudyard Kipling (1891)	Mark Twain (1895)
Russell Drysdale*	Douglas MacArthur (1942)	HG Wells (1939)
Prince Henry, Duke of Gloucester (1934)	John McEwen*	The Duke of York (later King George VI) (1927)
	Mary MacKillop*	

and Vietnam. For one exercise, the battalion had to move by troop train from Brisbane to Rockhampton and a siding near Shoalwater Bay Military Training Area. This proved an interesting logistical nightmare with much crowding owing to a lack of carriages for the task, and so I got the blame, although I think it was really Queensland Rail that was at fault.

In 1971, at age 24, I entered the New South Wales State Parliament, having won the seat of Sturt, which included Narrandera and Boree Creek, and later

Junee Junction but not Albury. Then in 1984 I switched to the federal level and won the seat of Farrer, which did include Albury and several rundown branch lines, such as Moama-to-Balranald (now closed) and Moama-to-Deniliquin, which still operates today.

Eventually, I became federal leader of the Nationals, deputy prime minister and trade minister, and when on official overseas trips used to make a point of visiting key railway stations, such as the ornate one at Pretoria in South Africa and the rundown one at Teheran in Iran, albeit counterbalanced by the new but underused station in beautiful Isfahan.

Australian ambassadors were sometimes annoyed at this, having to make protocol and security arrangements before starting out at dawn to see the early rush-hour commuters at the various main stations. But this practice certainly gave me a feel for the standard of living and quality of infrastructure in countries off the beaten track. In China, it resulted in my being seated in the 'Mao chair' in the lounge at Shanghai Station and also at Xian; this was the seat used by Chinese Communist Party leader Mao Zedong who, after he came to power in 1949, frequently used special trains around China.

On one occasion all this station-visiting backfired. I had run down to nearby

≫ One great day in May 2011 as this steam special, the *Caritas Express*, departed for Orvieto from the Pope's platform with St Peters in the background.

Pretoria Station to watch the early morning rush hour to Johannesburg via Irene and was much impressed by the electric narrow Anglo Cape gauge trains departing on time, with the odd steam locomotive attaching to the long-distance trains. Later that day, however, I asked then South African Deputy President Thabo Mbeki when he had last visited Pretoria Station, commenting how clean and efficient it looked. He replied that I should not ask as 'it was 20 years ago and I was trying to blow the place up'.

Today, many train rides later, and after a stint as Australian Ambassador to the Holy See in Rome, where in 2011 I helped create the *Caritas Express*, a steam train from the Pope's platform in the Vatican Gardens to Tuscany, I happily turn again to writing about 'steam'. On this occasion I do so to write mainly of steam travel in the Australian context.

Over the years, I have travelled on steam-hauled trains of many different kinds. In my youth, it was the South West Mail that I used most. Today, it is the occasional ride on the glorious Puffing Billy in the Dandenongs, east of Melbourne, or on the mighty Pichi Richi Railway that runs between Port Augusta and Quorn, plus a few others around the world. Wensleydale Railway in Yorkshire comes happily to mind, as does Steam Swindon and riding the Brunel ultra-broad gauge at Didcot Railway Centre, Swindon and Didcot being on the old Great Western Railway (GWR) route from Paddington to Bristol. In Baltimore it was the first USA railroad ever, which today leads out of the Baltimore and Ohio Railroad Museum in Maryland to the east.

So, all aboard for this journey through the story of steam railways in Australia, and of the great locomotives that crossed the huge Australian continent, over many different systems and 22 different gauges. Our main focus will be on the key steam locomotives that galvanised Australia during its critical phases of development and as it fought in two world wars. (Incidentally, the word 'galvanised' comes to us indirectly from Italy, a nation with a huge collection of steam locomotives at a revamped

⌃ Steam is always a joy to behold, even more so today than ever before, as evidenced by the crowd around locomotive No. 4472 *The Flying Scotsman*.

national rail museum, the Museo Nazionale Ferroviario di Pietrarsa near Naples. In 1737 the Italian physician and physicist Luigi Galvani was born in Bologna, the oldest university town in the Western world and today a busy rail junction. He studied at the University of Bologna, and later demonstrated, by using dead frogs, the effects of electricity on the nervous system. While Galvani was only nine decades ahead of train travel, his research led to breakthroughs in all directions, including ultimately with the use of electricity for many forms of transport.)

Of course, steam locomotives continue to operate today as a key part of rail heritage tourism in Australia and many other countries — often with internal adjustments made to ensure greater efficiency. In some cases, recycled cooking oil is now used to generate boiler heat to create steam; for example, the Grand Canyon Railway in Arizona, USA, where the big local fast-food outlets hand over huge amounts of cooking oil each month. Nowadays, the drive is on to boost fuel efficiency for those steam locomotives still being built and operated or, as with those giants of steam such as the *Flying Scotsman* (being revamped with new boilers) and the NSWGR 3801. Further research is also under way to create a steam turbine locomotive for freight haulage in the future.

The steam locomotives that startled the horses all those years ago helped create nations and their economies, but they also remain a great force of action and interest today.

TREVITHICK'S PORTABLE STEAM ENGINE:
Catch Me Who Can. Mechanical power subduing animal speed.
ADMISSION CARD TO RICHARD TREVITHICK'S RAILWAY, BLOOMSBURY, LONDON, 1808

CHAPTER 1

THE ARRIVAL OF
STEAM LOCOMOTION ON RAIL

<<< Locomotive 6029 hauling an ARHS train on the Wagga viaduct, 1980. This long viaduct across the Murrumbidgee River always had speed restrictions until it was completely rebuilt by the ARTC early this century.

⌄ The city terminus of the Melbourne and Hobson's Bay Railway Company, 1854. The company's modest beginnings led to much more over the decades.

Steam locomotion arrived in Australia in 1854. That year, the directors of the Melbourne and Hobson's Bay Railway Co, in what was then the Colony of Victoria, placed an order for the very first Australian-designed-and-built steam locomotive to run on Australia's first rail line. In fact, it was intended simply as a stopgap until some Stephenson locomotives could arrive from England. A strong case could be made that this was a 'Hobson's Choice'; as we will see, it was a jolly powerful little locomotive with English design aspects, but built entirely in Melbourne by Robertson, Martin and Smith Engineering Works, with a Langlands boiler installed. It had a 2–2–2 wheel arrangement. (Steam locomotive wheel arrangements are counted as the number of small leading wheels as a total, the number of driving – or coupled – wheels as a total, and the number of small trailing wheels as a total. A Pacific wheel arrangement is 4–6–2, where there are four wheels in the leading truck, six total coupled wheels and two wheels under the trailing truck, but a NSWGR 32 Class, for example, with no trailing truck, was a 4–6–0. Tender wheels do not count. More detail on these configurations is supplied in later chapters, including the peculiarity that steam locomotive wheel patterns were generally named after oceans.)

In the beginning, however, the word had long been around that steam propulsion was coming. Drawings of early incarnations of steam boilers on rudimentary sets of wheels had circulated widely throughout the world for centuries, in places such as China, France and Great Britain. During the

The City Terminus of the M. & H.B Railway Compy 1854

Renaissance, even the artist, inventor and architect Leonardo da Vinci, who had drawn versions of so many machines, came up with a simple steam engine design using a flywheel and crank.

Although rudimentary steam engines date back to the *aeolilipe* of Hero of Alexandria in the first century AD, there was arguably just one godfather of steam propulsion and ten outstanding fathers of robust steam locomotives. That godfather was a member of that meddlesome but dynamic religious order, the

⌃ Nicolas-Joseph Cugnot's fullsize *fardier à vapeur* (1770): French excellence on display just 500 metres from Gare du Nord, Paris, in a museum where you do not have to queue.

Society of Jesus. Father Ferdinand Verbiest SJ (1623–1688) was a well-travelled Flemish Jesuit who developed an embryonic steam engine. He also followed in the footsteps of Father Matteo Ricci, travelling along the Marco Polo trail to China. In 1672 Father Verbiest designed a toy steam trolley for the Kangxi emperor (r. 1661–1722) and copies of drawings of this trolley eventually found their way into circulation. In reality, this steam-driven toy trolley was neither a giant exemplar nor a progenitor like the Ford Model T, but it did point to early – indeed very early – thinking about using steam power as an effective method of propulsion.

In 1769 Frenchman Nicolas-Joseph Cugnot created what is generally regarded as the first steam-propelled vehicle, the *fardier à vapeur*, which was dominated by a large spherical boiler at one end. It could be argued that Cugnot was the first father of steam locomotion. Despite the horrendous disruption caused by the French Revolution in the last decade of the eighteenth century, both creator and machine survived; it can be seen today in an expansive museum setting at the Conservatoire National des Arts et Métiers in Paris.

Then, also in 1769, along came James Watt, up there on the border between England and Scotland. He famously invented the first big double-acting steam water pump, which was used to drain deep coal mines. This clearly established a new benchmark for the use of steam: no wasteful spurts of gushing steam on an external paddle wheel, but rather an enclosed piston driven by a vacuum on one side and a steam push on either side of the piston in turn.

There had been precursors to Watt's engine, however. Back in 1698, military engineer Thomas Savery had invented the 'miner's friend' as a fixed-location

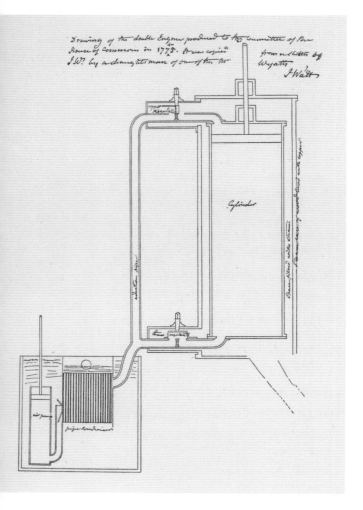

« The British House of Commons was always interfering with the development of rail. One amendment famously added half an inch to the Stephenson standard gauge, and so 4 ft 8½ in (1,435 mm) became the world's most popular gauge.

⮯ James Watt, one of the great pioneers of steam.

steam-driven pump designed to pump water out of coal mines, and in 1712 Thomas Newcomen devised the first practical steam machine, which was later improved by John Smeaton. These pioneering British engineers — and no doubt others — deserve mention, but it was the giant figure of James Watt who lifted steam power to entirely another dimension.

If Verbiest was steam's godfather, and Cugnot and Watt its first fathers, who are the other eight key figures? Once again, British and French names predominate: household names such as Isambard Kingdom Brunel and father and son George and Robert Stephenson (but also some lesser known ones from across the English Channel).

The early nineteenth century heralded massive changes in land transport. In the era immediately before hard steel rails came to the fore, a likely lad based in Cornwall was beavering away, creating rudimentary and heavy steam locomotives which had the bad habit of smashing or flattening iron rails. His name was Richard Trevithick and his most famous effort was to build a small demonstration locomotive that was dubbed *Catch Me Who Can*. It was used to haul a few open carriages in a circle behind some canvas hoardings as a kind of sideshow in London, but it pointed the way to more serious endeavours.

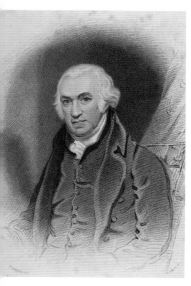

George Stephenson from Newcastle upon Tyne had sighted one of Trevithick's creations, a rudimentary locomotive called *Black Billy*, and that was enough for the self-educated George to get busy and build his own. It was called *Locomotion*, and it emerged in 1825 ready to haul what is regarded as the first railway ever (as opposed to plateways and tramways, which were mainly horse-hauled), the Stockton and Darlington Railway (1825–63).

In *Locomotion* Stephenson had most of the right ingredients, and it was a trail-blazer, but even before this George had been joined by his son Robert

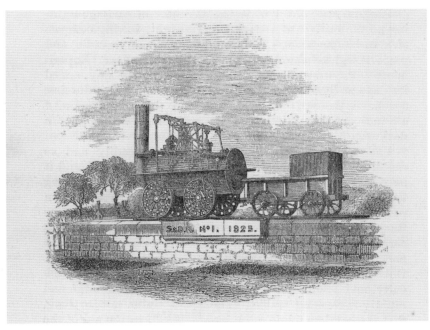

⌃ George Stephenson, c. 1847. His closest friend and business partner was his son Robert.

⌄ Richard Trevithick's London railway and locomotive of 1808. The novelty of rail meant steam haulage soon became the dominant way forward.

⌃ 'The No. 1 Engine at Darlington', 1859. So many Stephenson standard-gauge engines were exported from Britain to the world that the rail width had to be built to match.

⤵ Trial and error dominated many of Trevithick's creations: one blew up outside an inn where they were celebrating its inaugural run.

GEORGE STEPHENSON'S TRICK TRACK

There was another flourish added by George Stephenson with the Liverpool and Manchester Railway, which used a double Stephenson standard-gauge track from its inception; he cunningly designed the gap between the two sets of tracks to be also exactly 4 ft 8½ in (1,435 mm). This meant that, around midnight, steam trains carrying very wide loads could operate 'down the middle', so to speak, having entered this middle line by a special set of points. Unfortunately, no photographs or sketches exist of this set-up, which was later removed when the need arose to put more separation between the two main tracks.

One suspects that the need to compete against the canal barges with their capacity to carry wide loads may have been a factor that prompted Stephenson to devise the middle track in the first place. I am not aware of this type of track layout ever having been repeated anywhere in the world since then.

in building locomotives and creating railways. George was born in 1781, Robert in 1803, so only 22 years separated them; their engineering partnership became a true father-and-son business with both men working closely together.

Between 1825 and 1830 George was working on the huge Liverpool and Manchester Railway project, which faced trenchant opposition from the big canal owners and operators. Meanwhile, Robert was beavering away at the foundry and workshops at Newcastle upon Tyne, and looming large were the famous Rainhill Trials, intended to decide which type of haulage power and which brand of locomotive would be employed on the Liverpool and Manchester Railway. A £500 prize had been offered.

Much correspondence has been found dating from 1829 between the 48-year-old father and his 26-year-old son (who enjoyed a much better formal education than his father, who had still been illiterate at 19). They were finalising their entry for the Rainhill Trials, the sturdy 4-tonne *Rocket*. Built at Newcastle upon Tyne, it was totally dismantled for the long trip by wagon, barge and ship to Rainhill, which is located in Merseyside about halfway between Liverpool and Manchester.

George had built the Stockton and Darlington Railway and *Locomotion* to fit a 4 ft 8 in (1,422 mm) gauge, but this was found to be too tight a fit on the curves for this new project. So in 1828 he sought, and obtained, a famous amendment in the key legislation at Westminster that made allowance for an expansion of just ½ inch to 4 ft 8½ in (1,435 mm). This gauge would become a new worldwide benchmark.

In the twenty-first century a huge majority of the world's railways operate at the adjusted Stephenson standard gauge, but none operates at 4 ft 8 in — practical common sense played a big part in this, as did the concept of pathway dependency described by the American economist Douglas J Puffert in his authoritative history of railway track gauges. The notable exceptions today are Brazil, India and Russia, as well as Victoria and South Australia down under. In 2015 Ethiopia opened its new Addis Ababa metro in standard gauge, and in 2016 the country opened the new 700-kilometre-plus trunk railway from Addis Ababa down the Rift Valley to the coast at Djibouti on the Red Sea, also in standard gauge, thus walking away from the old French 1-metre gauge used previously. Gauge will be dealt with in more detail later, as it had a huge impact on steam locomotive boiler size and performance, not to mention overall cost.

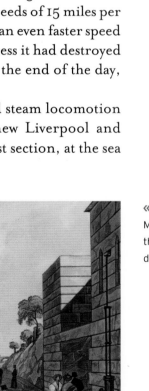

≫ The Stephensons' *Rocket*: absolute brilliance on wheels.

With that extra half-inch, plus a good boiler design, George and Robert Stephenson blitzed the opposition with the *Rocket* achieving speeds of 15 miles per hour (24 kph). Another locomotive, the *Novelty*, had reached an even faster speed on the day — an incredible 28 mph (45 kph) — but in the process it had destroyed its internal workings. By contrast, *Rocket* was still standing at the end of the day, ready to go again.

Rocket was declared the winner of the Rainhill Trials, and steam locomotion was declared the choice for providing haulage for the new Liverpool and Manchester Railway, although a rope tow was used for the first section, at the sea end, which took in a steep grade out of Liverpool Station.

≪ The Liverpool and Manchester Railway was the first real modern double-track railway.

The world now had its first reliable robust steam locomotive ready for trailblazing action — balanced on two rails, it could pull three or four times its own weight. But even the mighty *Rocket* was missing two huge improvements that would allow for greater performance. They were just around the corner, or in fact just across the English Channel. Two French engineers devised two essential components that allowed steam locomotives to really succeed. Both would be used ever after 1850, a fact which explains the renown of these French pioneers.

First, Marc Seguin had hit upon the idea of making more use of the heat from the fire of steam locomotives by sending it along tubes which passed through the water jacket of the boiler, thus creating more steam for each kilogram of coal or oil or wood burnt. Then the tubes would join the flue of the locomotive chimney and exit upwards, simultaneously creating momentum and helping the fire to

A Train of the First

Drawn by I. Shaw, Liverpool.

A Train of the Secon

TRAVELLING ON THE LIVE:

London, Published

draw properly. There is some debate over whether the Stephensons were already onto this aspect of the design, but on balance the French are usually given the credit. It certainly very quickly became mandatory in the design of almost all steam locomotives.

Then along came a certain lateral thinker, Henri Giffard. In 1852, aged 27, he created a steam-powered dirigible – a hydrogen-filled balloon with a steam engine underneath – capable of driving a propeller. Decades ahead of the Wright brothers in the United States, Giffard travelled more than 24 kilometres on the world's first propelled flight, near Paris, but the steam engine was not strong enough on the day to turn around and travel back to the starting point.

However, Giffard's big breakthrough came when he designed and built a robust water injector, which had no internal moving parts, to force the water

⩔ Leading the way: travel on the Liverpool and Manchester Railway, 1831.

arriages, with the Mail.   PLATE I.

RQUES OF STAFFORD MANCHESTER   LIVERPOOL TREASURER MANCHESTER   LIVERPOOL DESPATCH MANCHESTER   ROYAL MAIL
AILWAY-COMPANY   RAILWAY-COMPANY   RAILWAY-COMPANY

Aquat.d by S.G.Hughes.

r outside Passengers.

AND MANCHESTER RAILWAY.

N, 96 Strand, Nov.r 1831.

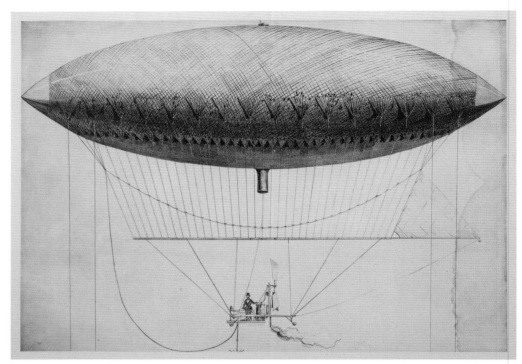

» Giffard was a trailblazer both in the air and on the ground.

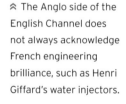

⌃ The Anglo side of the English Channel does not always acknowledge French engineering brilliance, such as Henri Giffard's water injectors.

supply back into the boiler against the built-up pressure of the steam already being held to supply the piston cylinders. The Stephensons had used a water pump for this purpose, but Giffard went one better with an invention so good that it took the world by storm and remains part of every steam locomotive today. At the time, accusations of 'black magic' were made, but it was soon widely accepted as the best and safest way to put water back into the boiler to make more steam, without losing any of the existing steam in the process.

It worked like this: steam from the boiler enters into the injector through a control valve. It passes through a venturi cone that decreases its volume and thereby increases its velocity. It passes into the combining cone, where it is mixed with fresh, cold water. The effect of the hot steam meeting the cold water not only heats the water but also increases the velocity. The mixture now passes through a third cone and its velocity forces it past the non-return valve (also known by railwaymen as a 'clack' valve because it clacks back into place), overcoming the boiler pressure that keeps that non-return valve closed. What adds to the momentum is the fact that as the steam cools it accelerates; then, as it releases from the cone past the point of maximum compression, it accelerates even more. Since this is as close as you can get to a form of perpetual motion, it is easy to see how some thought it magical. Just think about it: the steam, having exited the boiler under pressure, maintained a swift forward movement as it flowed through the cone of the Giffard injector, picked up the water flow and returned it all back into the boiler from which it had exited, by forcing open clack valves engineered for one-directional flow.

Over the decades, Giffard injectors have usually been made of brass; they are designed to last and are usually the least troublesome vital part on a steam locomotive – unless the cones have not been maintained and permitted to erode, thereby reducing the venturi effect, or unless there were hapless crabs or fish in the water tank, leading to unexpected blockages. Famously, this did happen once to the *Flying Scotsman* on a run from Leicester into London. The crew were desperately trying to get steam and water into the boiler, but some dead fish had completely blocked both injectors. The boiler water level was plunging, and there was imminent danger of an explosion. The crew coasted down the grade into King's Cross Station and just managed to stabilise the boiler, and then unblock the injectors, in time.

Cugnot and Watt, George and Robert Stephenson, Marc Seguin and Henri Giffard, these pioneers had all done their work. Enter now Isambard Kingdom Brunel, celebrated bridge-builder and steamship-builder but also the founder and chief engineer of the Great Western Railway (GWR).

The Great Western Railway, with its key trunk line from London's Paddington Station to Bristol and Penzance, was nicknamed 'God's Wonderful Railway'. It was initially built to an ultra-broad gauge of 7 ft ¼ in (2,140 mm). To match this, Brunel designed and built steam engines with a very wide frame and good stability.

The *North Star* was a 2–2–2 configuration, and in 1838 it hauled a special GWR directors' train. While it followed Brunel's design, the *North Star* was built by none other than Robert Stephenson and Co at Newcastle upon Tyne. It was originally due to be delivered to fill an order from the United States, but the deal fell over and so the design was adjusted to fit the GWR.

The subsequent Firefly class of locomotives was pure GWR from go to whoa, and one can be found operating today at the Didcot Railway Centre. The recreated *North Star* also has pride of place at Steam Swindon, the superb museum built using the old GWR steam workshop and foundry. Both Didcot and Swindon are magnificently maintained and well worth visiting today.

On reflection, Brunel, for all his brilliance and his glorious bridge, railway and ship construction projects, really did little with regard to the creation of steam locomotive power as such. However, after the Stephensons and the other pioneers, another brilliant Frenchman, André Chapelon, did come along just after the First World War. After serving as an

>>> J.M.W. Turner, *Rain, Steam and Speed* – The Great Western Railway, 1844. Turner's masterly paintings encompassed much more than ships and burning parliaments – rail was also in the mix.

˅ Now stored at Steam Swindon, the *North Star* is a masterwork of steam locomotive design.

⌃ Steam locomotive No. 1A at Wangaratta, Vic., c. 1900s. Once upon a time this was a busy dual-gauge junction.

artillery officer he went on to apply rigorous scientific standards to every aspect of steam locomotive design. In effect, he led the way in devising the modern steam locomotive, and the technical excellence of his designs greatly improved the performance of the steam locomotives of the Société Nationale des Chemins de Fer Français (SNCF).

Chapelon's improvements to steam locomotive exhaust systems constituted a major advance in efficiency; he designed and then refined the Kylchap exhaust system, and was forever improving and refining compound steam piston systems. The result of both these breakthroughs was that a lot less coal could drive locomotives further and further. So good were the Chapelon designs that they spread right around the world, notably to Argentina, but also had a great impact on the mighty Baldwin steam locomotives of the United States and beyond.

Sir Herbert Nigel Gresley was born in Edinburgh in 1876, and after a good formal education eventually joined the London and North Eastern Railway (LNER). These initials are well known to all model train operators as so much of Hornby and other stock—which enjoys such a strong market both in Commonwealth countries and in the United States—was based on the LNER design.

⌃ An LNER steam train in full flight always had a certain majesty about it.

MALLARD'S RECORD-BREAKING SUNDAY

There was tension on the footplate of No. 4468 *Mallard* of the LNER as experienced driver Joe Duddington opened the throttle as far as he could and fireman Tommy Bray shovelled coal furiously into the roaring firebox. It was Sunday 3 July 1938, and what would become the most famous of all steam speed trials was about to unfold near Stoke summit on the LNER main line, southbound towards Peterborough and London.

A dynamometer car (No. 902502) was attached just behind *Mallard*, and its swaying tender; then came six Coronation Pullman carriages with no paying passengers but rather a few officials now in on the secret plan: to beat the record of 114 mph (182 kph) set by the rival LMS, but also the German speed records of the era.

Soon enough, *Mallard* smashed through all existing steam locomotive speed records, peaking at 126 mph (203 kph) before having to brake for some awkward curves near Essendine. Shortly afterwards, it reached Peterborough where it got a check-over and a rest. Despite some dubious subsequent German claims, *Mallard*'s speed record stands to this day.

Gresley became the Chief Mechanical Engineer of the LNER and he not only built the famous 4472 *Flying Scotsman* (now renumbered), he also created the A4 Pacific fast steam locomotive designed for the express trains from London to Scotland via York and the LNER main line. In 1938, just north of Peterborough, the A4 *Mallard* reached 126 mph (203 kph) – the all-time world speed record for a steam locomotive.

One of the A4s is named *Sir Nigel Gresley* after its creator, and both the *Mallard* and the *Gresley* can be seen most summers around the National Railway Museum in York or other former LNER haunts.

There is no doubt Gresley lifted steam locomotive design and performance to new levels. Later the LNER placed long water troughs between the rails in level areas, about halfway between London and Edinburgh and added scoops to the tenders; it also created passageways to allow crews to change over at speed. As a result, a non-stop *Flying Scotsman* service running between London and Edinburgh began in 1928. Superbly designed and engineered, this world-famous train departed King's Cross at 10 am each day. It had originally commenced operating in 1862 and was steam-hauled for around 100 years of its working life.

The final steam supremo hails from the Southern Hemisphere. Livio Dante Porta, born in Argentina in 1922, deserves his place in the sun for devising two solid breakthroughs which boosted basic steam locomotive efficiency. He lived to the grand old age of 81, his life and work spanning two centuries. Porta's close liaison with André Chapelon led to the vital exhaust system design of steam locomotives being boosted for greater efficiency.

After the Second World War, Porta took Chapelon's original Kylchap ejector and created the Kylpor unit before going one further step with the Lempor ejector, which consisted of a

⌄ The *Flying Scotsman* leaves King's Cross. For decades, this scene was repeated as nearby Big Ben struck 10 each morning.

FATHERS OF THE STEAM LOCOMOTIVE

Here is the complete honour roll (in alphabetical order) of those who contributed a great deal to the worldwide creation of the steam locomotive. Their ground-breaking contributions paved the way for Australians to take up the cudgels and design and build Australian steam locomotives after the first wave of imported models arrived, many from the Stephenson works at Newcastle upon Tyne around the middle of the nineteenth century. The sizable contribution made by many Australian engineers of renown will be described later.

André Chapelon (1892–1978), French mechanical engineer

Nicolas-Joseph Cugnot (1725–1804), French inventor of the first self-propelled vehicle

Henri Giffard (1825–1882), French inventor of the first steam-powered airship

Sir Herbert Nigel Gresley (1876–1941), British steam locomotive engineer

Livio Dante Porta (1922–2003), Argentine steam locomotive engineer

Marc Seguin (1786–1875), French engineer who invented the wire-cable suspension bridge and the multi-tubular steam-engine boiler

George Stephenson (1781–1848), British civil and mechanical engineer, renowned as the 'Father of Railways'

Robert Stephenson (1803–1859), British railway and civil engineer, son of George Stephenson

Richard Trevithick (1771–1833), British mining engineer and inventor

James Watt (1736–1819), Scottish inventor, mechanical engineer and chemist

blast pipe, then a four-lobe vertical exhaust manifold, followed by a mixing chamber and diffuser. With Porta's design, each chug of the steam locomotive created maximum draught and vacuum, thereby boosting overall efficiency. In essence, it involved splitting the exhaust through four nozzles to great advantage; once again the effect of a cone is in play whereby the exhaust gases are concentrated as they move up through the vertical cone to its wide exit point before suddenly bursting free beyond the cone. This design generated extra exhaust momentum.

Later Porta concentrated on boosting the treatment of the water used in steam locomotives to greatly reduce scaling within the engine's various steam tubes and pipes, increasing efficiency and massively lowering maintenance costs in the process. It is known today as the PT system. In its heyday, Porta's narrow-gauge steam locomotive named the *Argentina* was a streamlined beauty.

After 1830, what was the driving force behind the need for the initial steam locomotives to become bigger, better and safer? Both the unfolding of the Industrial Revolution and the need to create new nations and secure their sovereignty played a key role, along with the pressures arising from increasing urbanisation, which created the need for essential items such as milk and other foodstuffs to be quickly and efficiently hauled to the markets of the growing cities. In France, the capital, Paris, was located a long way inland, requiring early rail connections to and from the coastal ports. And while in Great Britain there were numerous canals in the middle of the country, these were costly and plainly were not coping with the demands placed on them, so it was rail transport, in the form of trains hauled by steam locomotives, that was much in demand to meet rapidly growing freight needs.

The consignments of coffee and tea, and the heavy cotton and wool bales, streaming into the country from around the Empire and the Americas had to be sorted and despatched from the giant Port of Liverpool, with its many wharves, to Manchester and beyond. Much of this traffic flowed down the new rail network that led to an ever-growing London.

In Germany, it was the early rail networks that made possible the merger of various kingdoms and duchies and paved the way for Prussian Chancellor Otto von Bismarck to unify the country into a formidable military power. In North America, it was the need to provide east–west links with an eye to securing and maintaining sovereignty on the lucrative west coast that was a vital factor. Russia had established fishing villages as far south as Portland, and from the south Mexico and the Spanish had reached north of San Francisco to Sonoma near Sacramento.

The discovery of gold in places like California was one factor that prompted the building of the First Transcontinental Railroad to ensure that the governmental

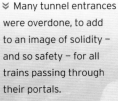

⩒ Many tunnel entrances were overdone, to add to an image of solidity – and so safety – for all trains passing through their portals.

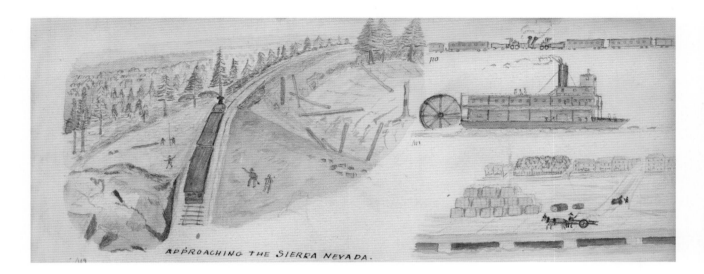

APPROACHING THE SIERRA NEVADA.

power base on the distant east coast might hold onto the vital resources of the rich Pacific coast states, such as California, Oregon and Washington.

In all these cases, hardy steam locomotives had to be built to operate up and down steep grades or around sharp corners. After the first decade or so of operations, safety and speed became factors demanded by the users. There was a degree of contradiction in boosting speed along lightly constructed main lines while at the same time trying to avoid derailments.

Because almost all the initial steam locomotives on the new railway networks and systems being established around the world originated from Robert Stephenson and Company, or from one of the other early locomotive factories in Great Britain, the nineteenth century saw the emergence of various common patterns and types.

The smallest type or category of steam locomotive was the 'tank engine'; it had no separate tender, and the water tank and coal or timber storage area was mounted on the main (and only) frame of the locomotive. These locomotives were often used for shunting and were easily recognisable with their water tanks sitting high on either side of the boiler.

The second, and main workhorse, type of steam locomotive was the 'Standard Engine' with its boiler and pistons and footplate on the main frame, with a separate wagon or tender for holding the coal or timber — as well as the most necessary item of all, the water tank.

The third and much larger type was the 'articulated engine', which came in three parts and was usually denoted as a Garratt (after the British locomotive engineer Herbert William Garratt, who developed the system), even when it had been built by another company in another country. This type initially had a water tank, followed by the main boiler and control footplate and then a tender for coal

⌃ The Americas abounded with vibrant rail images.

⟫⟫ At night-time, rail junction complexity always seemed to be magnified.

29

or timber, and in some cases for oil (if it was an oil-burner). The steam from the boiler drove two sets of pistons, forward and rear. This is best explained by the typical wheel arrangement such as with the locomotive 6029 of the NSWGR, namely 4–8–4 + 4–8–4, which makes for a total of 16 big driving wheels.

In the United States, there was one other variation: the 'Big Boy' class of the Union Pacific which had one huge boiler driving four sets of pistons (two sets on either side) on one long frame, and so this wheel arrangement: 4–8–8–4. The bogies allowed for a certain degree of articulation. Just 25 of these 500-tonne plus giants were built, all of them during the Second World War. By 1960 they had been pushed off the stage by the all-conquering diesel and diesel-electric units, although one is currently being restored to operational service, No. 4014.

This leads us into discussion of the various wheel arrangements of steam locomotives. Somewhat curiously, in many cases, these were named after oceans. Arguably, the most famous of all was the Pacific class of steam locomotive wheel arrangement (4–6–2), where the first number relates to the forward section, the middle one denotes the large driving wheels and the third indicates what is usually located under the footplate.

↳ A southbound *Spirit of Progress*, 1939. Sadly, all four S Class streamliners were scrapped around 1960.

The list of Locomotive Wheel Arrangements (p. 248) starts with the Adriatic 2–6–4 and the Atlantic 4–4–2 and works right through.

The overall dimensions of the various types of locomotives varied greatly, and this was driven by complex calculations such as that for crank pin velocity. The calculations for counter-balancing the extra weight on the driving wheels can run to pages, but they served to ensure the smooth running of each piston thrust. The valve gear that allows fresh steam into the piston chamber, and the old steam out and into the exhaust pipe system, also involves complex calculations; the

Valves: vital synchronisation

The ever-inventive Stephensons devised a type of link valve motion that was eventually named after them, but there was also the Walschaerts valve motion and later the cam motion associated with the poppet valve.

There were three overall types of valves quite apart from valve motion: first, the slide valve; second, the piston valve; third, the more enduring poppet valve. The trick was to get maximum use out of the expanding steam in the main piston cylinder, and then allow rapid removal of the spent steam on the reverse stroke. Almost all steam engines use both sides of the main piston to push with the expanding steam, or to remove the spent steam, and the more efficient the valve design and movement, the stronger and indeed faster the outcome will be.

When the *Mallard* shattered all previous speed records, the valve gear was hammering away to help deliver the new record, but after the big run it had to be carefully checked to ensure no damage had been incurred, as the valve gear had been tested beyond its specifications.

⌃ From its inception, the steam locomotive valve gear involved precision calculations and complexity.

All of this further demonstrates that your average steam locomotive is anything but a simple beast. Rather, they are exceedingly complex machines that can at times become cranky beasts if the driver and fireman do not possess intimate knowledge of their type of locomotive or the chosen rail route, especially its grades and curves.

valves operate in harmony with the pistons in a well-timed movement.

The factor that had the greatest impact on the size and shape of steam locomotives was the matter of gauge, which is to say the width of the rails on which the steam locomotive had to operate. (The next chapter will return to this crucial question of rail gauge in greater detail.)

Right around the world, the early steam locomotives of the first half of the nineteenth century ushered in 100 grand years of steam locomotive excellence. During the period 1850–1950, most haulage outside of urban electric rail systems was accomplished by steam-driven locomotives. It was the golden age of steam, soon to be comprehensively displaced by the advent of the diesel and diesel-electric locomotive. And yet, in every corner of the world, there are still some steam locomotives operating today.

One of the advantages of switching from steam locomotives to diesel or diesel-electric was that it meant there would be no more ugly black stains created by steam locomotives at rest in stations with large train sheds, such as St Pancras, London. It has a superb arched Barlow train shed, now painted in powder blue with not a black soot mark to be sighted anywhere. This was also a problem at the giant Milan Central and Sydney Central, and at various large underground stations such as New York's Grand Central Station.

In the case of Grand Central, the long-haul steam locomotives were replaced by electric locomotives just north of New York, for the run into the tunnels to and from the huge terminus. So the famous *20th Century Limited*, which operated daily between New York and Chicago for decades, always departed from its red carpeted platform underground in New York under electric power. Many stations had ventilator chimneys located above where the steam locomotives normally came to a halt, to ease the burden created by black smoke pollution, but to this day remnant black soot stains can be seen around some big station complexes.

In the golden age of steam there were big trains and small ones, streamlined and half-streamlined, and today steam continues to operate, albeit mainly for rail heritage and tourism efforts, but on many sugar cane networks steam locomotives are in full swing every day of the sugar harvest season.

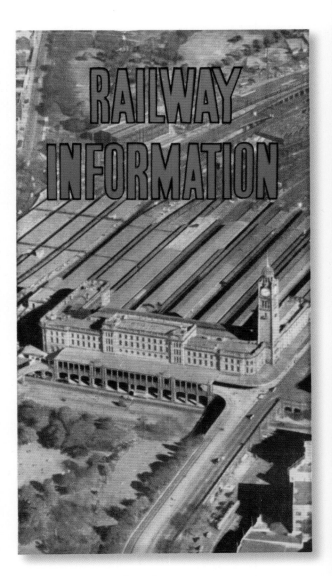

RAILWAY INFORMATION

⌃ Australia's grandest terminus station, Sydney Central.

⌃ The American Civil War had a great impact on railway gauges in the USA, leading to the Stephenson standard gauge being adopted.

Clearly, it was the steam locomotive that gave the world a huge breakthrough by delivering improved mobility for freight and passenger, by galvanising the hinterlands of so many nations, and by paving the way for modern economic development. And in time of war, fleets of steam locomotives were called upon to make even greater efforts.

During the American Civil War (1861–65) there was an element of competing rail systems, with the northern Unionist states extending their standard-gauge system ever southwards, in the process ripping up the Confederacy's Czar broad-gauge system of 5 ft (1,524 mm). As a result, the Confederacy's steam locomotives were rendered unusable unless time-consuming adjustments were made. The Unionist victory over the Confederacy thus meant that the main US rail networks would all be built in standard gauge. This included the key inaugural east–west Transcontinental Railroad, the two halves of which linked up at Promontory, Utah, on 10 May 1869. At last, the east coast and the west coast had a direct transcontinental rail connection.

Imperial Germany's extensive rail network played a crucial role in the nation's strategic policy in the years leading up to the First World War. Most historians now concede that it was the fact that the German troop trains hauled by steam locomotives were already moving west and north-west in the last week of July and first week of August 1914 that prevented Kaiser Wilhelm from avoiding the nightmare of war on two fronts, against both France and Russia. When he suggested halting the country's mobilisation, his Chief of the General Staff told him that it was too late to stop the troop trains heading west. And so Germany invaded Belgium (and then France), implementing the so-called 'right hook' strategy implicit in the Schlieffen Plan. Shortly thereafter, on 4 August 1914, Britain declared war on Germany, and British Empire countries such as Australia automatically found themselves at war. Ultimately, millions were killed outright or died of wounds and sickness over the four dreadful years of the so-called Great War.

The Australians played a key role in winning the war, perhaps none more than a former Australian railway builder and highly successful civil engineer, General

Sir John Monash of Melbourne and Jerilderie, who was appointed to lead the newly formed Australian Corps in 1918. He soon helped turn the tide on the Western Front through the exemplary success of the battle of Hamel on 4 July, and later the battle of Amiens where he used rail and combined arms in a holistic way to punch 16 kilometres through the German front line in just one day, 8 August, helped by the Canadians on the right flank.

Often Monash would issue orders that Decauville narrow-gauge track of 1 ft 11⅝ in (600 mm) be laid quickly but on standard-gauge sleepers, so that when operations and time permitted the railway carrying vital supplies and munitions could be easily upgraded to the full standard gauge. This, in turn, created the advantage of seamless connection with the French SNCF network, notably at the key rail hub of Amiens.

Operating on the Decauville mobile narrow-gauge railways were Hunslet locomotives made by the Hunslet Engine Company in Leeds, both before and during the war. They were sturdy tank engines, and one is preserved today in the National Collection of the Australian War Memorial in Canberra, although it is not always on display.

Throughout the nineteenth and twentieth centuries, steam locomotives were created and delivered massively in both war and peace, this was no truer anywhere than in the great island continent of Australia, as we shall now see.

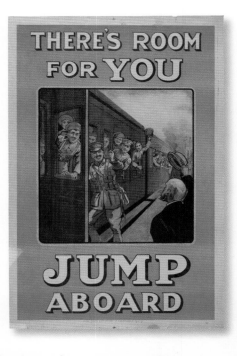

⌃ Rail travel promotion took many forms, as seen in this c. 1915 poster.

⌄ The giant German railway gun known as the Amiens Gun, seen here in a Canberra railway siding in 1927, was captured by the AIF during the great victory of 8 August 1918.

CHAPTER 2

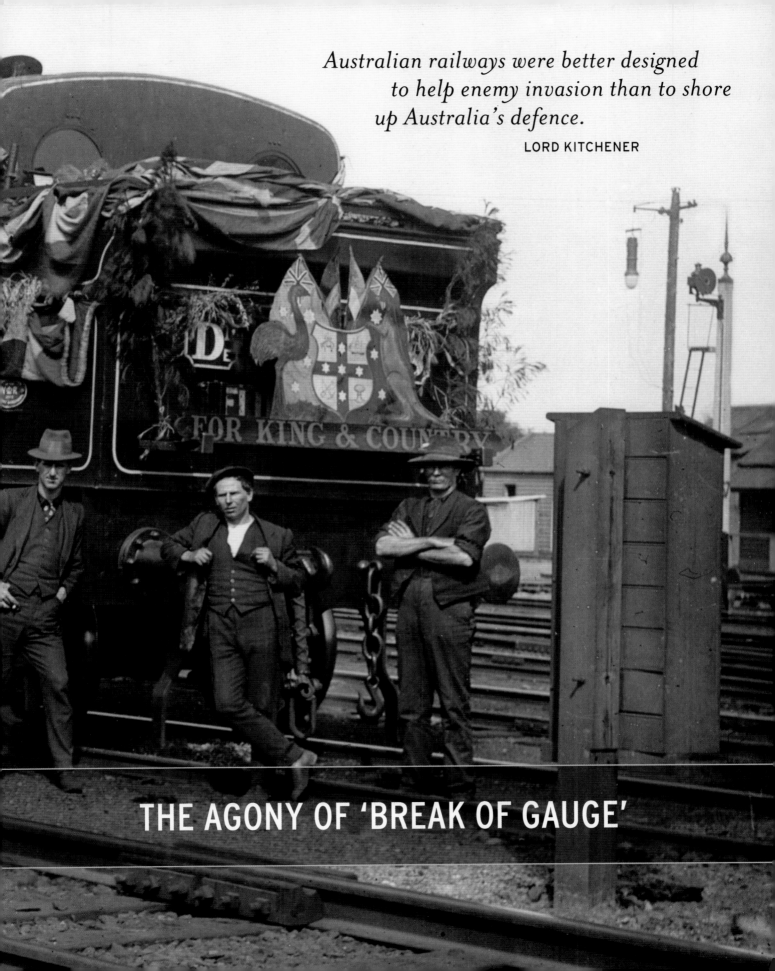

Australian railways were better designed to help enemy invasion than to shore up Australia's defence.

LORD KITCHENER

FOR KING & COUNTRY

THE AGONY OF 'BREAK OF GAUGE'

«« VR DDE Class locomotive carrying volunteers for the AIF, 1914. In both world wars Australian railways played a huge supporting role.

» Twenty-two gauges were developed and operated in Australia.

≫ India has much steam locomotion to this day.

Over the centuries, it was a worldwide tragedy that railway engineers and planners did not stick to just two gauges. These should have been just one narrow gauge and one standard main gauge: 1 metre/1,000 mm (3 ft 3⅜ in) for the narrow gauge, and the Stephenson standard of 4 ft 8½ (1,435 mm) for the main gauge – the one that carries all AVE, ICE, Shinkansen and TGV trains today. Some might argue that, given the capacity of modern earth-moving equipment, the Irish broad gauge of 5 ft 3 in (1,600 mm) might have been the best choice for a standard, but it was not to be.

However, the concept of pathway dependency held sway; once standard gauge had taken hold in Great Britain, and notably after the Stephenson steam engine building foundry at Newcastle upon Tyne began exporting in large numbers, it was easier to stay with 4 ft 8½ in. Countries such as Belgium and Egypt, to name just two, all went along with the dominant Stephenson dimensions.

Worldwide, some 18 different gauges dominated in the nineteenth century, and today ten of these continue to carry passenger trains daily. All used steam locomotives in the past, and the narrow-gauge ones among the ten continue to use steam almost daily; for example, in India steam trains continue to operate on the Darjeeling, Ooty and Shimla narrow-gauge mountain railway lines.

These famous three railways, with direct connection to the huge broad-gauge main-line network of India, each have their own gauge, and this has an impact on both the size and the height placement of the boiler for their steam locomotives. New steam locomotives for the Ooty are still being built today at a huge Government of India rail workshops located on the edge of Trichy in southern India. By sheer good luck, when visiting with Scott McGregor some years ago, I witnessed the roll out, for the 1-metre-gauge Ooty system, of a brand new steam locomotive complete with complex rack-and-pinion equipment for the steep grades. The Kalka–Shimla Railway, which follows a mountainous route in northern India, has narrow-gauge track of 2 ft 6 in (762 mm), and Darjeeling World Heritage railway is 2 ft (610 mm).

In Australia, some 22 railway gauge systems were initially developed, which meant that 22 different sizes of steam locomotive had to be developed to match them. And, of course, this meant 22 different sizes for the various steam locomotive key components. (Only one

Tim Fischer's

GREAT AUSTRALIAN RAILWAY GAUGES

Past and Present
1831-2004

No. 1 IRISH BROAD 1,600 mm : 5'3"
(VIC, SA and NT) ◪ ☐ ■

No. 2 STEPHENSON STANDARD 1,435 mm : 4'8½"
(now all mainland States/ACT/NT) ◪ ☐ ■

No. 3 DELORAINE STANDARD 1,372 mm : 4'6"
(Mersey to Deloraine, TAS) ◪

No. 4 STARVATION NARROW 1,219 mm : 4'0"
(Starvation Creek, VIC) ◪

No. 5 MISTAKE NARROW 1,131 mm : 3'8½"
(Mt Pleasant Colliery, NSW) ◪ ☐

No. 6 OUTER SYDNEY NARROW 1,080 mm : 3'6½"
(El Caballo Blanco, NSW) ☐

No. 7 ANGLO CAPE NARROW 1,067 mm : 3'6"
(all States at various times) ◪ ☐ ■

No. 8 RUBICON NARROW 1,029 mm : 3'4½"
(Rubicon Forest, VIC) ◪ ☐

No. 9 METRE NARROW 1,000 mm : 3'3⅜"
(Hartley Vale near Zig Zag, NSW) ◪ ☐ ■

No. 10 KOOLOOLA LOG GAUGE 991 mm : 3'3"
(East of Gympie, QLD) ◪ ☐

No. 11 LORNE LOG NARROW 940 mm : 3'1"
(Lorne Pier to Mill, VIC) ◪ ☐

No. 12 AMERICAS NARROW 914 mm : 3'0"
(Industrial including Newcastle, Portland NSW, Yarra Valley VIC) ☐ ■

No. 13 MONASH NARROW 900 mm : 2'11⅜"
(La Trobe Interconnecting, VIC) ☐ ■

No. 14 LECONFIELD NARROW 838 mm : 2'9"
(Greta, NSW) ◪ ☐

No. 15 SUEZ WALHALLA WHITFIELD 762 mm : 2'6"
(Puffing Billy/Walhalla, VIC) ◪ ☐ ■

No. 16 APPLETON NARROW 700 mm : 2'3⅜"
(Port Melbourne, VIC) ■

No. 17 GOLD NARROW 686 mm : 2'3"
(Woods Point, VIC) ◪ ☐

No. 18 CAPRICORNIA NARROW 661 mm : 2'2"
(Mt Morgan, QLD) ◪ ☐

No. 19 CANE NARROW 610 mm : 2'0"
(QLD, TAS) ◪ ☐ ■

No. 20 SONS OF GWALIA 508 mm : 1'8"
(Near Kalgoorlie, WA) ◪ ☐

No. 21 SEMAPHORE NARROW 457 mm : 1'6"
(Port Adelaide, SA) ☐ ■

No. 22 BEACH NARROW 381 mm : 1'3"
(Bush Mill, TAS/Bronte NSW) ◪ ☐ ■

LEGEND
◪ in use 19th century
☐ in use 20th century
■ in use 21st century

SCALE 1:10

Top left: Albury Station, Locomotive 3830

© *Tim Fischer* 2003

Top right: Walhalla Goldfields Railway

The gauges listed above reflect measurement of inside rail to inside rail and arise from railways which have operated or are operating 1 mile or more
(1.6 kiolmetres or more) in Australia since 1831 when Australian Agricultural Company built Australia's first railway in Newcastle, NSW to export coal.
Only Anglo Cape Narrow operates in all States, Stephenson Standard operates in all mainland States, and to Darwin with Freightlink and The Ghan in 2004.

Commonwealth Railways (CR) steam locomotive was developed with the capacity to switch gauges. However, this was not easily done: it involved major restructure of pistons, linkages and wheels, even if the firebox and boiler sitting above the bogies did not have to be altered.)

In all of this, chief mechanical engineers had to decide upon and impose the right basic specifications for their railways. Decades ago, one engineer wrote down a '3' instead of a '4', and this resulted in a 3 ft 8½ in gauge railway being built near Wollongong, New South Wales. It operated for over eight decades along a small colliery network of about 80 kilometres (50 miles). The oddity of this network meant that yet another different size steam locomotive had to be built.

In part, the 'break of gauge' fiasco was a matter of poor timing. If the railways had arrived in Australia a few decades earlier than when they did in the 1850s, the Colonial Secretary, Earl Grey, might well have ruled absolutely that a continent as large as Australia should have just one railway gauge. Or, had they not arrived until a few decades later, around the time of Federation, the chances are that just one gauge would also have applied. Unfortunately, the railways arrived in earnest at a time when the colonies were gaining more formal separate status. The various 'gold rushes', with the jealously guarded uplift for a colony's economy and population that inevitably followed, combined with an unfortunate lack of communication, resulted in the agony of the 'break of gauge' phenomenon, which led to some 22 gauges being developed in Australia, some five of these operating significant distances to this day.

⩔ Locomotive P458 and train at Wollongong, 1900. Coastal terrain made it difficult to provide fast services north and south of Sydney.

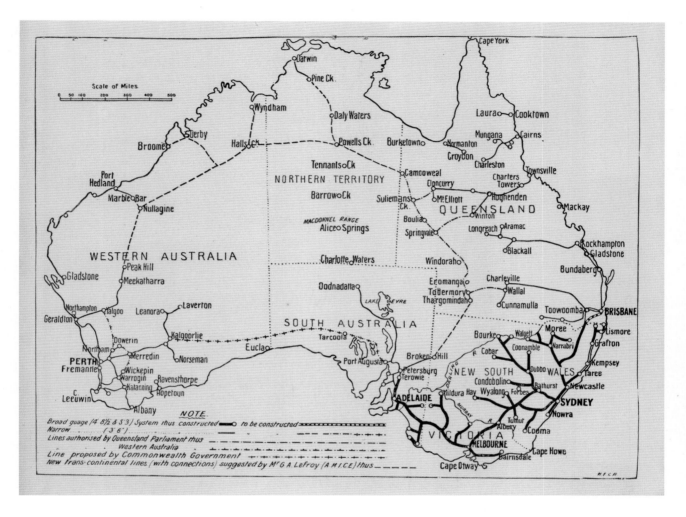

This 1911 collector's map points to a bizarre attempt to bring the colonial railway systems together.

Level terrain between Geelong and Melbourne led to reasonably fast services.

South Australian steam trains operated over long distances of all three main gauges: Irish broad, Stephenson standard and Anglo Cape narrow.

With the advantage of hindsight, it is of course obvious that just two gauges, and so two sizes of locomotives, should have been developed: standard gauge and 1-metre narrow gauge. This would have greatly added to efficiency and productivity.

There were two big factors driving the emergence of the 'break of gauge' saga in Australia: the biggest and most destructive factor was the split between New South Wales and Victoria; the other was the argument mounted by the large thinly populated mainland states — notably Queensland, South Australia and Western Australia — that they could not afford the extra costs associated with the larger standard gauge. Queensland, South Australia and Western Australia all opted for Anglo Cape gauge of 3 ft 6 in (1,067 mm) — in one sense, this was a trailblazing decision, but ultimately it simply created a nationwide headache.

In the mid-nineteenth century, Victoria took advantage of Westminster's support for its breaking out from the original colony of New South Wales, and the legislation authorising its creation as a separate colony was signed by Queen Victoria on 5 August 1850. New South Wales then passed enabling legislation, and on 1 July 1851 Victoria officially came into being.

Almost concurrently, gold was discovered lying on top of the ground and along creek banks within four days' walk from Melbourne, and so Melbourne and the colony of Victoria took off.

The success of the early Liverpool and Manchester Railway was already well known, it had been operating as a profitable trailblazing success for two decades. And in Victoria there was an urgent need for a railway that would run from the main shipping wharves on Port Phillip Bay via Sandridge into the centre of Melbourne. Driven by the Victorian gold rush, the Yarra River wharves had quickly become congested as freight and passenger volumes greatly expanded. And there was a pressing need to connect Melbourne directly to the gold-mining centres of Ballarat and Bendigo, and later to other parts of north-eastern Victoria.

EUROPE: MAINLY ONE DOMINANT GAUGE

You might think that, with centuries of conflicts and jealousies behind it, Europe would have at least 20 rail gauges, but this was not to be. In fact, Stephenson standard gauge dominated on the continent, followed by Iberian broad gauge (1,668 mm, or 5 ft 5⅔ in) in Spain and Portugal, and Czar broad gauge (1,524 mm, or 5 ft) in the European section of Russia, with one track of this Russian gauge also operating into Poland.

Holland, France, Great Britain and China all managed to develop just one main gauge (namely, Stephenson standard gauge), yet maddeningly this was not to be the case for Australia. Today you can travel by train from Brussels, sweep around Paris on the express TGV line to Lyon, then proceed to Geneva, Zurich and Vienna. After this, you can make an easy run over the Brenner Pass to Rome (Vienna to the Vatican). Even though these five countries have fought each other in various fierce wars since the

>> The promotion of rail was always very creative, as is evident in this 1927 poster for the *North Star*.

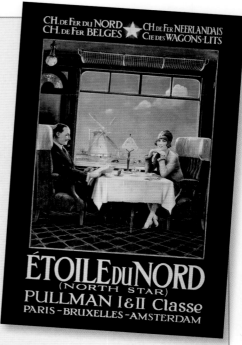

advent of rail, this whole journey across much of Continental Europe can be completed on the same standard-gauge set of networks.

The ugly truth is that, in regard to this aspect of its history, Australia has experienced more jealousies, petty differences and squabbles than have the grand nation states of Europe. And in some ways, this continues to this day.

In 1848 Colonial Secretary Earl Grey had written to New South Wales Governor Charles Fitzroy advising that Stephenson standard gauge should be adopted in Australia – as it had been in Britain following the recommendations of a Royal Commission in 1845; the commission also recommended that Ireland stay with its Irish broad gauge (5 ft 3 in, or 1,600 mm). The Great Western Railway (GWR) gauge of 7 ft ¼ in, created by Isambard Kingdom Brunel, was to be switched to standard gauge. (This was finally completed with a big burst of activity one famous weekend in 1892. The line from London's Paddington Station to Penzance in Cornwall was no longer Brunel broad gauge, but standard gauge throughout, with no longer any need to change trains at GWR network boundary stations such as Gloucester.)

In Australia, the privately owned Sydney Railway Company (set up in 1846) had employed an Irish construction engineer named Francis Webb Sheilds. Sheilds, who is alleged to have had a drinking problem, dallied with the idea of adopting the Iberian or Indian broad gauges (around 5 ft 6 in, or 1,676 mm), but eventually settled on Irish broad gauge. However, in 1850, for whatever reason, Sheilds departed the Sydney Railway Company. His replacement was James Wallace, an engineer of Scottish background who had worked with Robert Stephenson before migrating from Scotland to Sydney, and he understandably favoured standard gauge outright. Wallace persuaded the New South Wales Government to switch gauge from Irish broad to Stephenson standard. This

⩔ The first Australian railway was a turning point that called forth many works of art.

having been agreed, a note went to the new government in Victoria advising it of the switch.

In Melbourne, this switch was considered by the embryonic railway companies and by the Victorian Government who determined that, having walked away from standard gauge once they would not now revert. And so the first orders went off to Newcastle upon Tyne for four new steam locomotives, affirmed to be built in broad gauge. The damage was done, and in that moment the split over gauges was locked in between the two colonies.

Arguably, this crucial 'break of gauge' at Albury, Oaklands and Tocumwal in the Riverina held back efficiency and productivity with economic development, affecting not just the region but Australia more generally. This has proved especially so in time of war when large shipments of personnel and freight, as well as munitions, needed to be hauled; Oaklands, for example, had a huge multi-gauge military storage depot that could handle trains direct from Sydney and Melbourne. (Interestingly, the interstate Benalla–Oaklands branch line was switched from broad gauge to standard gauge, in one move, in the first decade of the twenty-first century, and today is a busy line conveying grain from the Riverina to the ports of Geelong and Melbourne, crossing the Murray River border at Yarrawonga/Mulwala.)

In 1909 Lord Kitchener visited Australia to inspect the state of defence preparedness of the young Commonwealth and advise on the best means of providing it with an adequate land defence. As part of this task, he reported on the nation's railways, noting that they were clearly better designed to help enemy invasion than to shore up Australia's defences.

Many decades later, the huge lingering cost of the New South Wales/Victoria 'break of gauge' continues having spilled over for good measure into South Australia, which has ended up with large distances of all three of the most popular gauges. To this day that state has hundreds of kilometres of broad, standard and narrow gauge track. In places such as Peterborough, railway points handling the three gauges were constructed at extra expense.

⌃ 'Break of gauge' created many headaches: locomotive No. 2517 at the dual-gauge turntable at Oaklands in the Riverina.

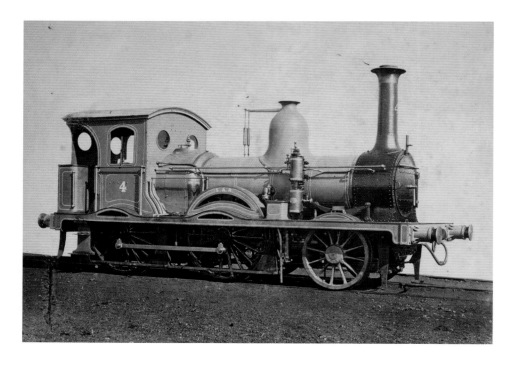

« The first locomotive manufactured at the Government Railway Workshops, Adelaide, 1875. Somehow copyright and intellectual property rights were overcome to allow for the rapid construction of steam locomotives around the world.

» Bridges and great viaducts, such as the Sleeps Hill viaduct in the Adelaide Hills were always eye-catching features.

In 1836 South Australia had been proclaimed as a free colony (that is, one without convicts). Population numbers increased, and the Parliament of South Australia was created in 1857, but the railway only came slowly — and in three gauges almost from its inception. (One unintended bonus arising from this has been the creation of the world's best multi-gauge railway museum, the National Railway Museum at Port Adelaide.)

Initially, South Australia faced the difficulties of building east through Belair and the Adelaide Hills past Mount Lofty towards Victoria. Perhaps it should not have proved so difficult: after all, this region is only about one third of the height of the Semmering Pass in Austria or the Brenner Pass between Austria and Italy. As early as 1854, the mighty Semmering Pass had been conquered by a brilliantly engineered double-track railway. By contrast, South Australia devised an awful pathway over the Adelaide Hills with many steep grades, and it took decades to complete.

Queensland started out as a penal colony under the activities of the exceptional explorer John Oxley, and in due course it had its own mini-gold rush. A petition to break away from New South Wales was lodged in 1851, leading to its formal establishment as a separate colony in December 1859. Once again, railways were in great demand, but mainly east–west ones designed to enable access from the big ports of Cairns, Townsville, Rockhampton and Brisbane into their productive hinterlands.

Little thought and planning was given to the 'national' dimension and indeed there were difficult border ranges to conquer on the NSW–Queensland border south of Brisbane, adding to the isolation factor and special interdependent status of Queensland. One of the last rail connections to be made was Cairns to Brisbane and then Brisbane to Sydney, the latter initially via Wallangarra and Tenterfield and later direct via Beaudesert and Casino.

Abraham Fitzgibbon, Queensland Railways' first chief mechanical engineer, was convinced the cheaper narrow gauge of Anglo Cape was the way to go as it allowed for sharper curves and lighter construction because narrow gauge hugs the ground and closely follows the terrain. Brisbane agreed, and so the north–south 'break of gauge' was launched with the building of the first line, from Ipswich to Grandchester.

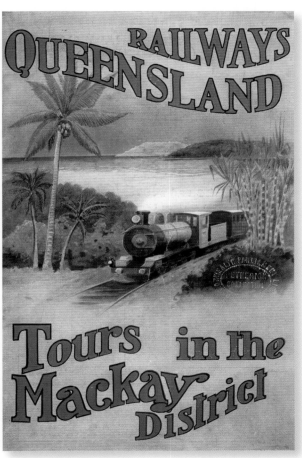

≫ The promotion of rail often included a regional focus.

≫ The giant Railway Workshops in Ipswich have been preserved as the renowned Queensland Workshops Rail Museum.

This choice, in turn, led to a series of narrow-gauge steam locomotives being built, many of them at North Ipswich Railway Workshops, which has today been converted into a magnificent set of galleries as the Queensland Workshops Rail Museum. This is arguably the best narrow-gauge railway museum in the world. Narrow gauge did not, however, preclude quite large and heavy steam engines being built and operated, including superb Garratt articulated engines designed to help pull loads over the Great Dividing Range.

But as we look back in hindsight, was the decision to go with a set of narrow-gauge main lines in Queensland correct? While it is not without merit, the narrow-gauge system today limits productivity and connectivity; for example, in Queensland coal trains 'max out' at around 12,000 tonnes, but on standard-gauge lines trains can easily be operated at twice this capacity. In the Pilbara region of Western Australia, the iron ore trains operate at around 32,000 tonnes carrying capacity — and as a 'one off' at the turn of the millennium they operated at as much as 99,000 tonnes.

In the west, the same thinking held sway, and so the Western Australian Government network was built at Anglo Cape narrow gauge. It was private enterprise that, with the support of the dynamic minister for industrial development (and later premier) Sir Charles Court, saw the introduction in the 1960s of standard gauge for the heavy iron ore haulage in the Pilbara, where trains had to travel around 200 kilometres from the big open-cut mines down to Port Hedland, Dampier and other places on the coast. This remains an independent network to the Western Australian Government Railways (WAGR) system, which operated mainly in the south of the state, around Perth and its hinterland (now known as Transwa for passenger services).

The massive Pilbara system has had huge diesel-electric locomotives from its inception but do not make the mistake of assuming there has never been a major steam locomotive in the Pilbara: for a few

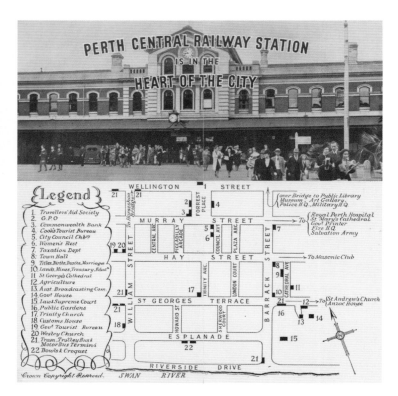

years a group of dedicated volunteers had the renowned *Pendennis Castle* locomotive from Great Britain operating on the Mount Tom Price or Rio Tinto system. Today this system is developing driverless trains where the huge iron-ore trains are controlled from headquarters in Perth.

South Australia had a huge mixture of gauges. At Federation in 1901 the proposal had been mooted to name the whole central area of the country, essentially from Adelaide right up to and including Darwin, the 'State of Albert', but instead the part from Alice Springs to Darwin became the Northern Territory under direct Canberra rule. Anglo Cape gauge was used from Port Augusta to Marree, and on to Alice Springs, until this was replaced in 1981 with the Stephenson standard-gauge link from Tarcoola to Alice Springs.

Likewise, Anglo Cape narrow gauge was used between the Port of Darwin and Adelaide River, and for the Katherine railway, the legislation for which — the *Palmerston and Pine Creek Railway Act* — passed in 1883. It officially opened in 1889 and helped the trailblazing Frances Creek iron ore mine. It eventually reached Birdum in 1929; however, it never reached Tennant Creek and Alice Springs, as originally promised — and, thank God for that, as it would have been in the wrong gauge. In 2004 the Stephenson standard-gauge link finally opened for business between Adelaide and Darwin; operated by Freight Link it quickly doubled freight volumes.

⌃ The Pilbara railway networks for hauling iron ore to port demonstrate world's best practice.

≪ Rail arrived just in time in all state capital cities – with space still available for above ground terminals.

51

Tasmania also was a mix of gauges and locomotives. Initially, some Irish broad gauge was built from Western Junction near Launceston through to Deloraine, but sensibly Anglo Cape narrow gauge was adopted for all private mining railways and the government network as well. Robert Gladstone McGowan surveyed some of the north-west main line past Burnie to Wynyard and beyond. A veteran of two world wars, he knew a great deal about getting the surveys done to produce grades of a manageable level.

The Tasmanian Government Railways (TGR) operated from 1871 until 1978, when it became part of the CR. All that was required of the system was a rail gauge and locomotives to match that could haul some coal traffic, regular container traffic from Bridgewater near Hobart to the Port of Devonport, mineral traffic and timber log traffic.

On the west coast of Tasmania there was an Abt railway connecting Queenstown and Strahan. (The Abt rack system — devised by Swiss locomotive engineer Roman Abt (1850–1933) — was just one of many rack-and-pinion or cog railways that were developed to negotiate particularly steep grades. The Abt system remains the most widely used for mountain railways.) Known as the Mount Lyell Mining and Railway Company, it officially opened in 1897 and carried mining produce to port. It ceased operation on 10 August 1963 — and the last train was hauled by the same locomotive that had operated on the very first service. Following a huge

≫ TGR locomotive B7 with a passenger train at Fitzgerald on the Derwent Valley line, 1937. Hobart to Launceston was one rail corridor that could have delivered much more in terms of fast passenger shuttle services.

New Zealand: one railway gauge today

New Zealand almost became a seventh state of Australia, with provision originally made for this in the Australian Constitution. Railways started in New Zealand with multiple gauges: Stephenson standard in the far south; Irish broad out of Christchurch across the Canterbury Plains; and Anglo Cape elsewhere, including the main trunk line on the North Island that ran from Auckland to Wellington.

Sir Julius Vogel (1835–1899), New Zealand's eighth premier, was a strong leader who imposed Anglo Cape as the national gauge. He also abolished the New Zealand provinces in 1876, a move that helped ensure the country had just one railway (and related ferry) system. Today KiwiRail is enjoying a surge in international tourists journeying on trains on both islands, notably with the *TranzAlpine Express* and the *Northern Explorer*. Alongside this, the Federation of Rail Organisations of New Zealand Inc. (FRONZ) is enjoying growing interest in the range of steam heritage train travel on offer, including the Weka Pass Railway near Christchurch to name just one.

Bicentennial grant of $26 million from the Federal Government, a reconstruction of the original railway today operates between Queenstown and Strahan as the West Coast Wilderness Railway with steam tank locomotives. The rack-and-pinion section is quite dramatic and contains some steep grades.

Australia not only developed more railway gauges than any other country in the world, it also had a more diverse set of steam locomotives than any country, to match the many different gauges. Normally, diversity is a good thing, but in Australia's case the sheer range of railway gauges and locomotives ultimately led to a costly set of errors and did nothing for economic efficiency, let alone steam locomotive uniformity.

» Mining ore and harvested grain were the two big staples of the early rail systems.

CHAPTER 3

Well, sir, I take it that your decision is reversed.
SIR JOHN MONASH

GOLD, COAL, WOOL AND WHEAT

⌃ Massive amounts of earth were moved to ease rail gradients, as with this railway tunnel through 'the big hill' near Mount Herbert, 1875.

⟪⟪ Steam locomotives coaling in Newcastle, 1930s. Coal from Newcastle was the nation's first bulk export to the world.

So far as rail development was concerned, it greatly helped that the discovery of gold was both well inland from the coast and in large quantities. As a result, decades of mining generated a great demand for improved transportation.

It was also serendipitous that the main early finds took place just as railway development was unfolding, both in Australia and around the world, when the steam locomotive was gaining acceptance. The first high-standard main line built in Victoria was the 164 kilometres uphill broad-gauge double track to Bendigo. Many bluestone bridges were quickly designed and built. Two tunnels were also quickly completed between Woodend and Bendigo, one near Elphinstone and another at Big Hill. Just six years after the Victorian Government had taken over the project, the Melbourne–Bendigo railway was open for brisk business in October 1862.

Given the fact the Elphinstone tunnel was 385 metres long and the Big Hill tunnel was 390 metres long, it can be seen that the building of this railway was a herculean effort, putting to shame more recent efforts which very often involve very slow construction, no tunnels and big budget over-runs.

Furthermore, local politicians and community heavyweights demanded that Clarkefield and Castlemaine be on the main through route. Hence this main line swerves to the right, or sharply north, to Clarkefield before swerving to the left towards Castlemaine, away from the direct route taken by today's freeway. To this day, this adds about half an hour to every train journey between Melbourne and Bendigo. When a big upgrade project unfolded around the turn of the millennium, these distance-adding swerves were sadly exactly maintained. Also,

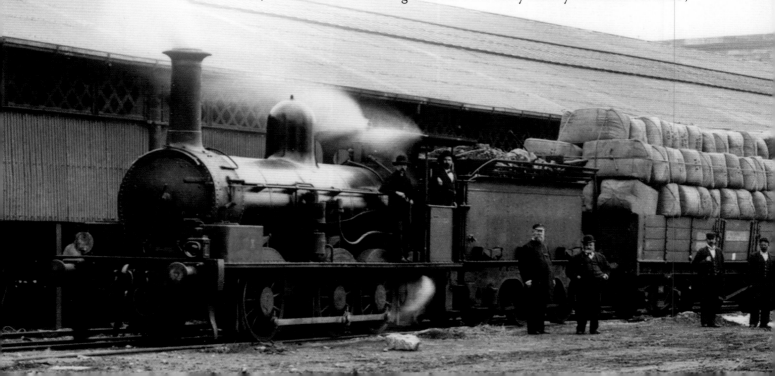

in an absurd move which is now greatly regretted, much of the main line was reduced to single track.

Bendigo passenger and freight trains were very popular and offered from inception a reasonably pleasant three- to four-hour journey between the two fast growing centres. Gold was underpinning the growth of Bendigo as a local hub, and a dignified city of substance with a big rail junction and steam locomotive depot quickly emerged.

Gold, not coal, had driven the construction of rail to, and through, Bendigo, but interstate jealousies and the rapidly expanding wool industry meant that Victoria was racing to build a railway onwards to the Murray River. While there were many branch lines, the most important was the one built through Elmore straight up to the Port of Echuca on the Murray.

During the first half of the nineteenth century, wool was Australia's biggest export industry, but it was one beset by problems associated with transporting heavy wool bales from far inland to the seaboard for export. The rapid spread of

⌃ For decades, good old semaphore signals successfully controlled much rail transport.

⌞ Darling Harbour, late nineteenth century. The revamping of old rail hubs continues all over Australia, especially close to CBDs.

merino sheep across all states meant that each year the bales of wool had to be transported to the selling centres and the ports. This trade drove the railway due west from Brisbane all the way to Quilpie, and due west from Sydney all the way to Orange and later Broken Hill and north-west to Bourke.

Down south, paddle steamers had found it easier to take the big wool cargoes down to Goolwa in South Australia, and then across to the big selling centre in Adelaide. The Darling and Murray rivers became major commerce corridors, favouring South Australia to the disadvantage of both Victoria and New South Wales. Intercepting the Murray River with efficient steam haul rail at a point only a half day's journey from Melbourne made strategic sense and actually reversed the

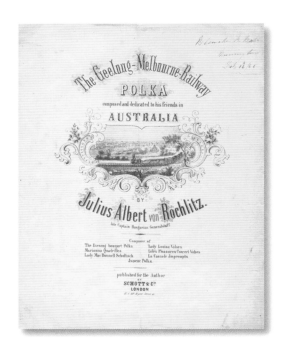

flow of wool produce from the big stations along the Murray between Echuca and Mildura. After the rail connection was made in 1864 to the Port of Echuca — in fact, right alongside the river at the huge red gum wharf — wool that always used to go downstream was suddenly able to be conveyed by paddle steamer upstream to Echuca, and so found its way into the huge wool stores in Melbourne the very next day. Interestingly, today both daily passenger and freight trains ply this route between Melbourne and Echuca, with an alternative rail route (via Seymour) that opened up later still in operation for freight trains today.

The triangle of Melbourne, Geelong and Ballarat was soon fully connected by rail: there was double track from Geelong to Ballarat, but crazily only single track from Ballarat direct to Melbourne via Bacchus Marsh. In turn, from this triangle the rail went west to service the rich wool-growing area of the Western Districts.

AMIENS BRANCH LINE — NOT FRANCE BUT QUEENSLAND

Sometimes special factors arose that led to the building of country tramlines and short branch lines. This was the case with the Pikedale Soldier Settlement, a development of small fruit farms, north by north-west from Stanthorpe, set up immediately after the First World War. An efficient link was needed to transport the fresh fruit to market quickly and without bruising.

In 1921 the Prince of Wales (later Edward VIII) opened the Amiens branch line; it took off from the main line just south of Warwick and ran for more than 16 kilometres through a series of stations – Fleurbaix, Pozières, Bullecourt, Passchendaele, Bapaume, Messines – to reach a small terminus at Amiens. After some debate, the locals and the authorities had agreed on this group of names, inspired by famous Western Front battles in which the AIF had fought as it helped to deliver victory to the allies. Within a couple of years, annual traffic of over 10,000 tonnes of fruit was despatched along the Anglo Cape narrow-gauge line with the wagons hauled by light steam locomotives.

It was another 'steam only' branch line. After a short trial with an evil petrol engine tractor –

» A bank of signs at the Stanthorpe Museum: surreal in any setting, albeit one far from the Western Front.

soon found wanting – the line reverted to steam locomotives, which were used until its closure in 1974. It was a different kind of line in many ways: apart from having stations and sidings named after battles in France and Belgium, it only operated on Sundays during its last ten years of operation.

Today the Southern Downs Steam Railway provides an excellent rail experience through the area using the few key railway lines that are still open. It traverses the same tracks that the Amiens traffic used en route to Warwick and Brisbane, the same tracks that Prime Minister Billy Hughes, Sir John Monash and many other famous people used to make interstate connections in the early years of steam train operation.

The Victorian pattern of branch lines was neat and strategic. At one point, there were eight branch lines running parallel north-west to south-east towards Melbourne and Geelong, covering the Mallee and Wimmera wheat-growing areas. Many branch lines were built to quaint places, such as Yanac, Carpolac, Casterton and Coleraine. All were serviced by steam-hauled trains for decades. Indeed, some of the early branch lines, which closed after just a few years' operation, only ever saw steam-hauled trains.

⌃ Coal was an early starter in the economy of both New South Wales and Queensland.

» Crane at Port Waratah, Newcastle. Over the years, various methods have been used for emptying wagons, including tipping them through 360 degrees.

With the arrival of Federation in 1901, and the improvements made to wheat varieties around that time by key scientists such as William Farrer, there was a big leap forward in wheat production across the boundless plains of most Australian states, especially in those parts where annual rainfall was adequate. This happened before the mass production of motor trucks, so rail branch lines were placed in such a manner that every wheat farmer was no more than a day's round-trip horse-drawn wagon haul from the grain silos at their nearest railway.

At the zenith of the rail networks, there were no fewer than eight branch lines and two regional lines covering the Riverina between the Murrumbidgee and Murray rivers of the New South Wales Government Railways (NSWGR) system and two Victorian Railways (VR) lines that had crossed the border at Echuca, to Deniliquin and to Balranald via Moulamein. Today there are just two surviving branch lines, Rock–Boree Creek and Echuca–Deniliquin, plus the Junee–Narrandera regional line.

Wheat and wool drove branch-line construction for decades after the initial flourish of the gold rush. Conversely, coal was first discovered in large quantities at Newcastle, near the mouth of the Hunter River, about 1797. Australia's very first railway was built by the Australian Agricultural Company to bring coal down to the wharfs from the pits that had been developed on the nearby hills, not far from where Newcastle's Anglican Cathedral is located today. Founded by a British Act of Parliament in 1824, AA Co is one of Australia's oldest still-operating companies. The line officially opened in 1831. The pitheads were a good deal higher than the wharf structure with its elevated railway, so the coal-laden wagons rolled down the track across Hunter Street and onto the wharf. Two horses were carried in the last wagon: once the train had been unloaded, these horses would be hitched up to drag the train back to the coal pits for reloading.

⩗ Australia's first steamer, the *Sophia Jane*, seen here in Charles Dickson Gregory's c. 1920 painting, conveyed the first coal exports from Newcastle to India.

Horsepower and gravity it was, then, and this was even used in late 1831 to fill the *Sophia Jane* ship with the first significant export load of coal from Australia, bound from Newcastle to India.

The good-quality black steaming coal found around Cessnock, Maitland and Newcastle had a strong domestic market for producing steam to heat large buildings, but above all else this coal was used to power the ever-growing number of steam locomotives being imported or built locally to operate rail in every Australian colony.

≪ Wheat bags were
often attacked by
mice, so the switch
to bulk storage was
accomplished quickly.

≫ 'Running wrong
side', as they say, but
maximising efficiency
in the rail systems of
the Pilbara.

The export figures point to the importance of gold, coal, wool and wheat to the early economic growth in the various colonies before Federation. Initially, it was wool that led the way, then the gold discoveries led to swift and dramatic changes; later came the big expansion in wheat, and finally the millions of tonnes of coal exported annually.

In 1938, just before the Second World War, the Federal Government imposed a total iron ore export ban, largely in response to public fears arising from Japan's full-scale invasion of China the previous year. In 1960 the ban was lifted, and so the Pilbara region of Western Australia saw rapid expansion of huge open-cut iron ore mines, initially by Broken Hill Proprietary (BHP) and Conzinc Riotinto of Australia Ltd (CRA), building on the exploratory work of Lang Hancock. During the decade that followed, Charles Court, Minister for Industrial Development, Railways and the North-West, who went on to become a very successful premier of the state, finessed the building by private enterprise of all the iron ore rail lines in standard gauge. An old Western Australian Government Railways (WAGR) branch line in the Pilbara, that from Marble Bar to Port Hedland, ran in the wrong location and with the wrong gauge (Anglo Cape), so did not play any part as an exemplar.

Because it was planned from the start as heavy haulage modern railways with diesel-electric locomotive haulage, huge iron ore trains were operated, today at around 32,000 tonnes. It was so well engineered that at the start of the millennium a 'one off' train operated by BHP created a world record at 99,000 tonnes, from Mount Newman to the coast.

Coming much later, none of the Pilbara iron ore effort had anything to do with the story of steam locomotives in Australia. However, the development of gold, coal, wool and wheat over time left decisive footprints on the layout of all networks in Australia beyond the capital cities, and it was the steam locomotive that had handled the transportation of these goods for the first 100 years. What was the main source of energy for the rapidly expanding fleets of steam locomotives that operated in all six colonies? There were some wood-burners, and later a few oil-burners, but the dominant energy source came from using high-quality black coal to produce the steam needed to drive the great engines.

In New South Wales coal had first been found just to the south of Botany Bay in the 1790s, then later at Newcastle around 1800. Queensland was lucky to find coal at Ipswich, near Brisbane, in June 1827, and later massive deposits were found on the Darling Downs (by the explorer Ludwig Leichhardt in October 1844) and in the Bowen Basin. As for Victoria, that state struggled to find black coal in sufficient quantity. A few deposits were located around Gippsland, and a Royal Commission in 1906 was set up to find ways to expand coal production. Things stalled somewhat with the intervention of the First World War. But afterwards things got moving again, driven in part by the need to find an energy source to help generate electricity for domestic consumption. In 1920, Sir John Monash, who had led the Australians to victory on the Western Front, was appointed head of the new State Electricity Commission (SEC).

Monash was both a brilliant engineer and army general who was discriminated against. Why did this happen? In part, because he was Jewish and also a reservist, not a graduate of Duntroon or Sandhurst. As a result, he was jammed at the rank

⩔ Both in the 1880s and today, Wollongong has run always second to Newcastle when it came to coal exports.

of lieutenant general from November 1918 until November 1929. However, he did not allow this snub to interfere with his brilliantly creative work. He threw himself into developing brown coal deposits at Yallourn in Gippsland, alongside of which he built large power stations to use the coal. In turn, he developed large transmission lines to carry the electricity due west to Melbourne.

Monash was clearly the right man for the job. In London in 1919 Monash had been given responsibility for overseeing the demobilisation and repatriation of the Australian troops, and Prime Minister Hughes would not allow him to come home until Boxing Day that year. So Monash authorised a crew to make a quick visit to the coalfields of defeated Germany to study methods used to harness the more difficult types of coal, such as brown coal with heavy water content.

Halfway through the construction phase at Yallourn, Monash realised that the scale of the project was not large enough and that there needed to be a big expansion not just in the capacity of the mine but also of the power stations themselves and of the conveyer belts that led to them. His revision was readily accepted, and indeed it proved to be the right call.

Then in 1928 Monash tackled head-on a Victorian Cabinet decision knocking back the request for an additional £1 million. He went straight to Parliament House and to State Cabinet; Premier Sir William McPherson allowed him in, and everyone stood – and remained standing – while Monash made what then state Attorney-General Robert Menzies described as a strong presentation. At the end of the discussion Monash said, 'Well, sir, I take it that your decision is reversed.' All agreed, and with that Monash produced the necessary Order-in-Council document, already drafted. It was immediately signed by the premier. This huge source of reasonably good-burning brown coal underpinned Victoria's industrial growth.

South Australia was less lucky in the early years, with useful quantities of copper found at Kapunda, but no coal. After the Second World War, Leigh Creek was drilled and developed as a huge open-cut coal mine requiring its own railway in standard gauge down to the power station at the top of the gulf near Port Augusta.

In Western Australia coal finds were made near Collie, 200 kilometres south of Perth and 60 kilometres inland from Bunbury. For its part, Tasmania had adequate coal near St Marys, on its north-east coast, which is still being mined today. Even the Northern Territory had some luck, but it was a deadly business, especially for those mining underground.

⌄ The TAM sleeping carriages were comfortable enough, and the great John Monash was not too crushed on arriving in Sydney from Melbourne in 1929.

« The Victorian State Electricity Commission, led by Sir John Monash, created a massive set of brown coal projects in Gippsland, as evidenced by this Frank Hurley photograph of a ditch bunker at Yallourn Open Cut transferring coal from trains to conveyors, which deliver it to the Yallourn briquette factory, 1947.

In 1908, as railways reached their zenith in terms of distances covered and density of operation, some 20,000 Australians were employed in mining coal, everywhere except South Australia. In that year, some 26 were killed in mining accidents, mainly underground.

New South Wales dominated coal production, and many an old steam train driver would say the best steaming coal was the black coal sourced from around Newcastle and the Hunter Valley. Coal production in 1908 across Australia was valued at £3,762,914, but the state-by-state figures from the Bureau of Statistics show the degree to which New South Wales dominated (see Table 1, below).

⌄ Loading coal bound for Japan, Port Kembla, c. 1970. Care had to be taken with bulk shipments of coal and wood chips to protect against the risk of explosive fires.

TABLE 1: COAL PRODUCTION ACROSS AUSTRALIA, 1908

1908 COAL PRODUCTION (IN TONS)	
NSW	9,147,025
QLD	696,332
WA	175,248
VIC	113,962
TAS	61,068
SA	0
TOTAL	10,193,635

TRANSCONTINENTAL:
RIGHT GAUGE, RIGHT TIMING

October 1917 saw the Transcontinental Railway open for business, but for the first few decades it stood alone without any seamless connection, owing to the bold decision to build the 'Trans' in Stephenson standard gauge. If travelling from Melbourne to Perth, you had to change trains at Adelaide, owing to South Australian Railways (SAR) policy and a dead-end grand station, then due to the 'break of gauge' you had to change at Terowie, Port Augusta and Kalgoorlie.

Eventually, the 'break of gauge' muddle was sorted out, and today freight trains can travel right through, from Melbourne to Perth and from Sydney to Perth, on standard gauge. The *Indian Pacific* luxury train operated by Great Southern Rail conveys passengers from Sydney via Adelaide to Perth and return.

So wise was the placement of the east-west Transcontinental that it provided a flood-free 'take off' point at Tarcoola for the standard-gauge south-north Transcontinental line to Alice Springs (and, since 2004, to Darwin).

On special occasions, steam trains, including the *Flying Scotsman*, have operated east-west across the desert – although not this century, and in any event never to Darwin on the new through line.

On weekends, freight traffic from Adelaide to both Perth and Darwin is very heavy, and some five operators pay the Australian Rail Track Corporation (ARTC) so that their super freighters can use the Transcontinental; in the main these long double-stacked container trains are efficient and profitable high-yielding units.

⌃ Crossing the Nullarbor, 1954. The Transcontinental Railway was a nation-building endeavour, and by the 1950s had been greatly upgraded since its opening in 1917.

⌃ For decades Port Pirie, South Australia, operated with all three main rail gauges.

» Unloading coal, Sydney, 1953. For decades, until the diesel engine emerged supreme, ships used coal as a primary energy source.

Initially, to allow steam locomotives to operate in South Australia, coal was imported from New South Wales and Victoria. But in 1917, when the Transcontinental Railway opened from Kalgoorlie to Port Augusta, Western Australian coal was used in South Australia, though mainly for use on the trains operating the Transcontinental line.

Coal has been described as black gold. It has certainly proved a valuable asset over the decades, especially for the valuable export dollars it earns. Today Newcastle is the largest coal export port in the world, with in excess of 150 million tonnes per year delivered down the Hunter Valley ARTC network. So busy is this network that large sections of it are triple track, and the last section, from Maitland eastward through Hexham to the port loop turnoffs, is quadruple track. The two southern tracks are reserved exclusively for coal trains, with more loops being built at Hexham to allow for a reshuffle of the trains so that they can approach the big unloaders in the correct order to match the shipping program.

All in all, the extent of rail development, and therefore the size of steam locomotive fleets, was greatly enhanced by the discovery in large quantities of gold, coal and other mining products, together with the advent of the great inland wool and wheat industries. For a while after white settlement in 1788 Australia, on its coastal fringe at least, remained a cottage economy serviced by the odd clipper and later steamship, producing just enough to be self-sustaining. Had things stayed like this, then the railway would never have taken off 'down under'. Instead, Australia became a great trading nation, based in large measure on a pastoral economy, in which valuable exports playing a huge role from 1800 to the present day; accordingly, various modes of land transport, notably road and rail, had to be created. (As the world's driest continent, Australia was never well-suited to the barge traffic and canal networks that played such an important role in Britain and elsewhere.)

While rail has waxed and waned over the decades, with massive competition, in particular from road, it is here to stay and in the twenty-first century it is in many ways a case of 'Trains Unlimited'. Alas, the number of operational steam locomotives that function as part of this equation today is limited mainly to various profitable tourist heritage operations, such as the Puffing Billy near Melbourne.

⌄ Loading wheat, Henty, New South Wales, c. 1965. While it might look efficient, the slow speed of loading grain often delayed trains for hours.

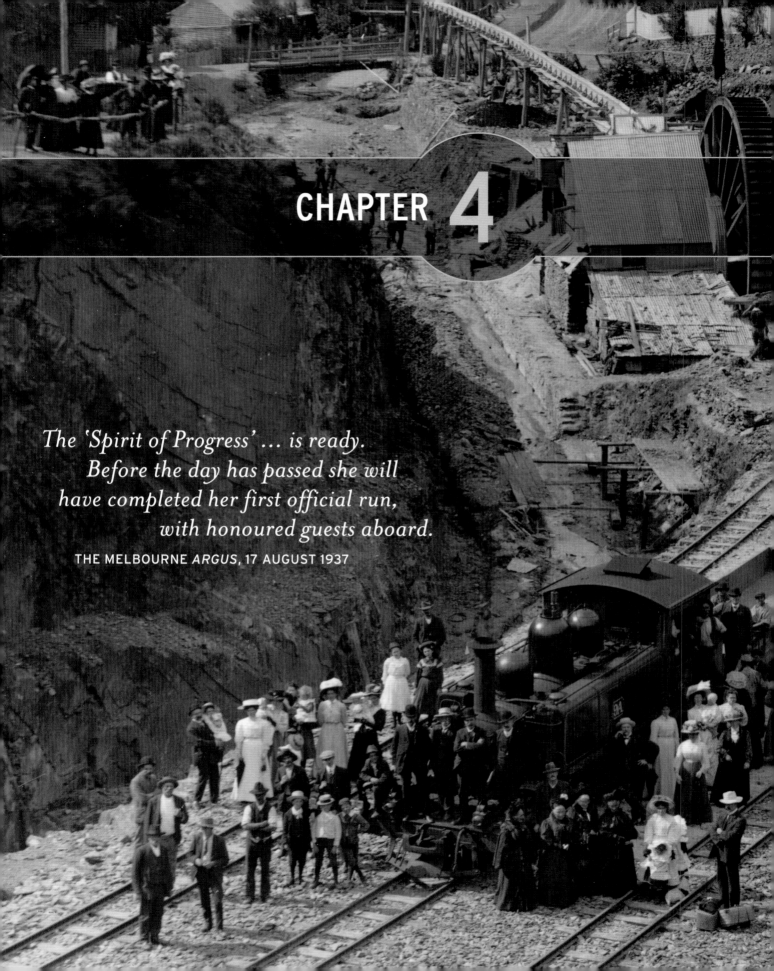

CHAPTER 4

The 'Spirit of Progress' … is ready.
Before the day has passed she will
have completed her first official run,
with honoured guests aboard.

THE MELBOURNE *ARGUS*, 17 AUGUST 1937

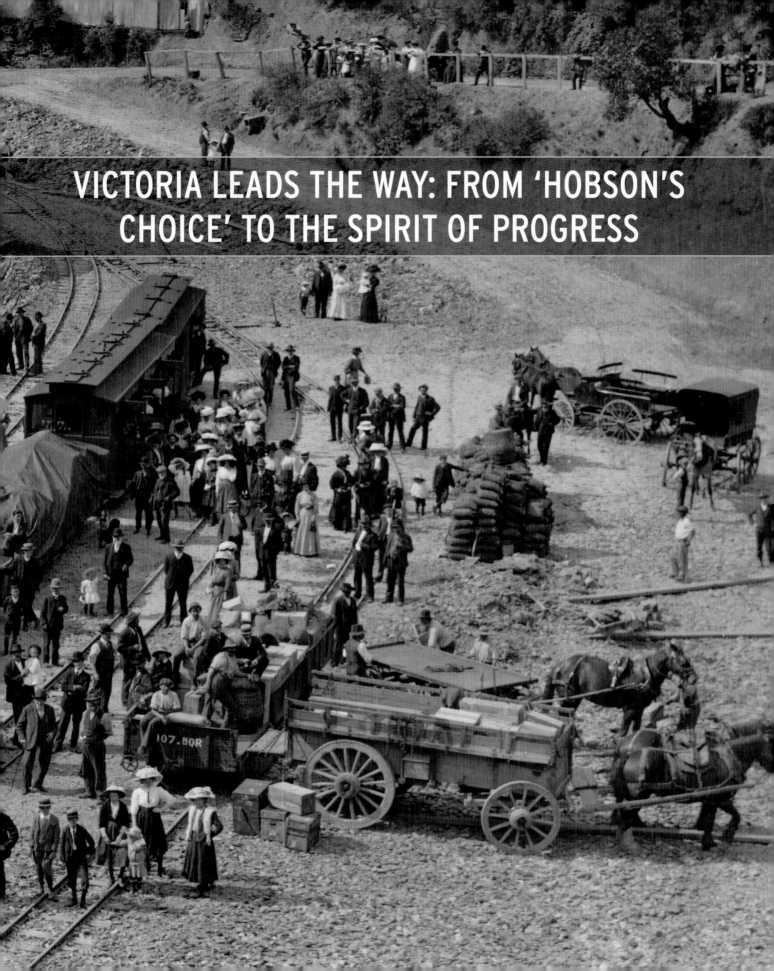

VICTORIA LEADS THE WAY: FROM 'HOBSON'S CHOICE' TO THE SPIRIT OF PROGRESS

≪≪ VR locomotive No. 9A with the first train from Moe to Walhalla, Victoria, 1910. A small section of this railway is in operation today.

≫ A few minutes before 8 am, it's all systems go for the *Spirit of Progress*, led by locomotive No. S300 *Matthew Flinders*, as it runs down the grade to the Murray River and into Victoria.

≫ Laying the foundation stone for the Geelong and Melbourne Railway, 1853. Every major town sought rail links to the state capital.

'The firing on the *Spirit* was hard and constant, and you need to go about it the right way — light and often, light and often.' This was the wise mantra of Bernie Greene, fireman on the streamlined S Class locomotives that hauled the *Spirit of Progress*, the famous express train that made the 191-mile (307-kilometre) run between Melbourne and Albury. For some, the *Spirit* was known as the 'Commissioner's Train'. In its heyday, it was one of the best trains in the world.

Fireman Bernie Greene was one of the best of the best, and he had the ace of a fireman's jobs, the top of the ladder, with nothing to match it in Australia or the United States. He applied the finely honed skills he had acquired in the RAAF to what many might think of as the dumb task of constant shovelling of coal. As we shall see, however, this task was anything but that.

The Victorian Government Railways (VR) had very humble beginnings. As happened in many places around the world, it was the collapse of a private company charged with building Victoria's first railway that led to setting up the state railway that progressively took over all existing embryonic rail effort in an early form of nationalisation.

In most of the Australian colonies railways had been started by private enterprise companies, such as AA Co in Newcastle and the Melbourne and Hobson's Bay Railway Company, which ran from Flinders Street Railway Station to Sandridge on Port Phillip Bay. However, huge start-up costs and wildly fluctuating economic times, not to mention the 'gold rush' dynamic, made the private enterprise rail company a difficult template to operate successfully. Inevitably, the government of each colony took over the task of railways, and this occurred earlier in some states than others.

In the 1880s the Victorian Government vertically integrated all aspects of rail in Victoria under the Department of Transport. Originally established over two decades earlier, VR by this stage dominated the market, operating as a governmental corporation. It took over all country lines, including the first regional line to Geelong, which had been built by the Geelong and Melbourne Railway Company and opened on 25 June 1857. Even around Melbourne, the initial suburban lines were built by numerous companies. These operated from Flinders Street,

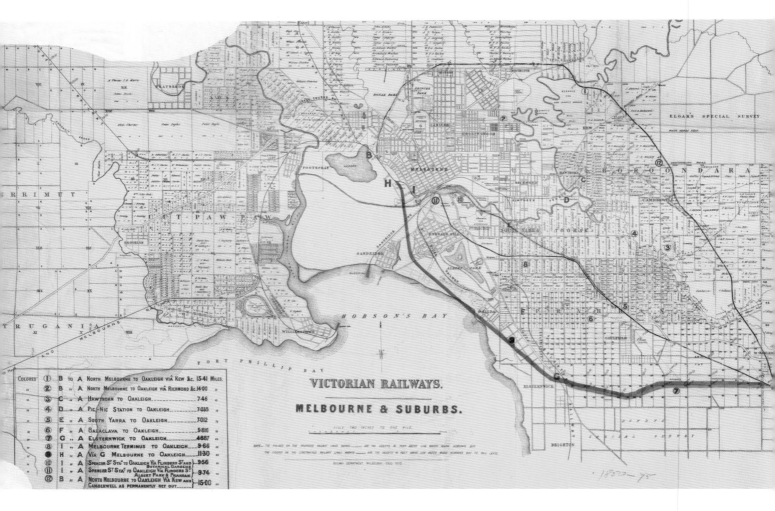

VICTORIAN RAILWAYS.

MELBOURNE & SUBURBS.

⌃ Victorian Railways, *Melbourne & Suburbs*, 1875. Radial hub and spoke dominated the Melbourne suburban system, but alas an outer circle section built by John Monash was ripped up after just ten years of operation.

« Incursions of broad gauge into New South Wales were few, totalling five distinct branch lines, plus Albury (seen here c. 1920) and Tocumwal 'break of gauge' stations just north of the Murray River.

and in 1865 they were amalgamated under one company, the Melbourne and Hobson's Bay United Railway Company, but it too was subsequently taken over by the government (in 1878).

Eventually, in 1883, the first interstate connection was made at Albury when the Victorian and New South Wales networks met, thereby creating the famous 'break of gauge' on the NSW–Victorian border which existed for the next 80 years. The 'break of gauge' was finally eliminated in 1962 when a single-track standard-gauge line was built between Albury and Melbourne, on the eastern side of the broad-gauge track.

The new standard-gauge track led to the extension of the *Spirit of Progress* service through to Sydney, and to the establishment of a new train, the smart-looking *Southern Aurora*. Both trains were hauled by diesel-electric locomotive throughout their years of service between Sydney and Melbourne. However, the 13-hour running time between Australia's biggest two cities meant that, once the Hume Highway was upgraded, it was quicker to drive – and also much quicker and

⌄ Bursts of rail construction in the late nineteenth century boosted local economic activities.

cheaper to fly. By the 1990s this had spelt the death knell for these two famous trains.

In 1887 a seamless link was established at Serviceton on the South Australian–Victorian border which resulted in the same broad gauge operating over the full length of the journey between Melbourne and Adelaide. This allowed for the introduction of the *Intercolonial Express*, which ran overnight between Melbourne and Adelaide – and which was used by Mark Twain on two occasions.

In the 1880s there was a new burst of railway construction in Victoria following the passage through the Victorian State Parliament of the *Railway Construction Act 1884*. This authorised almost 60 new regional railway lines and branch lines, with the notable guiding principle that wheat farmers should not have to cart their grain too far by horse and wagon to the nearest railway siding.

On the steam locomotive front in Victoria, the first four steam locomotives arrived from the Robert Stephenson and Company's huge factory at Newcastle upon Tyne and entered service around 1855. At last, with the introduction of these locomotives, the 'Hobson's Choice' which had trail-blazed passenger train haulage in Australia now had some back-up. Indeed, in the second half of the

Locomotives Nos 3830 and 3813 pulling the first standard-gauge *Spirit of Progress*, 1962. Crews needed a special skill set to coordinate the pulling power of two joined steam locomotives.

'This Curious State of Things':
Mark Twain travels by train down under

By rights, there should be a bronze plaque at the Albury Railway Station to record the occasion when the famous American humorist and author Mark Twain had to change trains there before dawn on 26 September 1895. In his 1897 travel memoir, *Following the Equator: A Journey Around the World*: Twain wrote of this experience:

> *Now comes a singular thing: the oddest thing, the strangest thing, the most baffling and unaccountable marvel that Australasia can show. At the frontier between New South Wales and Victoria our multitude of passengers were routed out of their snug beds by lantern-light in the biting cold of a high altitude to cars on a road that has no break in it from Sydney to Melbourne! Think of the paralysis of intellect that gave that idea birth, imagine the boulder it emerged from on some petrified legislator's shoulders.*

Twain reflected on the cause for 'this curious state of things':

> *One is, that it represents the jealousy between ... the two most important colonies of Australasia. What the other one is, I have forgotten. But it is of no consequence. It could be but another effort to explain the inexplicable.*

In all, Twain undertook 16 train trips in Australia in 1895 as part of his famous lecture tour, but it is this experience that seemed to impress itself more firmly upon his mind.

Australia's 22 railway gauges were a costly madness, to be sure, and defied every bit of common sense − just as Twain rightly observed.

nineteenth century, many more locomotives were imported, not only into Victoria but also into the other railway systems of Australia. Steam locomotion continued to develop, notwithstanding two world wars, and in fact reached its zenith with the massive transport demands created by the Second World War.

In 1854 the Phoenix Foundry had set up at Ballarat as a private enterprise endeavour, and after a few years it found that steam locomotive production was both practicable and profitable. The foundry won a key VR contract in 1871, and within two years it had produced 100 steam locomotives. It made a big bid for the crucial DD Class Steam locomotive, but after a Royal Commission had investigated the tendering process, the company was ruled out in favour of VR's Newport Workshops.

Eventually, there were 260 DD Class locomotives in the VR system, and many regarded the DD Class as the very best that VR operated. At last, there was some uniformity of class and type of steam — in contrast with the three main decades of Phoenix steam locomotive production. From 1873, Phoenix rolled out 352 steam locomotives for VR, but at its direction these 352 involved 38 different types — a costly absurdity.

≈ Phoenix-built S Class locomotive No. 197 and staff on the platform, Ballarat Station, 1885. This rare train shed is still standing today.

Author AE Durrant, who has studied steam locomotive production around the world, favours the 4–4–0 Phoenix steamer produced in the late 1870s. Phoenix had turned out eight of these, following Beyer, Peacock & Co. design from overseas, and they gave good service. It is not exactly clear the extent to which patents were honoured, and intellectual property rights paid for, given the many steam locomotive refinements around the world in the early years, and it is difficult to trace every breach or possible illegal copying of design. Of course, some foundries and steam locomotive works held licensing rights from Robert Stephenson or Beyer, Peacock.

After about five decades in business, the Phoenix Foundry went into liquidation, but it left behind as its legacy nearly 40 different types of locomotives. This was an outcome great for train-spotters, but it hardly made for an effective rail system.

In 1943 the Victorian Railways owned 577 steam locomotives, including the heaviest ever built, H 220 *Heavy Harry*, which entered service in 1941. *Heavy Harry* weighed in at over 260 tonnes and was designed for the Adelaide–Melbourne line, but it worked all over the VR network where axle weight of 23.5-tonne operation was permitted. Today, *Heavy Harry* is stored or preserved at Williamstown; it is not operational but does have heritage orders applying to it. On at least one occasion, it hauled the *Spirit of Progress*, arriving ahead of schedule at Albury.

⌄ Locomotive No. H220 *Heavy Harry* and goods train at Wodonga in 1956. This locomotive still exists today, but is out of service.

» Equipment complexities abounded with the railways from inception. Here a VR employee checks the staff exchanger with a gauge, Sunshine, c. 1950.

⩗ VR locomotive No. 3A hauling potatoes over a trestle bridge near Wright on the Gembrook Line in 1947. Modern road trucks put paid to countless rail freight services.

⌃ VR Locomotive 3A stranded during the infamous 1954 landslide at Upwey, Victoria, the effects of which took years to rectify.

« Signal systems vary enormously, state by state; for example, VR used this three-aspect colour light system.

» Today the *Puffing Billy* in the Dandenong Ranges is the most visited and travelled tourist heritage rail service in Australia.

The locomotive's wheel configuration was 4–8–4, its driving wheels were 67 inches (1,702 millimetres) in diameter, and its overall weight was 150 tonnes, with a tender (weighing an additional 115 tonnes) that could carry 9 tonnes of coal to fire the engine and 64,000 litres of water. The firebox was a huge 16 square metres, and there were three pistons with a stroke of around 2 feet (711 millimetres). Today *Heavy Harry* would make a grand sight steaming into the sunset up the 1-in-48 Ingliston Bank between Sunshine and Ballarat, Unfortunately, for this to happen, massive work would be required on the boiler, and indeed on every other part of Australia's heaviest steam locomotive.

It was of course incredibly stupid to create 22 different rail gauges in Australia, but the various main railway networks were not much better when it came to creating a simplified numbering system. Indeed, there were several stabs made at sorting out a complex system which initially featured odd numbers for steam locomotives hauling freight trains and even numbers for those hauling passenger trains. At one stage in 1866, for example, on the VR register there were 46 passenger steam locomotives numbered '2-92' and 32 freight steam locomotives numbered '1-63'. Around 1880 the VR's Spencer Street rail lines linked up with the Flinders Street suburban railway lines, so it became necessary to revamp the numbering system. Letters were introduced ahead of the triple number. All of this was necessary to avoid duplication of numbers.

⩔ VR locomotive H220 in the erecting shop, Newport Workshops, 1940. The internal components of a steam locomotive were much heavier than diesel locomotives.

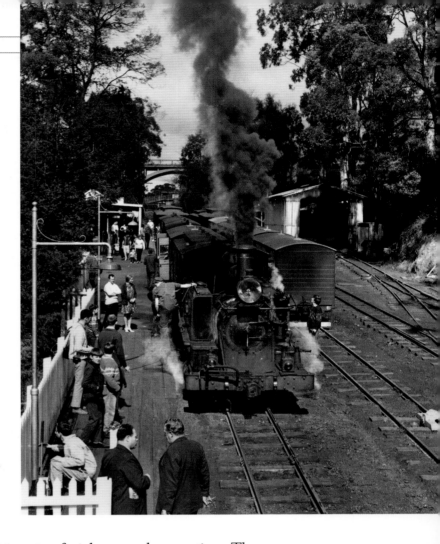

Narrow-gauge steam locomotives were simply numbered consecutively. This was helpful as many of the narrow-gauge trains were mixed passenger and freight trains. Victoria had a small narrow-gauge system operating in the Otways and from Moe to Walhalla in Gippsland. There was also a narrow-gauge line between Wangaratta and Whitfield, and of course there was Puffing Billy in the Dandenongs. All four were built in 2 ft 6 in (762 mm), and occasionally steam locomotives were ferried between the four systems to meet demand.

In 1911 the system of odd numbers for freight locomotives and even numbers for passenger locomotives was finally done away with. Over 50 years of use it had become unnecessarily complex and cumbersome, to the point where there were eventually 836 so-called passenger steam locomotives and just 529 freight steam locomotives. The truth is that before the First World War VR operated many broad-gauge mixed passenger freight trains, sometimes swapping the use of many locomotives as various demands arose in the steam locomotive fleet of 1,365.

In 1951, with the advent of Operation Phoenix (a program to modernise rail after years of wartime neglect), the system was further revamped. This was just ahead of the large-scale introduction of diesel-electric locomotives into the VR fleet. Over the years, various bureaucrats had allowed an unnecessarily complicated numbering system to hold sway. From the very start, the allocation of one or two letters regarding the class of locomotives followed by the actual locomotive number in chronological sequence would have sufficed.

The most memorable of all steam locomotives were the S Class locomotives that were built at the Newport Workshops in the roaring twenties, with each weighing around 220 tonnes and, when streamlined and with added coal capacity in the tender of 7 tonnes, they were a smart unit.

These four streamlined S Class locomotives became legendary, and each had an increase in tender size, from four-axle to six-axle, to enable them to handle their special *Spirit of Progress* purpose which required them to carry

⌄ In light of modernisation, VR's Operation Phoenix was in many ways too little and too late.

OPERATION PHOENIX

more water and the 7 tonnes of coal. They were as follows: S300 *Matthew Flinders*; S301 *Sir Thomas Mitchell*; S302 Edward Henty; S303 *CJ Latrobe*.

These were locomotives of fame and precision performance that drew attention from the public standing safely alongside the line, whenever they operated at speed on the Melbourne–Albury interstate main line. Arguably, they were the most famous steam locomotives ever developed in Australia, but not without some faults, including barely enough coal capacity to allow for non-stop operation between Melbourne and Albury. In terms of maintenance, it is not generally realised that these locomotives had a third piston in the middle, forward of the boiler, to which it was difficult to gain access. These pistons generated a huge amount of power as they were over 20 inches in diameter and had a long 28-inch stroke. The boiler had the capacity of 200 psi steam pressure, and the locomotives could travel up to 70 mph (113 kph) as they made their dash between Melbourne and Albury, with priority given to them over all other rail traffic.

On occasions these four locomotives would be allocated to freight trains, but it remains one of those great tragedies of railway modernisation that all four locomotives were scrapped as part of the so-called modernisation drive.

Leon Oberg, a prominent steam train driver and renowned rail historian, declared: 'All four were all too quickly scrapped and it was sheer vandalism that, despite at least one attempt, an example of the S Class was not preserved for posterity.' Destructive negative forces were at play; over and over again, this has been the case during the contracting railway phase as steam was replaced by diesel locomotion.

≫ The *Spirit of Progress*, seen here in 1939, was arguably Australia's smartest looking steam streamliner.

The *Spirit of Progress* itself was the brainchild of a famous VR Commissioner, Sir Harold Clapp. Clapp was born in St Kilda in 1875 and had transport in his genes, owing to family connections with Cobb and Co as well as the tramways of Melbourne and Brisbane. After a stint working in the United States, Clapp became Chairman of Commissioners of VR and reigned supreme for two decades.

Clapp undertook an inspection tour around the world in 1934, experiencing the latest developments, including such famous trains as the *20th Century Limited*, which operated on the superb 'Water Level Route' between New York and Chicago. Upon his return, Clapp drew up plans for the *Spirit of Progress*. One suspects there was some interstate jealousy involved. Clapp wanted to ensure the passengers travelling between Sydney and Melbourne realised that the best train was to be found south of the border. Accordingly, he created an all-steel and all-air-conditioned train, deep blue in colour on its exterior and with comfortable leather fit-outs in the interior. In a bold stroke of marketing genius, the train was called the *Spirit of Progress*. It had a trial VIP run from Melbourne to Geelong on 17 November 1937 before commencing regular service between Melbourne and Albury six days later.

With an expansion of the S Class streamlined steam locomotive tenders, sufficient water and coal could be loaded for a non-stop run more than 190 miles (306 kilometres) at an average speed of 52 mph (84 kph). This meant a 3-hour 40-minute journey and required an express pathway without any signal delays or waiting in passing loops on the single-track section for train traffic coming in the opposite direction to cross.

As domestic air travel was in its infancy and Canberra, Australia's national capital, was growing, Clapp saw the importance of extolling a quality VR brand on the route used by senior businessmen, parliamentarians and public servants. They could all enjoy either a sumptuous dinner or a hearty breakfast in the large dining car and make use of the luxurious lounge car.

Clapp may have created this trail-blazing train, but it was the drivers and firemen who had to step up and deliver to meet its exacting requirements. In physical terms, it was the fireman in particular who had to shovel almost 7 tonnes of coal for each journey — all the while watching out for the signals as a double-check, operating the vital water injectors to ensure enough water was always in the boiler, and exchanging the staff or key on the single-track sections.

⌃ Early in his career, Chief Railways Commissioner Harold Clapp worked in the United States then applied the lessons he learnt there to the VR.

⌄ Rail was so dominant for decades that it engendered a good deal of culture; for example, this 'pathetic ballad' (c. 1908) that tells 'an engine driver's story'.

GARNISHEEING THE *SPIRIT OF PROGRESS*

Around 1950, a young lad, aged 16, was travelling on a VR train into the Melbourne CBD after school. The train jolted violently as it passed over a set of junction points, causing him to fall from the carriage. At the time the rustic red Tait electric train carriages of the Melbourne suburban system did not have automatically operating doors, and so doors often remained open between stations – in warmer months, this allowed some ventilation in the un-air-conditioned carriages.

The lad suffered a significant injury to his arm that required a partial amputation. His parents consulted Doyle & Kerr in Queen Street, where instructions were taken by a revered law clerk, the late Bill O'Callaghan. O'Callaghan explained to the parents that legislation (later repealed) limited VR's liability to £4,000 in damages for injury resulting from its negligence.

O'Callaghan wrote the usual letter to VR giving notice that proceedings would be commenced on behalf of the injured lad, alleging that his fall resulted from defective points in the rails. He asked that an engineer inspect the site of the accident. This request was denied. Despite the refusal, Bill attended the accident site with a VR engineer who confirmed that the points were indeed worn and therefore likely to result in severe jolting to a passing train.

Fortified with the engineer's report, O'Callaghan commenced proceedings in the Victorian Supreme Court seeking unlimited damages from VR. VR's insurer and its solicitors treated the proceedings with a level of disdain, highlighted by a complete lack of communication.

When the case went to trial, a jury found that there had been negligence and awarded the plaintiff substantial damages. Because of the legislative limit to liability, the trial judge entered judgement for the plaintiff in the sum of £4,000 plus costs (or around ten times a clerk's annual salary at this time).

Over the following months, O'Callaghan wrote a number of letters to VR headquarters and its solicitors, demanding payment without receiving any form of acknowledgement. He then decided to up the ante. A garnishee order was obtained against VR, and O'Callaghan cast his eye westwards to Spencer Street Station where the *Spirit of Progress* was readying to depart for Albury. He wrote a final letter to VR's solicitors advising that he had a garnishee order which would be handed to the sheriff to affix to the *Spirit of Progress* that evening if the judgement sum was not received at his office by 5 pm.

Shortly before the deadline expired, a cheque arrived and the folk on the *Spirit of Progress* were able to sit back and enjoy their dinner as the train ventured north. Justice had been served, albeit a little slowly. (I am indebted to Tony Doyle, formerly of renowned Melbourne legal firm Doyle and Kerr, for this account.)

» Good copies of the *Spirit of Progress* menus are priceless today.

"SPIRIT OF PROGRESS"

In which you are travelling was constructed at the Railway Workshops, Newport, Victoria. It is hauled by one of four streamlined Pacific locomotives, also built at the Workshops, which are named after men famous in Victorian history—Matthew Flinders, Sir Thomas Mitchell, Edward Henty and C. J. La Trobe.

Travelling non-stop daily in both directions between Melbourne and Albury, "Spirit of Progress" is Australia's premier train. It is built of special steel and is air-conditioned throughout. The air-conditioning equipment regulates temperature and humidity and completely eliminates dust. Selected insulation materials have reduced noise to a minimum and special gear prevents vibration even at the train's top speed. On its daily run, a mile a minute is averaged for much of the 190½ mile journey. 80 m.p.h. was exceeded in tests, but in normal running a 70 m.p.h. restriction is imposed.

A feature of the express is the ultra-modern kitchen with walls and equipment of stainless steel; a slow-combustion stove being an important part of the equipment. This kitchen has earned the warm praise of visitors from all parts of the world.

The first passenger run of "Spirit of Progress" was made on November 23, 1937.

We thank you for your patronage, and solicit your help in our efforts to cater for the present heavy demands upon Dining Car service. You can give this by leaving the Car as soon as you have finished your meal—a courtesy that will be appreciated by others who are waiting.

VICTORIAN RAILWAYS—DINING CAR SERVICES

... Menu ...

DINNER 6/-

Clam Chowder
Consomme Pearl

Boiled Flathead – Parsley Sauce
Roast Lamb and Mint Sauce
Boiled Leg of Mutton—Onion Sauce
Roast Chicken and Bacon

Vegetables in Season

Steamed Victoria Pudding
Compote Peaches and Custard
Vanilla Ice Cream

Savory or Cheese

Tea   Coffee

PLEASE DO NOT SMOKE IN THE DINING CAR

⌃ The *Spirit of Progress*'s dining car, c. 1945. In 2018 the rail dining car has returned to Victoria, between Drysdale and Queenscliff.

↘ After the Second World War, the *Overland Express* was modernised, but it still suffered from air competition between Adelaide and Melbourne.

» The *Spirit of Progress*, depicted here with locomotive No. S302 in 1937, was masterful, but facing headwinds with a maximum coal load of 7 tonnes it barely made it non-stop from Melbourne to Albury.

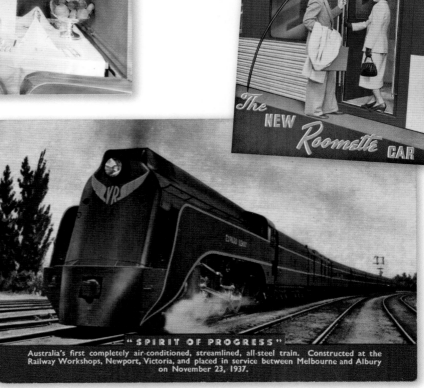

"SPIRIT OF PROGRESS"
Australia's first completely air-conditioned, streamlined, all-steel train. Constructed at the Railway Workshops, Newport, Victoria, and placed in service between Melbourne and Albury on November 23, 1937.

>> Demonstration of dropping and picking up the staff, c. 1950. Single-track working required this equipment, especially on busy main lines.

≫ Most rail traffic control systems have centralised to hub locations.

⌃ VR locomotive No. 6A shunting passenger carriages at Belgrave, 1968. This Melbourne suburb remains the terminus for both metro trains and the *Puffing Billy*.

»» VR Beyer-Garratt articulated locomotive No. G42 leaving Moe with a goods train bound for Erica, 1947. Fortunately, this Garratt still operates on the *Puffing Billy* system.

Bernie Greene was as good example as you will get of an ace fireman who worked the *Spirit of Progress* in the last of the golden years of steam in the period after the Second World War. Rail author and renowned photographer Nick Anchen has detailed Bernie's incredible life in his recent book *Enginemen of the Victorian Railways: Volume II* (2013).

Born at Ballarat on Christmas Day 1921, Bernie grew up listening to the big steam locomotives of the era making the grade towards Ballarat from Melbourne. He recalls the haunting sound of the *Overland Express* on its priority run between Melbourne and Adelaide. At age 17, he applied to work as a labourer with the railways and was accepted, initially at the Newport Workshops, where he saw *Heavy Harry* under construction, then at the big steam locomotive depot at North Melbourne.

As in most instances of climbing the career ladder, and aiming high, Bernie soon worked out how to get the ace job he wanted, which was to be fireman on 'Blue', as the drivers nicknamed the *Spirit of Progress*. As its permanent crews were based at Wodonga, he would have to move there, which he did in 1940.

By then, however, the Second World War was dominating the news and calls were going out for recruits, so Bernie joined the RAAF as a signaller and served around Australia, including up north before being posted to Laverton, where he met his wife-to-be, Isobel; they were married just after the war in St Augustine's Catholic Church in Bourke Street, near Spencer Street Railway Station.

⌄ Locomotive X.27 near completion in the old erecting shop at VR's Newport Workshops, 1929. Giant workshops were needed to underpin the railways, especially locomotive production.

Wodonga beckoned again and a chance to fire the *Spirit of Progress*, which was rapidly approaching its zenith in the postwar operation. As usual, Bernie had to work his way up the ladder. This included some work helping on freight trains along the highest Irish broad-gauge railway in the world, that from Wodonga to Cudgewa via Shelley.

At 781 metres above sea level, Shelley stood at the summit of this mountainous branch line, and the firemen on this route had to work really hard on the open footplate of the steam locomotives. (Today there is a superb restful picnic ground at Shelley Railway Station, just off the highway to Corryong from Wodonga.)

Finally, in 1947, Bernie landed a permanent position as fireman to driver Tommy Black on the S Class locomotive hauling the *Spirit of Progress*. On this roster, this meant leaving Albury at 7.50 in the morning, or alternatively platform 1, Spencer Street, at 6.30 each evening. For the crew, the early starts began with a sign on at 4.45 am, and after the S Class had been prepared and checked, with full water tanks and 7 tonnes of coal on board, it would move from the Wodonga Depot to the 'break of gauge' platform at Albury.

Few passengers or members of the public realised the enormous task facing the crew of the *Spirit of Progress*: absolute alertness was needed for almost four hours, with no access to a toilet or any form of break because the *Spirit* ran non-stop — a true express. Any crew running late, or maybe stopping owing to say a lack of steam pressure, were interrogated by the VR managers. They had much to answer for, much to explain, immediately after the run. Standards were set very high for what was a seamless operation, timed to the half-minute.

Once the *Spirit* departed on its journey the weights were on; the fireman began shovelling the coal but with a pattern to maximise the efficiency of the fire and steam production. The fireman had to place his foot on the treadle at the right

⌃ Wodonga was the terminus for trains from Cudgewa, the highest Irish broad-gauge line in the world.

⌄ Some say the steam train driver required a level of skill equal to that of a jumbo jet captain.

moment to open the firebox doors and then carefully direct the coal first to the back of the firebox and then to the corners and all other parts. All of this was done on a swaying footplate open on the sides to the elements.

The driver was on absolute alert as he sorted out the bevy of semaphore signals and ensured he had track clearance and on the single-track sections, ensured the key staff granting approval for access to the relevant section was on board and checked.

SIGNALMAN POWER AND DRIVER SHENANIGANS

As in all large transport and business units with over 20,000 employees, there was a small group of people who were good at gaming the system. Now if you were the driver of the 'fast goods' due out of Wodonga, southbound, at 4.15 pm on a weekday, you knew you had to cross the northbound *Spirit* before you reached the double track at Mangalore.

⌃ VR signal box, c. 1950. Its miniature electric levers were easier to use than the long levers of yesteryear, and halfway along the path to the mini switches and keys used today.

With just a minute or two of slow running for each southbound section, suddenly the planned efficient cross with the *Spirit* at Euroa was not achievable, so the 'fast goods' ended up being put into a loop further back at Benalla. This meant a good 45-minute extra break and smoko for the crew as they knew they could not get the staff and green signal until after the northbound *Spirit* had roared through.

Furthermore, hot pies were available at Benalla, if not at the station then across the road at the Terminus Hotel. Now, if the signalman was in on the act – this lark of deliberate slow running – then suddenly the 'fast goods' was running over an hour or more late, and the driver would be paid extra overtime.

In some places, signalmen became law unto themselves, such as at Cootamundra, New South

Wales, where there were steep grades in and out of the station. There was a very costly practice where express freight trains would be brought to a standstill even when they had no need to stop to drop or collect wagons, or change crews. Ten seconds later, the signalman would then change the signal to green, and hundreds of tonnes of train would move off, using a great deal of extra fuel in the effort to gain momentum up the grade. It was a case of pure bastardry.

However, no signalman was game enough to delay or hold the *Spirit* unless there was an absolute reason to do so.

There was not much time for conversation between driver and fireman, as both were very busy. About the only time for this was when the key or staff changed and there had to be a calling out of the station names on the key or staff as required by safety regulation; for example, Mangalore to Avenel at the start of the single-track section on the northward journey.

To this day, Bernie Greene will often join his friends at a coffee shop at the Spencer Street end of Bourke Street, just a hop, step and jump from platform 1 where he once departed on the *Spirit of Progress* and a stone's throw across the street from the church where he married.

He recalls the climb out of Melbourne as the train headed up the grades to the mainline summit at Heathcote Junction:

> *The grades up Pretty Sally were as steep as 1 in 50 and you'd be firing continuously all the way to the summit, with both injectors full on, the whole way. Some of the drivers would offer to take the shovel and give the fireman a spell up this long grade, but I was worried that the drivers would muck the fire up and I'd spend the rest of the trip trying to recover, so I usually kept firing. By now, the fire was glowing white hot and the engine was working at full capacity with the regulator full open, and we were really powering uphill. They were wonderful engines alright.*

⌃ From two tracks to now six tracks between Flinders St and Spencer St (Southern Cross Station), with planning for another two tracks under way.

95

His precise recall of events from his time as an ace fireman is a joy to behold. Take, for example, the story of how, on one of his last runs on a northbound *Spirit*, the key staff exchange at Wangaratta went awry: the staff went flying into the night (it was eventually to be found 50 metres away). Luckily, the staff being collected for the single-track section on to Springhurst had been safely collected, allowing the journey to continue and be completed on time.

It was not Bernie's fault, but a sharp letter was issued all the same. Nothing was meant to interfere with the running of the *Spirit*; nothing was allowed to delay the VR's 'Numero Uno' train in the decades before it was gradually eclipsed by dieselisation, standardisation and increasing reliance on aviation. The *Spirit of Progress* ran for the last time on 2 August 1986.

Some passengers would wander down to thank the drivers, and even offer them the occasional meat pie or a small monetary tip. Many members of the public would step outside to give the *Spirit* a wave as it sped through the suburbs, at various points along its route, or when it slowed down to pass through Wodonga, cross the Murray River and pull up to the dead-end platform at Albury Station.

After quite a few runs doing the hard yakka, Bernie decided to retire from VR and start a small electrical business, B.D. Greene Television and Radio Service, at Ballarat; he did well out of the advent of television.

⌄ Rail anniversaries remain big events to this day.

He had had thoughts of staying on the trains, but the looming dieselisation was enough to cause him to move on. He took with him, however, a rich store of railway memories.

All in all, Victoria developed 66 different classes of locomotives – 67, if you include the original unnumbered 'Hobson's Choice', the machine that paved the way forward in so many ways. But it was a case of far too much diversity and this added to maintenance costs and spare parts or inventory holding costs. Of necessity, huge inventories were established relating to each class of locomotive.

One truly bizarre class was the saddle tank VR steam engine that became known as the L Class; eventually, there were ten of these, all imported from Britain. Many historians give the distinctly shaped L Class a special mention as a good performer, and rightly so. It was a locomotive with a distinctive shape. The saddle water tank, shaped in a half curve, was mounted on the 2–4–0 frame, and the main funnel took the form of a large cone. These locomotives did a lot of work on the Williamstown route, but also ventured out into the countryside, operating on the Geelong–Ballarat direct route through Lal Lal until larger locomotives became available. Eventually, heavy maintenance costs overwhelmed these sturdy and flexible units which weighed in at 36 tonnes.

Curved-saddle tank steam engines existed on other systems in Australia, including the NSWGR. Many non-government business networks developed this type of locomotive; BHP, for example, developed one for shunting duties around Newcastle as late as 1948, but in Victoria the only one of this type was the L Class, and after about five decades they vanished into the scrap-metal heap.

Sadly, far too many steam locomotives suffered a similar fate, including, as we have seen, all four streamlined S Class locomotives. It has been claimed that this was due in part to a clause in the VR contract for purchasing diesels which stipulated that these four had to be destroyed, lest they emerge again as some form of rival. In effect, though, it was destructive vandalism.

Today all V Line passenger trains between Melbourne and Albury are hauled by diesel-electric locomotive, but all of them with timetables that run slower than did the *Spirit of Progress*, so it can be asked whether any real progress has been made over recent decades. The truth is that, while steam locomotives were dirty beasts, in their heyday they did set a high standard of performance that provided a stimulus for so much of the early economic development of Victoria.

« The S Class locomotives were serviced at VR's North Melbourne engine shed.

« Locomotive No. 465 *City of Ballarat* passenger train at the 'break of gauge' platform at Albury.

CHAPTER 5

*A large number of persons were assembled
who cheered lustily as the first passenger
carriage was started in New South Wales.*

ILLUSTRATED SYDNEY NEWS, 2 JUNE 1855

FULL STEAM AHEAD IN NEW SOUTH WALES

<<< Locomotive 3612 hauling a passenger train up a steep grade, 1940s. The huge exhaust smoke plume was great for photographers but caused pollution around busy stations.

≫ Builder's plate from locomotive No. 1. Such plates are now major collector items.

Unlike Victoria, the very first steam locomotive in the colony of New South Wales was correctly numbered, and carefully preserved after it had operated successfully from 1855 to 1877. Locomotive No. 958 was built by Stephenson and Co in Newcastle upon Tyne in 1854 — which tells us that the Stephenson works were close to having produced 1,000 locomotives by 1854.

But New South Wales decided that this locomotive would be NSWGR 'Locomotive No. 1'. It arrived at Campbell's wharf at Sydney's Circular Quay on 13 January 1855, along with three other locomotives. They were then hauled by horse to the Eveleigh workshops in Redfern, where William Scott, the engineer who had overseen their construction in Britain, then brought them and the other locomotives out and readied them for service. All four were designed for Stephenson standard-gauge operation, and soon enough they were hauling ballast and various other trains.

There is no evidence of Locomotive No. 1 having been designated with a name. There may have been a missed opportunity here: given William Scott's role in its history, perhaps 'Great Scott' might have been an appropriate name, or at least a nickname, for No. 1.

History records the first passenger train in the colony ran on 28 May 1855, departing from where the first Sydney Central terminus was to be, near Redfern, and heading out towards Parramatta as far as Lewisham. Later that year the line to Parramatta officially opened; the 50-minute service proved instantly popular, with thousands travelling on the first day.

⌃ A Stephenson locomotive dating from 1855. NSWGR started off with some good imported Stephenson locomotives.

At 26 tonnes locomotive No. 1 was relatively heavy, with plenty of power for the easy run to Parramatta and later on to Campbelltown. It had a 0–4–2 wheel configuration and owed its design to James McConnell who gave it four driving wheels of 5 ft 6 in (1,676 mm) and two large internally located cylinders or pistons.

The pistons and linkages were hard to maintain. Big pits were built at Redfern to allow the maintenance workers access to them, and both pistons were balanced to ensure a smooth output.

The driver and fireman were well exposed to the elements as the cabin had no roof and small portholes through the 'spectacle plate' at the front, facing forward, through which the driver could observe the setting of the various semaphore signals and closely monitor track ahead. It is recorded that No. 1's first driver was William Sixsmith, who went on to become a senior driver with NSWGR, and its first fireman was William Webster, who was later an inspector based at Goulburn.

⌃ The arrival of the first train at Parramatta from Sydney, 1855: one of many great moments in NSWGR history.

⌄ Across the world horizontal signals meant 'Do not proceed'.

⌃ Locomotive No. 1 in
Redfern Yard, c. 1889.
Built to last – and last
it did, for many years.
(Today the locomotive
is on display at the
Museum of Applied Arts
and Sciences.)

Creature comforts for both driver and fireman were never a great priority in the early days of steam locomotion. Until the arrival of enclosed diesel driver cabins in the middle of the twentieth century, crews required a certain degree of stamina and dedication to cope with the exposed conditions. Long tunnels were especially hard going.

Locomotive No. 1 carried a maximum of 4 tonnes of coal, so it could cover considerable distances before having to reload, but it needed to top up its water supply more frequently. The trailing tender could only carry 2,000 imperial gallons (9,100 litres). Perhaps this was a deliberate choice: installing large-capacity water tenders would only add to the amount of coal that would have to be burnt to haul the added load around.

The NSWGR workshops and engraving shops at Eveleigh soon began building local versions of Stephenson steam locomotives, and later private companies, such the Atlas Engineering Company, to name one, and then Clyde Engineering, also stepped up. As for engineer William Scott, he eventually rose through the ranks to have huge sway on NSWGR locomotive output, some of which came from Eveleigh, others from abroad, and eventually as many as 60 in one order from Clyde Engineering.

After the usual pattern of excessive diversity with class and types of steam locomotives, steam locomotion reached its pinnacle in New South Wales with the (P6) 32 Class, through to the mighty 38 Class streamliner and then, in the dying days of steam, the huge Garratt built by Beyer, Peacock & Co. in Great Britain —

« On the photographic
front, steam beats diesel
every time.

103

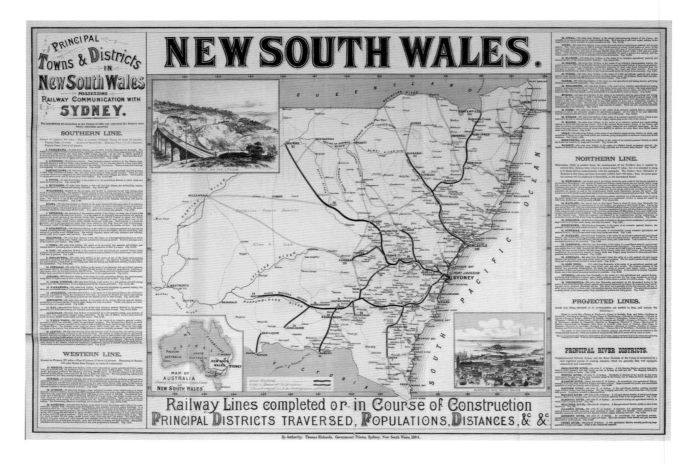

NEW SOUTH WALES.

Railway Lines completed or in Course of Construction
PRINCIPAL DISTRICTS TRAVERSED, POPULATIONS, DISTANCES, &c &c.

⌃ John Whitton's decades of loyal service were not fully appreciated.

264 tonnes of raw energy in an articulated vehicle of 4–8–4 + 4–8–4 wheel arrangement. From the first steps taken to build railways in New South Wales, it took a long time and the dedication of a great many to reach this stage. The role of Yorkshireman John Whitton was pivotal for over three decades.

It was John Whitton's experience as a civil engineer in building quality railways in Britain that helped him to obtain appointment as effective head of the NSWGR in 1856. It was a position he would hold until 1899, during which time thousands of miles of standard-gauge railways were built in the colony.

Before coming to Australia Whitton had been involved in railway construction near Manchester and near Oxford, but that was across reasonably level terrain with no big mountain barriers. To get out of the Sydney Basin, however, he had to cross the Blue Mountains west of Sydney, uneven terrain to the south coast and the Great Dividing Range towards Yass and Albury. To the north the mighty Hawkesbury River was a large barrier to reaching Gosford and Newcastle. This was finally conquered on May Day 1889 with a single-track bridge that effectively allowed trains to operate seamlessly from Sydney to the Queensland border. Whitton also showed a dash of boldness with climbing spirals and also a famous 'zig-zag' near Lithgow.

« 'Hub and spoke' was the dominant pattern out of Sydney.

» For beauty, the Zig Zag Railway on the escarpment near Lithgow (seen here in an engraving by Albert Charles Cooke, c. 1869) is hard to beat.

⨠ Opening day of the Hawkesbury River bridge, 1889 – finally, a rail link between Sydney and Newcastle.

≫ Oil-burning locomotive 5614 hauling a goods train in 1955. Firemen liked the oil burners as there was no coal to shovel.

≫ Troy Junction, near Dubbo, is still busy today but now under CTC signal systems.

» The *Vintage Train* being hauled by two locomotives, 1960s. From front or back, steam trains made for a great sight.

⯒ Locomotive 3082, 1950s. Black soot from steam locomotives was always a hazard, especially for those in sleeping accommodation carriages.

GLEAMING LOCOMOTIVES ON DISPLAY

To see New South Wales's first ever steam locomotive is to behold an icon of rare beauty. While it is not operational, it has been well preserved for over 120 years. With a gleaming brass safety valve and so much more, it looks almost new and yet it spent 22 years out and about on the NSWGR network. Today (2018) it can be found on the third level of Sydney's Museum of Applied Arts and Sciences.

But it's not the only train to see there. Carefully stored down on the first level is steam locomotive 1243 built by Atlas Engineering Company in Sydney in 1882. It was a much-loved train that steamed over 2 million miles on the NSWGR network during its 100 years of service. With a simple 4–4–0 wheel pattern and two external pistons, 1243 was easier to drive than most engines of its era.

Currently the locomotive can be found in a corner near track once connected to Sydney Central Station, alongside the governor's carriage and in front of the old manual 'destination board' from the main concourse of Sydney Central, as it was set for trains operating in 1937. There you can see the Kosciuszko Express, Temora Mail,

⌃ The McConnell-designed, Stephenson-built locomotive No. 1 at the Museum of Applied Arts and Sciences, Ultimo – a great setting for a great workhorse.

Orange Mail, Through Mail, South West Mail and North West Mail departure times, plus a choice of overnight trains to Brisbane (either via Casino or Wallangarra – a destination board evoking many memories of the great overnight mail train era).

Sadly, 1243 will not be in steam again anytime soon, but it is well worth a visit to see it and the heritage carriages alongside.

Good chief railway engineers had to have their wits about them, as their political masters in the nineteenth century were often very demanding, such as a kink here to reach a town where the local MP lived or a detour there to put in a siding for a local MP on his family wheat farm. Even the vice-regal representative William Denison weighed in suggesting narrow gauge for the western parts of the colony beyond the Great Dividing Range. In other words, he and others wanted another 'break of gauge', this time in central New South Wales. Whitton strongly disagreed, and instead stayed with standard gauge, but went for lighter rails and less ballast on some country branch lines, imposing slower speeds on these for safety reasons.

It is said that Whitton briefly considered switching to the broad gauge, as adopted in Victoria, by having dual gauge for the line from Sydney to Liverpool but broad gauge for the southern main line and the rest of the NSWGR network. Unfortunately, this solution was not to be, and so the last chance to correct the 'break of gauge' was lost forever.

Whitton was one of the world's 20 best railway civil engineers of the nineteenth century; his high standards helped ensure a strong foundation for the NSWGR system. As a result, in some years, the system showed a profit, generally in big harvest years when there were large shipments of grain from the hinterland to the main ports.

However, as the system grew, a new powerful position came into play: the chief mechanical engineer, based in Sydney, who was responsible for locomotive construction. Here were to be found the executives who designed and produced the working beasts that hauled precious freight over mountains and across plains, or faster steam locomotives pulling express passenger trains.

After the first shipments from Stephenson and Co., the steam locomotives were improved in various ways: first, fully roofed cabins; second, Giffard water injectors; third, external pistons to help maintenance; and finally, better braking systems.

For a period after Whitton, the affairs of the NSWGR drifted along, not helped by the sudden death of Commissioner EMG Eddy while attending a rail conference in Brisbane in July 1897. The steam-hauled funeral train from Brisbane to Wallangarra and then to Sydney drew huge crowds on its arrival at Redfern. Eddy Avenue near Sydney Central is named after him.

⌃ A large funeral was held for NSWGR Commissioner Eddy in July 1897, and it required a long funeral train all the way down from Brisbane, where he died, to Sydney.

Many of the key NSWGR executives were recruited from the railway companies of Great Britain, and one such person was Ernest Edward Lucy, who was attracted to Australia by the prospect of finding a better climate for his wife's health. He had gained vital experience in the Great Western Railway system, and played a leading role at the Wolverhampton Workshops.

David Burke in his penetrating and well-researched 1986 biography of Lucy, *Man of Steam*, records how he sailed into Sydney with his young family to become assistant chief mechanical engineer of the NSWGR on 2 January 1906. Despite various controversies after the grand Whitton era, and the clashes between railway commissioners and leading ministers and premiers, Lucy replaced William Thow as NSWGR chief mechanical engineer on 1 July 1911. For the next 21 years, this genteel Englishman, who always wore a bow tie, played a key role in developing steam locomotion in the state.

» Maroon-liveried 3265 carries the *Hunter* nameplates as it heads a Newcastle express in the 1930s.

The P6 Class had been introduced in 1892 as a well-balanced 4–6–0; it proved a strong and reliable work horse for New South Wales that gave Lucy some breathing space as he swung into action. Within three years of taking office, however, he had to deal with the particular challenges created by the outbreak of the First World War. In 1924 the P6 was rebranded the C32, and there were some four different builders of the C32; for example, Clyde Engineering built 45, before the construction schedule was completed in the middle of the Second World War.

Named locomotives were few and far between with the NSWGR, but one of these trains, No. 3265, was named *Hunter*. However, there was nothing to match VR and S300 Matthew Flinders or S301 *Sir Thomas Mitchell*, and many more.

≫ Pioneer Locomotive P6 at the head of the *Melbourne Express*, c. 1892. Many famous VIPs rode this express.

The C32 locomotives found their way all over New South Wales, and survived a decade or two of the dieselisation era before most were scrapped; in fact, the last restored steam service on the NSWGR was hauled by a C32. However, at least four have been preserved to this day, two of these at the NSW Rail Museum in

Thirlmere, south-west of Sydney near Picton. (Previously known as Trainworks, this is a brilliant complex with a connection to the main southern line.) Whether sitting at rest in the Tumut Station yard awaiting duties, or plying the branch line through Lockhart and Boree Creek to Urana and Oaklands, the C32s had a certain grandeur about them.

Fitting the same pattern, but with a 2–8–0 configuration was the T524 or post-1924 D50, plus the N928 (later C34), modified under Lucy's watch just after the First World War with a steam superheater of the Schmidt type and greatly improved performance.

⩓ Located in sight of the Sydney CBD, the giant Eveleigh railway workshop complex has today given way to modern housing and conference facilities.

Overall, Lucy made a stellar contribution, balancing railway politics, railway commissioner politics and state politics, but always working to improve the steam workhorses of the NSWGR. He also improved the physical conditions of the huge Eveleigh railway workshops.

As well as Lucy, there was the equally capable Harold Young who became a dominant chief design engineer. Lucy laid the basis of key steam locomotive designs and Young brought them onto fruition. Variously the two men were responsible for the big three steam locomotives: the D57 Class, which emerged in 1929, and the C36 were mainly Lucy's work, and the C38 was mainly Young's work. In their respective heydays, all three locomotives were the pride of the NSWGR fleet, especially during the years when it made a net profit from its steam and some of its electric locomotive haulage.

Steam locomotion reached its zenith in New South Wales with the D57, the C36 and the C38 – and, of course, in the closing moments before the curtain came down on steam, the mighty Garratt. There were many other types and classes of steam locomotives on the NSWGR system, especially smaller versions for the 'start-stop' suburban system until electrification finally took over. (It was the driving force of Sydney Harbour Bridge–builder John Bradfield that helped deliver much needed suburban electrification.)

In retrospect, greater harmonisation of locomotive types might have added to efficiency as locomotive numbers climbed, from around 600 at the time of Federation in 1901 to 1,600 during the Great Depression, and even more in the Second World War. In this regard, apart from the small tank engines needed for shunting, the D57, C36 and C38 would have carried the NSWGR adequately through to dieselisation, albeit with some adjustment for the track standards.

In parallel with the key locomotive developments, Lucy moved quickly to provide TAM sleeper carriages with polished wood compartments and corridors, as well as corridor 'sitting up' carriages, complete with toilets and washrooms. Many of these have been preserved with their gleaming wash basins and pressed-iron decorative ceilings; for example, at the huge Lachlan Valley Railway Roundhouse at Cowra.

Even into the 1970s, the grand TAM sleeper carriages were employed on the South West Mail between Sydney Central, Junee, Narrandera and then on to Griffith, with railmotor connections to Tocumwal and Hay. Except in heatwaves, they were very comfortable to sleep in. The TAM brought improved passenger safety, as previously up to six or eight passengers were all sealed in the one compartment for long periods of time when the gap between station stops was frequently over half an hour. Safety and security were only as good as the weakest character in the compartment, even if others were present, and of a mind to intervene in any situations that might arise.

The D57 was rolled out just ahead of the Great Depression,

⮟ One of the reliable D57 Class workhorses starting out after servicing.

« Overturned engine of the *Brisbane Limited* that crashed at Aberdeen, in the Hunter Valley, in 1926. Before the Casino-Kyogle-Brisbane standard-gauge link was opened, all northbound rail traffic went via the Hunter Valley.

after the design work had been finalised by Lucy and cleared by the chief commissioner. There was approval for 25 locomotives of the class, and once the normal teething problems had been overcome performance was adjudged to be another step-up in the quest for more power.

The huge D57 tender could hold 14 tonnes of coal and 9,000 gallons (40,900 litres) of water, twice the amount of coal that the VR S Class carried for the relatively short runs Melbourne to Albury. Soon the D57 was pounding out of Sydney in various directions, notwithstanding the downturn in rail activity associated with the dire effects of the Great Depression on the national economy.

Extra strength in tractive power also meant the need for better couplings, and better braking systems were also required and gradually installed. Often installation was sped up after big train runaway fatal accidents, such as the Ardglen Tunnel tragedy in July 1926 when, on the steep grade up to the tunnel, a coupling broke and several freight wagons rolled down the main line with increasing speed to smash into the North West Mail train, killing 27 passengers and injuring 41 others. All too often in that era there were fatal railway accidents followed by Coroner's Courts and even Royal Commissions.

The C36 was a stepping stone from the older designs to a more modern approach; with its 4–6–0 configuration, it was built for passenger train haulage and had simple maintenance requirements, helped by its having only two external cylinders. Between 1925 and 1928, 75 were produced by Eveleigh and by Clyde Engineering; once again, early kinks had to be removed, but their performance was so good that the new Commonwealth Railways adopted the design for 18 of its fleet. The 14-tonne coal capacity for its tender became a benchmark with NSWGR: both the D57 and C36 carried 14 tonnes and thus excelled through the extra range this entailed between coal refuel stops. Even when loaded by gravity from overhead bins, such stops always took some shunting and valuable time.

»» Train smash at Cootamundra, 1885. Visibility for steam locomotive drivers was about one-fifth that diesel ones, which may have contributed to many accidents.

« An old 0466 Class (later Z23 Class) locomotive off the turntable at Binnaway, c. 1930. Driver error can play a part in accidents, as was clearly the case here.

« Signal boxes were everywhere before CTC and centralisation.

» By day, semaphore signals were easy to read; by night, with kerosene lamps, it was another matter before electric signals were introduced.

≫ One of the boilers
going into a C38 in 1945
– some would say this
was the best steam
locomotive type of
the NSWGR.

The C38, which arrived in the middle of the Second World War, was of the Pacific wheel alignment, namely 4–6–2, and was regarded by many, including steam locomotive connoisseurs David Burke and Leon Oberg, as representing 'Steam Australia' at its zenith. By that time, roller bearings were in common use, conferring safe running; other modern dimensions were also added to allow solid performance from these 200-tonne beasts as they hauled named expresses in all directions.

Once again, the C38 had a 14-tonne coal capacity, and its driving wheels were standardised at 5 ft 9 in (1,753 mm), the same as those on the C36. Clyde Engineering produced the first five, C3801 to C3805, with cone streamlining and after the war they sported a lively light green colour. Chief Harold Young vigorously defended his role as overall designer and was quietly proud of all the Australian aspects of this futuristic locomotive. Young had previously tried to win approval for a radical Garratt design, articulated with one boiler and two sets of pistons, intended for use as an express passenger locomotive. However, the powers that be were not bold enough to accept this radical design. As a result, a bigger and better C38 emerged. With its graceful full (or half) streamlining, it was a sight to behold in the late afternoon as it swept past places such as Kapooka on the southern main line with the Riverina Express. In all, 30 were built, with the first five coming from Clyde Engineering, but only after some wartime delays. Clyde's initial bid had been for £20,000 per locomotive, but this quickly doubled to well over £40,000 by the time they arrived.

The ultimate claim associated with the C38 (and the class leader, 3801) was that its boiler pressure was the highest in Australia at 245 psi; however, this was not much good if all this heat and steam created did not flow properly. Only after

ON BOARD THE SOUTH WEST MAIL

As a frequent user of the South West Mail in the days when I was New South Wales state MP for Sturt and Murray, I would often enjoy a comfortable sleep travelling up from Narrandera on a Monday night for the state parliamentary sittings and coming back on Thursday night. The only refreshments available en route were to be had at the heritage Junee Station refreshment rooms. I recall that at breakfast mashed potato was always served with the sausages, not a great help in the battle of the bulge.

As for overnight train travel, to this day my great tip is always to get on board having had at least one, but no more than two, nips of Scotch – or one or two beers – in other words, slightly under the influence to allow the body to ease into the rocking movements of the train and hopefully sleep through the various noisy whistle stops between Harden and Goulburn in the middle of the night.

With a 7.05 pm departure from Narrandera and a mini-beerhall on the platform, known as the 'Rail Ref Room', it was an easy tip to follow. It allowed you to mix with a set of regulars and so catch up on the latest local gossip and gather feedback on how the government was travelling. After pulling into Sydney Central 12 hours later, at 7.26 am, there would be a quick dash down to Parliament House on Macquarie Street, followed by a shower and breakfast – and you'd be ready to take on the sitting week.

At week's end, it was a 10 pm departure from Central, surrounded as it was by many watering holes, and a 30-minute breakfast at Junee before arriving at Narrandera at 10.11 am, ready for a busy weekend in the electorate.

I and a few other MPs used the South West Mail, but the North West Mail to Werris Creek (and thence Moree and Inverell, with another section going to Tamworth and Armidale) was another matter. A large group of state MPs were regular users of that service. Bill Chaffey, the long-serving Member for Tamworth and a Second World War veteran, would generally smuggle on board a bottle of Scotch, then demand company from his parliamentary colleagues well into the night, even if all they wanted to do after the first hour was sleep. Chaffey always insisted 'Come and have a drink with me' to his fellow MPs travelling the North West Mail.

It was a reasonably reliable way to travel, especially when winter fog closed the Riverina airports. Back then, blissfully, there were no mobiles, and I certainly learned much from conversations with the guards or conductors, especially about proposed changes to the NSWGR and their concerns about possible downsizing.

Nowadays, no MP could afford to allocate 12 hours to a train trip twice a week, so rarely do you find a state or federal member on any train today, except for Prime Minister Malcolm Turnbull who is often spotted on short urban runs. It was another era.

>> 'Train Yourself to Relax in Comfort', 1940s. Yes, relax if on time, and if air-conditioned.

TRAIN YOURSELF TO RELAX

IN COMFORT

some initial kinks in the piping were redesigned did the C38 outperform the other locomotives in so many ways. I recall one driver on the Riverina Daylight Express deciding to 'go for it' between Picton and Moss Vale. The buffet car crew were not impressed when the crockery went flying, but the driver had the satisfaction of claiming an informal speed record on that occasion. The C38 was so good that it was able to compete successfully with diesels for a decade or more before being retired around 1970. (Famously that year, 3801 helped celebrate standardisation from Sydney to Perth by hauling the *Western Endeavour* across the Nullarbor, a return journey distance of close to 8,000 kilometres.

What overall assessment should be made of these bigger, bolder locomotives, notably the D57, C36 and C38 (and later the Garratt AD 60 Class)? First, it is important to note that they came into existence in part because of the NSWGR's profitable years in the 'Roaring Twenties'; there were three years when modest profits were obtained as freight volume jumped through the 16-million-tonne barrier in 1926-27, peaking at 19 million tonnes in 1928–29. Second, they engendered huge roundhouses and related workshops all over New South Wales, not just at big main-line junctions such as Junee or Casino. At Cowra, between Blayney and Harden on the regional line (now closed), rail had arrived in 1886 from the south and in 1888 from the north, connecting the two big systems and

≫ *Western Endeavour*, 1970. Steam ran right through east-west after standardisation was completed, but it was never allowed to run up the transcontinental line through Alice Springs to Darwin.

offering alternative pathways for trains between Melbourne and Sydney on busy occasions such as Easter.

In 1924 a new Cowra Locomotive Depot, complete with huge roundhouse and carefully balanced turntable, opened just south of the stately Cowra Railway Station; it was designated Depot No. 26 and had an initial staffing of 180 NSWGR employees to keep all those steam locomotives in the area properly serviced. A bonus feature was a set of beautiful internal gardens, including a nice fountain dedicated to staff who had lost their lives in the Great War. Today it is the home of the Lachlan Valley Railway; it is kept in amazingly good shape and is well worth a visit, along with the nearby famous Japanese peace gardens.

⌃ Preparing locomotives 3237 and 5917, 2009. The Lachlan Valley Railway trains were a cut above, and it is hoped they will operate again to Woodstock and Blayney.

Soon the Great Depression would hit hard, but around this time road transport was also greatly improving and becoming more competitive. Freight volume plunged from 19 million tonnes in 1928–29 to barely 10 million tonnes in 1931–32. Neither the railway managers nor the state government ministers and departmental officials fully anticipated the various transport changes rapidly unfolding.

After the sacking of Premier Jack Lang and his 'radical' NSW state government in 1932, the conservatives were back in power. Lieutenant Colonel Sir Michael Bruxner, from the electorate of Tenterfield on the Queensland border, was deputy premier (a post he held for nine years), Minister for Transport and Leader of the Country Party. The colonel was a steady and solid cabinet minister, but the drumbeats of the Second World War and the harsh economic times meant the capacity to be bold – for example, to follow some of the great ideas and plans of that brilliant engineer John Bradfield – was no longer possible.

As a result, the zenith of steam was short-lived. The NSWGR found annual profits more and more difficult to obtain, and wartime shortages threw the system into a degree of drift and decline. It was a tragedy, and it meant that vital shortening of routes on the main line, especially near Picton and between Goulburn and Yass, never occurred – which explains why so many crazy grades and sharp curves or kinks still exist today.

The last throw of the steam dice in New South Wales came with the long-overdue arrival of the Garratt – or, to be formally correct, the 260-tonne Beyer Garratt. The wheel configuration was 4–8–4 + 4–8–4 and the long central section, complete with firebox and large boiler, had no wheels directly underneath its middle section. This very factor conferred a huge natural advantage on the Garratt's cornering as it negotiated the many sharp curves and reverse curves on the state

THE CULLERIN RANGE

As a new backbencher in state parliament in the 1970s, I pleaded with then transport minister Tim Bruxner, son of Sir Michael Bruxner, to ensure that when the Hume Highway was upgraded between Goulburn and Yass it be done holistically. In other words, the opportunity should have been taken to place the main southern rail line alongside the superb new dual-carriage Hume Highway. This would have led to massive energy savings for every train between Sydney and Melbourne and up to a 30-minute reduction in travel time.

But the NSW Department of Main Roads (DMR) would not have a bar of this joint approach, and so while the Hume Highway, with its gentle curves and small gradients, cuts past the Cullerin Range today and past Gunning with ease, the railway continues with its agony route through the range. Experts such as Professor Phil Laird and others continue to push the case, but so far without luck.

It was silo mentality at its worst. Nine extra kilometres of sharp curves and grades remain in place, causing every train between Sydney and Junee today to burn extra energy and miss out on saving time.

Professor Laird contends today that, apart from the DMR, NSWGR itself has to take some of the blame as it was not that keen on finding its share of the project budget to get the job done. It might have seemed a 'no brainer', but once again the best rail option was ignored.

network. The very centre of the central section always slewed several millimetres to the inside of every curve, thus enabling the central section to act as a stabilising anchor as the Garratt came around each corner (either quickly or slowly). This allowed for faster operation, and it was also helpful that the Garratt had a very large number of axles (16, in fact). This meant it could operate as a designated 16-tonne axle weight along regional tracks and even some branch lines. The C36 was designated 20 tonnes axle weight, and the D57 and C38 were heavier again.

The order for the Garratts was placed with the expert in the field, Beyer, Peacock & Co. in Great Britain, and 45 arrived between 1952 and 1957, some coming in the form of non-assembled spare parts as the NSWGR powers tried to reduce their order when dieselisation proved to be an instant success in so many ways. It was a pity the wishes of Harold Young had not been followed, and that the Garratt had not been introduced decades earlier.

History records that it fell to the New South Wales Garratt to be the last steam locomotive in regular government system service (until March 1973, although by then diesel and diesel-electric locomotives dominated almost all services, with electric locomotion filling the rest). The last Garratt I saw working was hauling a

» Two 60 Class Garratt locomotives at the Junee Roundhouse, which now anchors a museum and a rail festival.

freight train near Harden, and it was back to front, operating tender first. Usefully, the Garratts were fitted with sand boxes that could apply grip sand in front of the driving wheels to handle grade while travelling either forwards or in reverse. It was a magnificent sight as it hauled many carriages of sheep heading to market in Sydney. (Sadly, however, livestock haulage vanished from the NSWGR system around the same time steam locomotion did.)

It remains almost a miracle that the Canberra Railway Museum, part of the ACT Division of the Australian Railway Historical Society (ARHS), succeeded in restoring 6029 to mainline operation, helped by a boiler retrieved from a log mill in Victoria. Now called *City of Canberra*, since early 2015 it has been hauling very popular excursion trains around Canberra and Goulburn and during Steamfest, around Maitland, as well. This giant Garratt 6029 is now housed at the NSW Rail Museum in Thirlmere (after ARHS ACT went into receivership in late 2016). Arguably, 6029 is now the only operational standard-gauge Garratt in the Southern Hemisphere, and you have to salute the epic work of the many volunteers who have helped bring this about. It means that almost the last one to come into service (in 1954) is now the last still in rail heritage service.

From the Museum of Applied Arts and Sciences' locomotive No. 1 to locomotive 6029, a hugely diverse range of steam locomotives has reigned supreme in New South Wales. In retrospect, there was perhaps far too much diversity, but this cannot detract from the fact that steam locomotives did much to enable economic development across the state.

≪ History being made by a polished Garratt locomotive 6029, although ownership of this great machine has a habit of changing.

Faugh-a-Ballagh: 'Get out of the way!'
QR STEAM LOCOMOTIVE NO. 3

CHAPTER 6

QUEENSLAND RAIL:
THE TRIUMPH OF NARROW GAUGE

«« Locomotive B15C 237 halfway up the mountain from Cairns to Kuranda, c. 1936–39.

Even to this day, many people still believe that during the Second World War a 'Brisbane Line' was developed to allow for a fall-back position in the event of a feared Japanese invasion of the mainland. No documentary existence for such a line has even been found.

Nevertheless, some might contend that a form of Brisbane line exists in a subtle way today, but it is one that starts at the state border. It is only a decade or so since Queensland standardised secondary education to a six-year structure, and there is no daylight saving north of the Queensland border. And it could even be said that the concept of the Brisbane line first emerged back in the mid-nineteenth century when Queensland deliberately established its railways using a narrow-gauge track (3 ft 6 in [1,067 mm]) for its main line — a gauge totally different from the NSWGR standard-gauge railway system it adjoined to the south.

Queensland was thus the first Australian colony, and the first major railway system in the world, to have narrow gauge at the core of its rail network. As a consequence, lying in the grass just north of the border, at Wallangarra, is the world's only dual-gauge railway triangle — or at least it did until a few years back, when an imbecilic road engineer dismembered part of it to better align a minor connecting road. Imagine levelling one of the mighty Glass House Mountains near Brisbane to make room for a freeway, or chipping off a corner of an Egyptian pyramid for a tramway, or even obliterating the eastern terminus platform of the

Steam locomotive crossing a viaduct, Mackay, c. 1875. Good steam drivers knew when to throttle back and maximise safety.

ENTER AN IRISH ENGINEER

It was a colourful Irish-born engineer, Abram Fitzgibbon, who stood up for Anglo Cape narrow gauge from the inception of the railways in Queensland. He had had experience around the world, notably in Ireland, Canada and Ceylon (Sri Lanka). However, his most recent work before he arrived in Queensland in June 1863 to take up the post of engineer-in-chief had been working on narrow-gauge railways in New Zealand. So successful was he there that short sections of Stephenson standard and Irish broad gauge track were ripped up and replaced with the Anglo Cape narrow gauge after NZ premier – and keen railway builder – Julius Vogel went all out for railways in narrow gauge.

In August 1863 Fitzgibbon, complete with bow tie, was called to give expert evidence to the Legislative Council in Brisbane, and after a few parliamentary wrangles, the issue was eventually settled in favour of his proposal. The main enabling legislation to set up Queensland Railways initially only made it through on a casting vote of the Speaker. After a dissolution and new election, held later that same year, in which the key issue was railways, the legislation went through by a narrow three-vote majority.

Fitzgibbon went on to become the first commissioner of Queensland Railways, so the die was cast and for the first time in the world the railways rolled out with the narrow gauge applying to main lines. In time, he found the local politics around the ridges of Brisbane not to be his cup of tea, so after a couple of years he parted ways with the government and returned to England.

To this day, the debate on Queensland gauge goes on: should Townsville–Mount Isa be converted to standard gauge? Should the new railway required from the Galilee Basin to Abbott Point be standard gauge? Were he here today, I feel Fitzgibbon would agree that the wider gauge was best, especially given the big earth-moving equipment readily available to ease grades.

original Liverpool and Manchester Railway. (In fact, the eastern terminus of that famous railway is being destroyed – perhaps because modern-day rail designers and town planners do not know how to use a simple protractor and are wedded to computers and crass solutions. I suspect George and Robert Stephenson are turning in their graves.)

Unfortunately, all over Queensland, famous lines have been obliterated – or at least truncated: the colourful Dirranbandi mail line, for example, is no more. To be fair, Queensland Rail (QR, formerly Queensland Railways) is building some extra track to further assist the movement of cattle by rail along the western system at Miles, facilitating Oakey Beef's return to rail, and it is trying to reverse recent trends by making a serious effort to keep some cattle movement on the main rail corridors and not have all of it go by road.

⌃ Hundreds of kilometres of narrow-gauge sugar cane track are still operated in Queensland today.

⌄ Transporting sugar cane, Nambour, c. 1965. Some sugar cane locomotives burnt cane to raise steam, completing a neat circle.

And at least today there remain hundreds of kilometres of operational 3 ft 6 in track in Queensland: from Cairns to Brisbane along the coast and then the main east–west corridors from the hinterland to the big ports, such as Brisbane, Rockhampton and Townsville.

The 2 ft sugar cane system in Queensland is also very extensive and intense around the big sugar mills located up and down the coast, driven by the fact sugar cane needs to be processed within 12 hours of cutting to capture maximum sugar extraction. Sugar cane freight only has an amazing 19 separate networks, all of them feeding the big mills that steam away into the night in the high season. One small section near Port Douglas is used for a tourist train operation, but the main purpose these systems serve is to get the sugar cane harvest delivered to the hub mills as quickly as possible.

While the average distance of haulage of the 36 million tonnes of sugar cane each year is 35 kilometres, some sugar farms are over 100 kilometres from their mill (the longest haulage being 119 kilometres). It has to be said that that is a long way on a 2 ft narrow-gauge track. Still, on the better sections of the networks, trains up to 1 kilometre long can operate carrying 2,000 tonnes of sugar cane (equal to about 50 B double truckloads).

In places, the 2 ft sugar cane railway crosses the north coast main line via a diamond crossover – something rail engineers hate – but gradually these crossings are being eliminated. One diamond crossover (now out of service) can be found in the grass at the small but impressive Bundaberg Railway Museum.

Pioneer Mill has a network that uses the Queensland narrow gauge; as a result, for one 25-kilometre stretch, the 2 ft narrow-gauge sugar cane track ran alongside the 3 ft 6 in Queensland main-gauge line. Only in Australia would we have so much dual gauge, including two large sections in Queensland and Western Australia.

For decades, steam haulage dominated the sugar cane networks. One veteran type of locomotive that had survived the First World War, the sturdy Hunslet, formed part of this system. Produced mainly for the Western Front, the Hunslet operated on the Decauville gauge, which was often laid down quickly after battles in which land was captured from the Germans. At places such as Clery, after the big advances following the successful battle of Amiens, Sir John Monash, commander of the Australian Corps, would issue instructions that standard-gauge size sleepers be laid down and narrow-gauge track on top to expedite transport; after the area settled down, then ballast would be brought along and the track converted to the SNCF standard gauge. This allowed for ammunition and food resupplies to be sent forward and for wounded troops to be brought back by rail quickly — all hauled by the two-piston Hunslet locomotive, which weighed a mere 14 tonnes but could pull heavy loads and was rarely derailed. Visiting senior generals could sometimes be found in the rear carriages of Hunslet-hauled trains, generally a few kilometres back from the actual front lines.

≫ The value of these builder's plates continues to climb every year.

In 1920 the Queensland government purchased six Hunslets repatriated from valiant war service; later this fleet grew to 15. All were destined for sugar cane haulage along the various networks running to the mills, such as at those at Innisfail.

One Hunslet was rescued and eventually ended up in the Australian War Memorial in Canberra. It looked marvellous when it was displayed alongside the big Lancaster bomber 'G for George', but unfortunately this meticulously restored Hunslet is currently locked away in a warehouse, at least for the time being.

But what of the other rail systems in Queensland? As we have seen, the legislation to form the fully government-owned Queensland Railways (QR) was carried in the colony's Lower House, by the casting vote of the Speaker, in 1863. After a huge public campaign, the legislation passed in both houses.

In turn, this led to QR becoming the all-powerful behemoth. It was fully government-owned and covered all Brisbane metropolitan, country passenger and freight operations for more than a dozen decades. Over this period, well over a thousand QR steam locomotives were created. Like all other colony- and later state-based systems, QR went down the familiar path of using too many types of locomotives and too complex a numbering system — but with the odd Irish twist or two.

« A worker 'laying the dust' at Central Station, c. 1950. This is not the main terminus station in Brisbane – that is Roma Street.

⩗ Locomotive No. 401 standing on a timber trestle bridge near Ipswich, c. 1970. By definition, a tank engine had no tender wagon behind.

≫ QR PB15 Class locomotive with a freight train, c. 1950. It was a brave decision to go narrow gauge with QR main lines – but it worked.

≫ QR Locomotive No. 888 with a test train of long-distance passenger cars, c. 1926. To this day QR still operates trains that take more than a day to reach their final destination.

↟ Faugh-a-Ballagh, 1865.
Ah, the Irish influence can
be found everywhere.

An initial batch of four imported locomotives came from Avonside Engine Company, Bristol, in England, and the first of these was used to steam from Ipswich North to Bigges Camp and on to what is today known as Grandchester. It was called Faugh-a-Ballagh, from an Irish term meaning 'get out of the way' or 'clear the way'. On the official opening in 1864, all four were in use.

For some reason Faugh-a-Ballagh was designated 'Train No. 3' and crewed by J Kenna as driver, J Hough as fireman and George Moore as the all-important conductor. These early crews soon learnt to hang on at any speed or risk being hurled out sideways by a big lurch into thin air. The rough early tracks ensured there were many such lurches.

The first four steam locomotives from Avonside were denoted with the letter 'A', meaning that they had two driving axles joined together. In turn, the letter 'B' denoted three axles, and 'C' four axles — so QR's famous C Class was 4–8–0. Ultimately, it was the mighty C Class that emerged triumphant.

« 'Cow-catchers' (as seen here on locomotive No. A12, c. 1890–1902) were unusual in Australia, but desirable on outback lines.

» Locomotive Class B: one of QR's great steam workhorses.

Burleigh Heads.

Stoney Creek.
Cairns Railway.

Millstream Falls.

LOCOMOTIVE, CLASS B, 17 INCH CYLINDER,
first of its kind built in Queensland.

Gallial Creek, Cairns-Mulgrave Railway.

Parlour Car
Queensland Rlys.

Cattle Creek. Mackay District.

Printed and Published for the Brisbane Newspaper Company, Limited, by William James Bonscott, of Sandgate-road, Clayfield, Brisbane, at the "Queenslander" Office, Queen-street, Brisbane, Queensland.

Queensland manufacturers stepped up to produce some 908 of the 1,311 QR steam locomotives eventually produced. Among many, Walkers Limited of Maryborough were big locomotive builders, used by the authorities to keep up a level of competition by providing a benchmark against which the government's huge North Ipswich Railway Workshops could be measured.

Later, the first four A Class locomotives were joined by the Baldwin, Fairlie, Ipswich and Nelson ones, along with others; as ever, there were too many types and not enough uniformity. This situation was not helped by the geography of Queensland, with its many big rivers that were difficult to bridge near the coast, and with the need to build networks quickly linking the ports to their hinterlands. By 1890 some 11 different separate systems had been established: (1) Brisbane–Charleville, Warwick and Yandina; (2) Cooroy–Gympie–Maryborough–Bundaberg; (3) North Bundaberg–Mount Perry; (4) Rockhampton–Longreach, Clermont and Springsure; (5) North Rockhampton–Emu Park; (6) Mackay–Eton and Mirani; (7) Bowen–Guthalungra; (8) Townsville–Hughenden; (9) Cairns–Mareeba; (10) Cooktown–Laura; (11) Normanton–Croydon.

The two big steam locomotives that truly ignited the economy of Queensland were the PB15 and the C17, sturdy fellows that stood the test of time, and did so on some very rugged track. Only later versions of these models enjoyed the advantage of having had roller bearings installed.

The PB15 was the earlier model, emerging from Walkers at Maryborough in 1899. Walkers went on to build 92 PB15s, almost half the QR fleet of this robust locomotive type that weighed in at around 35 tonnes. The fact that the PB15s were so sturdy meant they could handle rough track, and so allowed them to operate over all QR lines once the network was connected, and it was these engines that often led the mail trains out of Roma Street, Brisbane.

Over the early decades after Federation, improvements were made to the basic PB15; in particular, a switch was made from the Stephenson link valve motion to the better Walschaerts valve. By way of example, rail historian Leon Oberg highlights how No. 744 — known as *Miss Cairns* — was allocated to the tourist run from Cairns to Kuranda. Each morning *Miss Cairns* ground its way up from the coast at Cairns, climbing 330 metres to Kuranda.

⌃ 'Queensland Railways: Southern Mail Train', 1910. The industrial art of yesteryear is now a collector's item today.

Many drivers allude to the occasional lurch the PB15 could deliver, ensuring the need for driver and fireman to be sure their feet were firmly grounded at all times, preferably in heavy QR work boots. Remember the PB15 was operating on narrow gauge at main-line speeds, and arguably on an index calculating the amount of lurch or sway. Nevertheless, the PB15 broke all records compared with the standard- and broad-gauge steam locomotives travelling on much wider track.

The C17, which weighed in at around 80 tonnes, was designed for the heavy QR workload. These locomotives emerged in 1920, initially from Walkers but also from the North Ipswich Rail Workshops and three others. The fundamentals of the C17 was so good that they went interstate; for example, to the Zig Zag Railway in the Blue Mountains. But 25 were also built in Castlemaine, Victoria, for the Commonwealth Railways' northern operation through Marree to Alice Springs on narrow gauge.

The magnificent Pichi Richi Railway heritage operation in the Flinders Ranges still steams a C17 or NM25 between Port Augusta and Quorn today, one of a total 227 built between 1920 and 1953. Well designed and well built, the oldest C17 can be found near the Causeway in Townsville, under a roof but otherwise open to the weather, gently rusting away in that dynamic city with a huge army base. Perhaps some of the capable army engineers based there can step up to help de-rust this key locomotive and apply the necessary sealants.

≫ Good ballasted track being used by locomotive PB15 548 at Bethania Junction was essential for smooth running.

« The Garratt type of locomotive operated on four different gauges in Australia.

During the Second World War, Queensland came under direct threat as the Japanese bombed down the coast to near Townsville. In this period, the C17 came to the fore as QR resisted efforts by the federal government to create an Australian Standard Garratt (ASG) for narrow-gauge use. QR headquarters in Brisbane held out for their decided preference to build more C17s: better the beast that had a proven record than some new radical double-articulated locomotive. QR did operate a few ASGs, but hated them and so parted company with them.

Eventually, Queensland turned to Garratts, but not to the ASG. Instead, after the war ended, QR ordered their Garratts straight from Beyer, Peacock & Co., with deliveries starting from 1950. In all, 29 were built, and they were the heaviest steam locomotives north of the border, weighing in at around 140 tonnes.

» Locomotive No. 927 welcoming No. 926 on the northbound *Sunshine Express*, 1947. In Queensland very long-distance trains meant there was a need to change locomotives along the route.

⌃ Locomotive No. 3610, hauling the *Brisbane Express*, departs Sydney Central, c. 1940s. Once when riding this train, I shared the buffet car with a Queensland premier.

The smart-looking QR Garratt had a wheel configuration of 4–8–2 + 2–8–4, which was superb for climbing from Grandchester to Toowoomba, even if they were not easy to operate in the tunnels on that route. In due course, the Garratts were mostly based at Rockhampton and used for the coal mine traffic to its west.

Luckily, one QR Garratt (No. 1009) was preserved and put back into steam service for a period commencing in 1995. On one occasion, while at Roma Street Station to catch a suburban, I chanced to see this Garratt loading for a special run to Wallangarra. It had mainly British tourists on board. (I was jealous, but had to stay with my work schedule for the day.)

As late as 1968, there were thrice-weekly train services between Sydney, Tamworth, Armidale, Tenterfield and Wallangarra (where all changed for the QR train through to Stanthorpe, Warwick and Toowoomba before it turned down the range for Brisbane). You could depart Sydney Central at 3.10 pm on a Monday, Wednesday or Friday and arrive at 7.32 am the next morning at Wallangarra, just in time for a quick breakfast. After walking across to the QR platform, you could board the train departing at 7.55 am which was due to arrive in Brisbane at 5.15 pm. Dame Nellie Melba and Sir John Monash used this route — as did Mark Twain back in 1895, although he only reached Scone where he gave a lecture before turning back to Sydney.

The 2016 QR timetable shows the Westlander departing Roma Street at 7.15 pm to climb the range and reach Toowoomba at 11.05 pm, for a journey time of 230 minutes; by way of contrast, the 1968 timetable for the connecting train to Wallangarra shows a Brisbane departure at 8.15 am and Toowoomba arrival at 12.01 pm, so a travel time of 226 minutes. This means the trip on that vital but badly aligned railway was four minutes faster almost fifty years ago.

Queensland has shown considerable resourcefulness in welding 11 different systems into ten linked plus one, the one being the lonely Normanton–Croydon railway, which although not connected to the QR network still operates today, mainly for tourists.

An end to steam?

There is a real possibility that 'through' steam locomotive operation will end between Brisbane and Toowoomba, with tourist steam trains banned.

Both proposals for the Inland Freight Rail direct from Brisbane to Melbourne go through a proposed 7.6-kilometre tunnel under the Great Dividing Range near Toowoomba, intended to greatly ease grades and build efficiencies. It is envisaged this will be a dual-gauge tunnel with plenty of height clearance to allow double stacking of containers.

With this super tunnel opening, the existing steep main line through Helidon and Spring Bluff will most likely close, although there is a strong case to be made for keeping open the section from Toowoomba down as far as Spring Bluff, especially for the annual flower and garden activities each spring.

Owing to ventilation problems, trains will not be permitted to operate under steam through any tunnel more than 7 kilometres long, although they could be towed through at middle-range speeds by diesel-electric locomotives.

Essentially, this signals the end of the occasional steam train special travelling up and down the range between Brisbane and Toowoomba. It reflects progress, but once again it will come at the expense of the magnificent sight of a steam locomotive chugging up steep grades and trailing a lovely flume of smoke.

« QR locomotive No. 702 after its completion as the 100th engine to be built at Ipswich Workshops, 1922. Producing 100 of these C19 Class locomotives involved much precision work on the lathes and other machinery.

» In its current maroon colours, locomotive No. 1105, the last of this Garratt type, is a great sight.

⌃ Garratt locomotive G23 hauling freight to Townsville in 1944. The ASG was a product of the Second World War, and there is one of these Garratts left in Queenscliff, Victoria, today.

ONE LAST TOUCH OF THE IRISH

There are few rail giants still around these days, few people up there with the vision of a Brunel, a Clapp, a McCusker or a Whitton. Vince O'Rourke was born in that great railway town of Bathurst on 21 April 1936 and found his first job sweeping the longest platform in Australia, the 'break of gauge' one at Albury (where his father was stationmaster). After studying economics and finance at UNE Armidale, O'Rourke worked his way up the NSWGR management ladder.

In 1991 O'Rourke was appointed as QR Commissioner. He managed QR's corporatisation and became the first CEO of the newly structured body. He was probably the last rail chief to create a new luxury passenger train, the Great South Pacific Express, which was a joint venture between the Orient Express and QR. (Unfortunately, it arrived in difficult times and can now be found in that new vibrant luxury train market of Peru.) Under his watch, QR thrived, with huge increases in coal tonnages, bedding down electrification extensions and much more over the last decade of the twentieth century.

Senior rail management requires a very specific knowledge base along with the usual leadership and managerial attributes. The decades of service that such great exemplars as O'Rourke, and operations manager and rail strategist John Hearsch, formerly of Queensland but now back consulting in Victoria, have given to rail travel deserves salutation.

In 1996 O'Rourke created a special steam train run in the middle of Brisbane for then state Governor Peter Arnison, then Deputy Prime Minister (the author) and others. It gave us an opportunity to inspect track work and salute rail, both vintage and modern.

In a sense, QR started with one Irishman in Abram Fitzgibbon and ended up 140 years later being run by another. It is a curious fact, however, that Queensland is the only state (other than Western Australia) that never at any stage used Irish broad-gauge track.

Around the turn of the century, an Abt rack railway, with a notched middle rail, was built from Kabra to Mount Morgan, not far out of Rockhampton, initially driven by mining activity in the area. But after some 50 years of operation a longer route was developed on an easier gradient. Diesel locomotives replaced steam in the mid-1960s, but they failed to win much business back from the more convenient road link. Passenger services were withdrawn, and this branch line was eventually closed in 1978. Today there remain just two operating Abt railways in Australia, one in Tasmania between Queenstown and Strahan and another near Thredbo, known as the Ski Tube.

In 2010 Aurizon was set up to take over the QR freight operations and most of the existing track network. The company successfully floated on the stock

<< Abt rack railway near Mount Morgan, c. 1895. Mount Morgan had its golden years but soon was mined out, and so both railways servicing it are closed today.

exchange and today operates also in other states, including stand-alone operations shifting coal down the Hunter Valley to the port of Newcastle. It is today Australia's largest rail freight haulage operator and has been very profitable since inception. For its part, QR continues to operate passenger services and much more, but the huge freight effort of yesteryear has gone across to Aurizon. To its credit, QR has retained an in-house 'official historian', more particularly a holder of a wealth of corporate knowledge that helps maintain continuity. This position is held by the capable Greg Hallam, who knows all there is to know about railways in Queensland.

The process of electrification in Queensland was done on an unusually large scale, not only for the Brisbane metro system (from 1979), but also on the key coal lines in central Queensland, and, as an extra effort, the Brisbane–Rockhampton main line via Gladstone. A more efficient 25,000 volts AC was adopted, as opposed to the older 1,500 volts DC as used in Victoria and New South Wales. Brisbane bureaucrats worked out that rail electrification initially saved more than $100 million in diesel costs each year, which also means the state didn't have to pay tens of millions of dollars of annual fuel excise payments to the federal government. It was a smart move and combined with a new rail bridge connecting Roma Street with South Brisbane across the Brisbane River, electrification proved a huge boost to all kinds of rail traffic over the last three decades.

For 100 years, steam locomotive haulage had been to the fore, albeit with far too many types of locomotives. They did much to open up the hinterland of Queensland and help build the modern economy of the state of Queensland today. They also helped the defence of Australia during the Second World War.

⌄ A somewhat surreal portrayal of a rail scene.

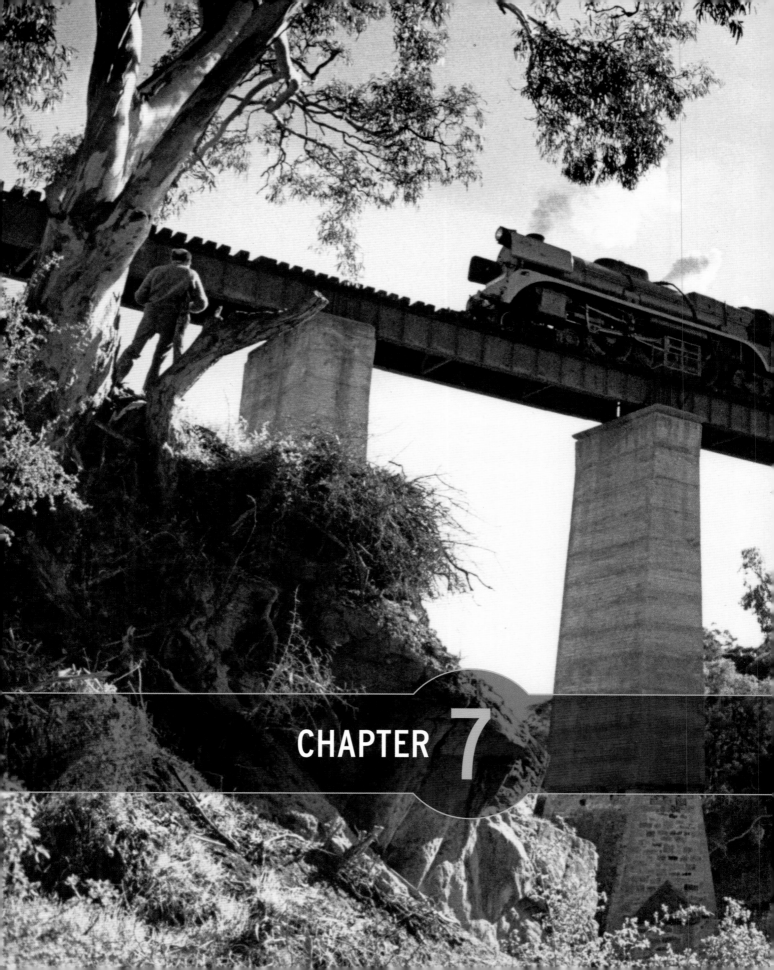

CHAPTER 7

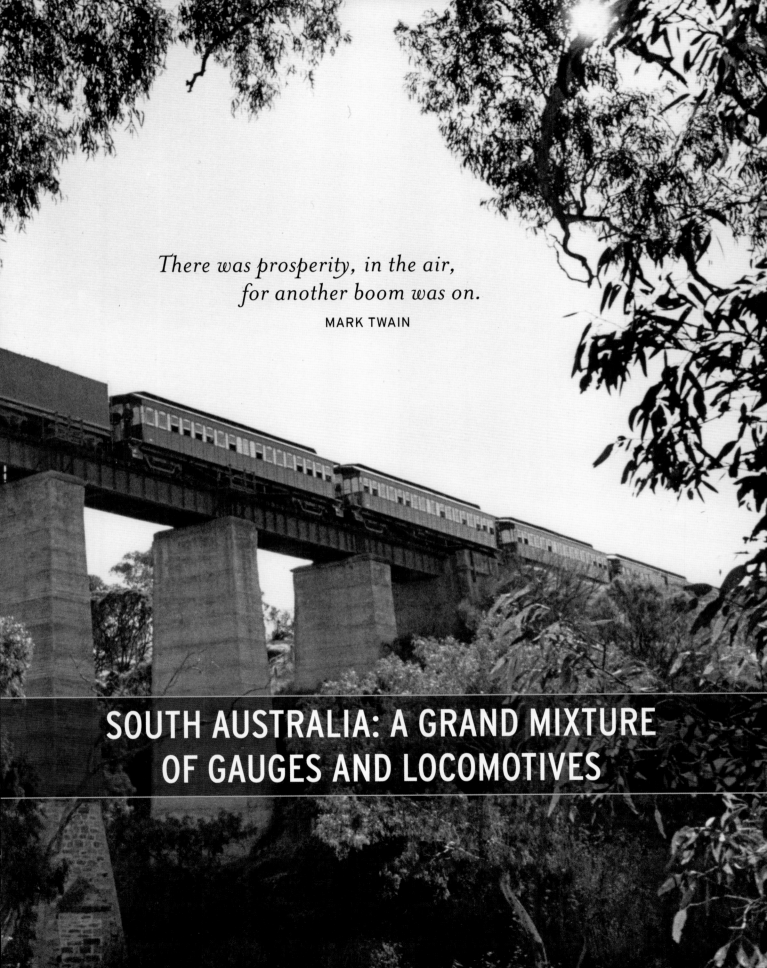

There was prosperity, in the air,
for another boom was on.
MARK TWAIN

SOUTH AUSTRALIA: A GRAND MIXTURE OF GAUGES AND LOCOMOTIVES

When Mark Twain arrived in South Australia in 1895, he came by steam train and departed by steam train. On his journey from Melbourne he absorbed much, alighting at Belair, on the outskirts of Adelaide, and then proceeded by carriage:

We descended and entered [Adelaide]. There was nothing to remind one of the humble capital, of huts and sheds of the long-vanished day of the land-boom. No, this was a modern city, with wide streets, compactly built; with fine homes everywhere, embowered in foliage and flowers, and with imposing masses of public buildings nobly grouped and architecturally beautiful.

Already Port Adelaide had been set up, and the Glenelg Railway that would later become a tramway was operating; the strong grid pattern of the Adelaide CBD was well established. Mark Twain entertained many on his lecture tour but he also wrote extensively about what he saw. Twain captured a great deal of the essence of Australia, as is evident from his earlier description of the blue hills and mountains of Australia: 'It was a stunning colour, that blue. Deep, strong, rich, exquisite: towering and majestic masses of blue — a softly luminous blue, a smoldering blue, as if vaguely lit by fires within.' Of course, near the main railway tracks, the masses of blue — whether mountain or sky — would occasionally be punctured by plumes of white steam or black coal smoke.

South Australia's first city railway ran from the Adelaide CBD to Port Adelaide; it had been authorised by legislation in 1851, and officially opened in 1856 to large crowds and much banter and bunting. Three steam locomotives were imported from William Fairbairn of Manchester, gravitas was extended when highfalutin names were appended to these 2–4–0 tank engines (A Class), later operating with tenders: No. 1 Adelaide; No. 2 Victoria; No. 3 Albert. Alas, not one of them was preserved, which is a great pity: No. 1 would draw huge crowds if once a year it was put back into steam at the National Railway Museum, Port Adelaide, but all too often so much from our early locomotive stables has been scrapped or ditched.

These three locomotives gave good service for around 15 years, although it has to be said that the predominantly level terrain made the steaming easy and did not hugely strain these early birds. They were later replaced by a B Class 2–4–0 and one or two other types, notably the X Class 2–8–0 in 1880, imported from the Baldwin Locomotive Works in Philadelphia, Pennsylvania, USA. As always, there was a plethora of types of locomotives used.

The mostly level Adelaide terrain saw other easy tracks built, including from the CBD via the famous racecourse at Morphettville to the jetty at Glenelg Beach. In 1871 the Parliament of South Australia had passed *The Adelaide, Glenelg, and Suburban Railway Act*, and away the rail mania went, along with a related land

⌃ Pacific-type locomotive at Adelaide Railway Station, 1927. In its heyday, this was a grand terminal, but long-distance passenger trains now leave from nearby Keswick.

» King William Street, Adelaide, c. 1909. Trams are back in Adelaide with a vengeance, with more route expansion planned for 2018.

» Concepts for double-
decker carriages have
been around a long time,
as this nineteenth-
century Adelaide and
Goodwood Motor and
CGL testifies.

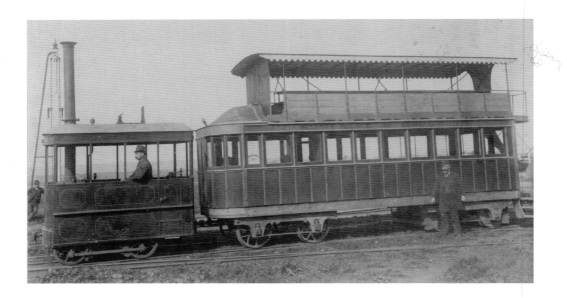

boom in proximity to the key routes. Significantly, the act stipulated Irish broad
gauge from inception.

The first steam locomotive for the Glenelg Railway was a Stephenson tank
engine; numbered No. 1, it did years of faithful service, helping the railway to
generate annual profits early on. There was regular commuter traffic, but on big
race days at Morphettville the trains were so crowded that some rode 'Indian style'
— namely, on the carriage roof, with no action taken against them.

The initial timetable had a certain flourish about it, with eight passenger
trains listed in both directions, correctly in the eyes of all diehards and history
students of rail showing Glenelg to Adelaide as 'UP' trains and Adelaide to
Glenelg as 'DOWN' trains. It has always been thus, with curious twists; for
example, 'The Fish' and 'The Chips' running to Sydney Central down the lower
slopes of the Blue Mountains and across to Parramatta — more or less downhill all
the way — is of course listed as the UP train. The governing rule worldwide is that
all trains to London are UP trains, all trains from London, or a central hub
station such as Sydney Central or Adelaide CBD, are DOWN trains. The famous
Bradshaw's Guides of yesteryear affirmed this. Where double track is involved,
one is invariably designated the UP track and the other the DOWN track.

The Glenelg Railway was a gold mine, profitable from inception. However, it
was accused in the local press of ripping passengers off and failing to meet rising
demand, especially on race days. In 1878 this prompted the Parliament of South
Australia to approve a rival, to be known as the Holdfast Bay Railway Company; it
commenced operations in 1880, but proved to be a flash in the pan. Merger talks
soon broke out, and in 1881 the parliament approved a merger under the
combined banner of the Glenelg Railway Company Limited.

» Cities with large
central grids, such as
Adelaide, Melbourne and
Turin, have many
advantages when it
comes to transport.

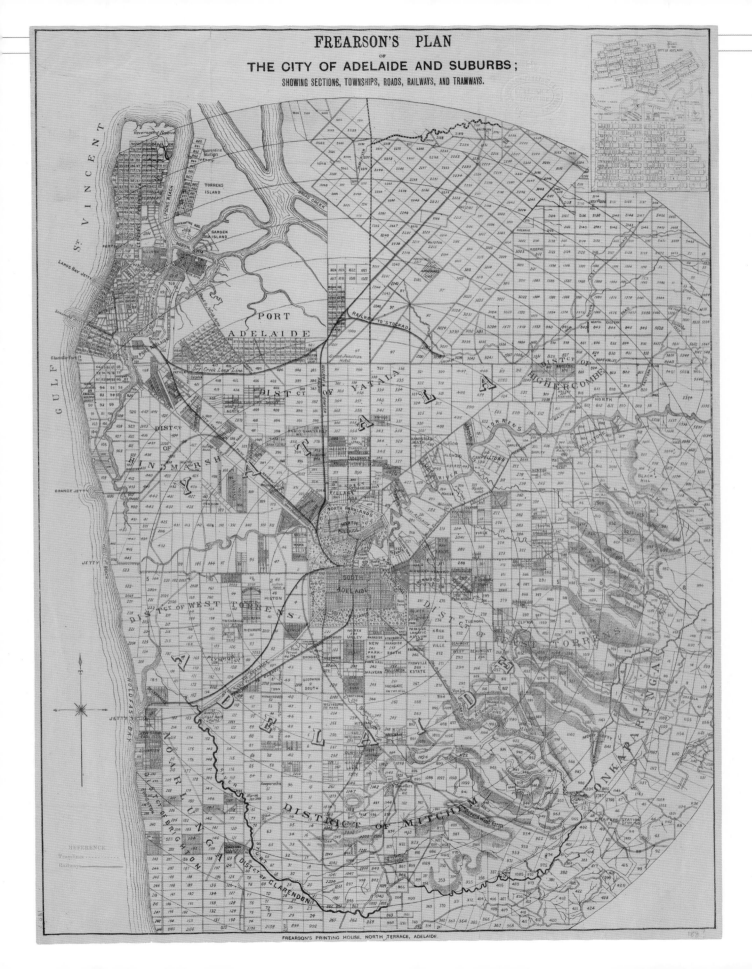

FREARSON'S PLAN

OF

THE CITY OF ADELAIDE AND SUBURBS;

SHOWING SECTIONS, TOWNSHIPS, ROADS, RAILWAYS, AND TRAMWAYS.

DOUBLE-TRACK RAIL

What was it to be – would the very British colony of South Australia opt for British left-side running or French right-side running? Do not think for a moment that, when it comes to the crucial matter of which side of a double-track main-line trains should run on, they automatically follow the roads. In Belgium, France and Italy, for example, they drive cars on the right side in the direction of travel, but their double-track rail systems all operate on the left side, mainly because rail development in Europe was dominated by the influence of the Stephensons *père et fils*. (In ancient times, all passing horse traffic tended to pass on the left side – in the direction of travel – to keep the right arm or sword arm ready for instant action if need arose. Sweden was the last big European country to switch from left- to right-side, which they did one famous weekend in 1967.)

The SNCF railways of France have always been thus, including with the high-speed TGV (Train à Grande Vitesse). Right from the start the TGV used sections of conventional double track from Paris Gare de Lyon to Lyon; as a result, the TGV system operates broadly on the left side. It was fortunate that the French swallowed hard and went the British way on this matter: when the direct Paris–London (Chunnel) service eventually opened, there was one less area of debate.

In Australia, there may have been no unanimity on gauge, but at least there was on which side to operate double track. In recent years, many sections of double track allow for bi-directional running to maximise efficiencies, though unfortunately not at Bethungra, between Cootamundra and Junee, on the Sydney–Melbourne main line. With increased locomotive power, all rail traffic should be

» Adelaide Horse Car and Electric Tram, South Australia, 1909. Electricity was a lifesaver, particularly for light rail.

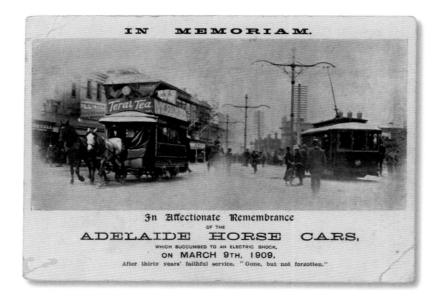

IN MEMORIAM.

In Affectionate Remembrance
OF THE
ADELAIDE HORSE CARS,
WHICH SUCCUMBED TO AN ELECTRIC SHOCK,
ON MARCH 9TH, 1909.
After thirty years' faithful service, "Gone, but not forgotten."

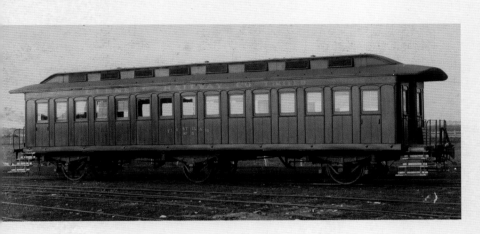

« A nineteenth-century first-class car of the Glenelg Railway. Weight and its distribution played a big part in the size of bogies.

and the expenditure of extra energy) to stop and restart a fully loaded coal train.

In South Australia, there were tangles around Adelaide, but broadly speaking, on double track, it was left-side running. The fact that the early Glenelg Railway Company used actual streets for sections of double track helped lock in this practice.

Today, between Crystal Brook and the junction at Port Pirie, there is a short section of standard-gauge double track leading into a 2-kilometre-long Australian Rail Track Corporation (ARTC) passing loop at Coonamia. Trains can, and do, occasionally run 'wrong-side' in this loop.

switched to the much shorter DOWN line when there's no conflicting traffic, but a lack of points at Bethungra, and at the top of the now largely unnecessary spiral, preclude this from happening.

On the busy main line between Rockhampton and Gladstone, with many coal trains on the go, there is often 'wrong-side running' on sections; this is all about reducing the need to stop loaded coal trains – with good reason, as it costs about $1,000 (owing to wear and tear on the brake gear

Other means of transport entered the fray, including not just improved horse-drawn coaches but also trams (initially, steam trams operating on standard gauge). After various investigations and parliamentary reports, notably the report prepared by William Goodman, momentum grew for the obvious solution. This was to switch the Glenelg lines to standard gauge (which was already being used by trams elsewhere in Adelaide), and electrify them to eliminate the pollution being caused by the busy tank engines in relatively narrow streets. In 1929 the last steam train ran to Glenelg. It was the end of an era, after more than 50 years' service, but not before large crowds waved it farewell.

The first true railway in South Australia had started up in 1854, to capture the busy trade on paddle-steamers up and down the Murray–Darling river system. It ran between the river port hub of Goolwa and Port Elliot, a distance of 11 kilometres, but was later extended another 7 kilometres to the safer Victor Harbor. For the first three decades, it was horse-hauled, with mighty Clydesdale

South Australia's first rail link: a horse-drawn tram on the Goolwa to Port Elliot Railway, c. 1860.

horses to the fore. (I suppose they could be designated '0–4–0'.) The actual mouth of the Murray River is rarely deep enough to be navigable, and so this horse-drawn railway was the solution.

It was not until 1884 that steam locomotion was introduced at Goolwa, concurrent with the rail connection from Adelaide via Mount Barker and Strathalbyn. All of this was built in Irish broad gauge from inception. In 2004 there was a great 150th celebration of the Goolwa-to-Victor Harbor railway, with steam trains operated by the SteamRanger Heritage Railway running frequently and huge crowds attending. (SteamRanger had stepped up in 1986 after Australian National withdrew from operating this railway two years earlier.)

The ultimate insult hurled at South Australia's first railway was to come in 1995 when the main line from Melbourne to Adelaide, through the Adelaide Hills, was standardised; this left the Mount Barker–Victor Harbor line stranded because of a failure to retain a few kilometres of broad-gauge connector track. It could have been a compromise, with a few kilometres of dual gauge, but it was not to be. The result is that the SteamRanger Heritage Railway cannot offer a smart gourmet day service from Adelaide terminus through the Adelaide Hills and down past the Murray River and on to Victor Harbor. Operating on the first Saturday of each month, it would have been a sell-out: an easy three-hour run down in the morning, with brunch served and back in the late afternoon with an early dinner. But instead there are services between Goolwa and Victor Harbor; at a distance of 18 kilometres, these are close to the absolute optimal length recommended by the European Federation of Museum & Tourist Railways (FEDECRAIL) for heritage rail.

SAR locomotive No. Rx207 and VR locomotive No. K190 with a special passenger train at Roseworthy, SA, 1981. Use of special trains fluctuates, but these can be useful revenue-raisers.

For most of its life this very scenic line that runs alongside the Southern Ocean for a few kilometres near Victor Harbor was operated by South Australian Railways (SAR), and the steam locomotive most used was the R Class, the most numerous early workhorse of the old SAR broad-gauge system.

The first six locomotives were originally imported from Dübs & Co. in Glasgow, Scotland; ultimately, a total of 84 R and Rx Class were built for South Australia alone. In the early days, shortly after the first six had arrived and gone into service in 1886, James Martin & Co. of Gawler, South Australia, built another 24. The R Class went on to give decades of superb service. Interestingly, orders for more were shared around, as far afield as Walkers in Maryborough, Queensland, and with the North British Locomotive Company, plus the local Islington Workshops of the SAR. The HQ elements and State Treasurers obviously had an eye to competitive tendering helping to keep tender prices down.

The R Class, which was upgraded to a larger boiler between 1898 and 1913 and designated the Rx Class in the process, was able to do the big hauls from Adelaide to Serviceton on the SA–Victorian border for the connection through to Melbourne and after 1917, from Adelaide to Terowie in the north for the connection to Broken Hill (for direct Sydney traffic) and the connection to Quorn and Port Augusta for the east west Perth traffic.

One or two are preserved and still capable of operation today but most were scrapped as a wave of modernisation took shape in the twentieth century. It has to be stated there was a great deal of intelligent mechanical engineering around the railways of the colonies, decisions at the time of Federation to think big and upgrade the R Class boiler was both wise and delivered successful outcomes.

As is often the case, there are critical turning points with railways and the year 1887 saw the rail link between Adelaide and Melbourne completed and the introduction of an overnight express on 19 January of that year, along with rail freight services.

Sometimes turning points involved new talent being appointed at the top. In the case of both SAR and Victorian Railways (VR), it was the arrival of railroad talent from the United States that shook things up.

⌄ SAR goods train at Victor Harbor, c. 1908. Victor Harbor was a key port for the lower reaches of the Murray River.

⌄ A 'mystery hiker' train, locomotive No. 712,
c. 1935 – presumably on another run up into
the delightful Adelaide Hills.

≪ SAR locomotives Nos T248 and 522 transferring passengers from the *Pichi Richi Pathfinder* special train, Terowie, 1962. To this day, the Pichi Richi Pass is one of the great train corridors of Australia.

≪ SAR locomotive G100 on a turntable at Victor Harbor in 1887. Turntables were essential to ensure steam locomotives were pointing in the right direction.

» SAR locomotive No. 603 with an Adelaide-bound passenger train, Riverton, c. 1930. The wayside stop to use local rail refreshment rooms was vital when no buffet or dining cars existed.

≫ Ballast being unloaded from a freight train, 1936. Bad ballast meant derailments; good hard ballast meant rail sleepers or ties, and the attached rail lines, being held in place.

INTERCOLONIAL EXPRESS

As luck would have it, there was no 'break of gauge' between Melbourne and Adelaide, so the moment the two rail systems joined at Serviceton both Victoria and South Australia moved quickly to create a seamless overnight express. Operating from 1887, it was the very first seamless rail connection linking two capital cities in Australia.

⬈ At least, this Adelaide–Melbourne rail corridor was the same gauge from its inception, so no midnight change of trains was ever required.

The new train was named – appropriately enough – the *Intercolonial Express*, and it was much faster than travelling by the Cobb and Co. coach service or by coastal steamer. All trains on this service were steam-hauled. Dame Nellie Melba, Mary MacKillop and John Monash were just some of the VIPs who used it regularly, along with various state premiers.

Strangely, each state system did not trust the other when it came to catering, so each night at Ararat the VR dining car was detached and at Serviceton the SAR dining car was unhooked; both were then readied to be hooked on the train coming the other way in time to serve breakfast. The dining car service was cancelled in the Great Depression, but one remnant Pullman broad-gauge dining car from the United States can be found, in all its glory, at the National Railway Museum. To assist with smooth dining, it has a lump of concrete weighing several tonnes below its floor.

Comfortable sleeping cars were updated from time to time, with air-conditioning introduced from 1949 along with stainless steel streamlining. In 1936 the name of the train was changed to the *Overland*. Today it continues as a daylight service aimed at the southern tourist market. It only operates a couple of times per week – but once again you can get a meal on board.

« Diesel power meant the capacity to accelerate quicker than with steam power, and to achieve greater average speed.

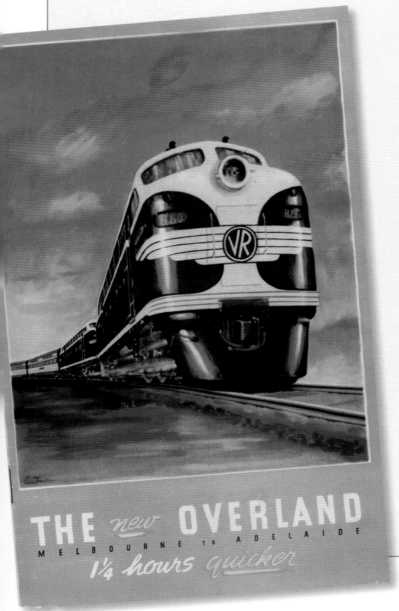

THE *new* OVERLAND
MELBOURNE TO ADELAIDE
1¼ hours quicker

While Sir Harold Clapp had been born in Melbourne in 1875, he had spent two critical decades working in America before his decisive stint as head of VR, beginning with his arrival in Melbourne in September 1920. Likewise, American William Alfred Webb, who had worked on railroads since the age of 12, was a railway person through and through, working his way up through Colorado Midland Railways and later Texas Central Railway and various US government railroad positions during and after the First World War.

Just a couple of years after Clapp had come across the Pacific to Melbourne, Webb arrived in Adelaide on 18 November 1923, ready to deliver a huge shake up. Although he was on a huge salary of some £5,000 a year, somehow he managed to avoid income tax on his annual payment. Worse still, in the eyes of both state and federal treasuries, he carried out necessary big revamps, but as if there was a bottomless bucket of money around to be spent.

William Alfred Webb, Chief Commissioner of Railways, at his work desk, c. 1923. Somehow, he had wrangled a deal where he did not have to pay income taxes.

Webb soon figured out that the SAR needed stronger locomotives, improved heavier main lines and greater decentralisation; even if South Australia was not then in a boom time — and there were no big mines on the horizon — Webb was nevertheless going to spend up big.

In 1937 an extension of the Transcontinental Railway from Port Augusta to Port Pirie in South Australia opened for business. The original east–west Transcontinental had joined at Ooldea on 17 October 1917, with trains operating shortly afterwards. The new key link meant the elimination of a grand circle connector whereby all passengers travelling from Adelaide to Perth initially went to Terowie, just west of Crystal Brook, and changed to narrow gauge to Peterborough, then on through Quorn to come down through Pichi Richi Pass to the island platform at Port Augusta. There all changed again from the narrow gauge to the Transcontinental standard-gauge express to travel to Kalgoorlie, where there was a change back to narrow gauge for the final leg into Perth. This meant that, in the era of steam, passengers from Sydney to Perth (whether going via Melbourne or via Broken Hill) had to change trains at least three, if not four, times. After 1937 this situation was greatly improved, with fewer changes between Sydney and Perth via Broken Hill and Port Pirie, and likewise between Adelaide, Port Pirie and Perth.

Webb's problem was having no locomotive for the dash from Adelaide to Port Pirie, some of this on light rail, because this new key link had not been properly installed to main-line standards. And so to help handle the growing east–west traffic Webb ordered the 500 Class and later the 620 Class, some very smart looking 4–6–2 locomotives. In ordering the 500 class, he took the first big steps towards steam modernity in South Australia. Designed by Fred Shea, these locomotives started out as 4–8–2 but were later converted to 4–8–4 for better weight distribution and tracking guidance.

Ten of these handsome steam locomotives were built by Armstrong Whitworth in Newcastle upon Tyne, complete with tenders that could carry some 12 tonnes of coal. Under the watchful eye of William Webb they went into operation, handling the heavy grade out of Adelaide to Tailem Bend on the Melbourne main line – 30 kilometres of steep climbing – before descending to cross the mighty Murray River.

All ten 500 Class locomotives carried names of famous South Australians; as luck would have it, No. 504, bearing the name *Tom Barr Smith*, is the only one that has been preserved. Barr Smith was a wealthy grazier and philanthropist whose father had been a successful South Australian pioneer and whose mother was an Elder, and so part of the family that started the huge wool trading firm known as Elders Limited today. Some of the Barr Smith family properties were over the border, near Wentworth in far south-western New South Wales, and in good seasons they produced a great deal of wool which, as we have seen, went by paddle-steamer to Goolwa, near the mouth of the Murray River, and then by steam train

⩒ South Australian light Pacific 620 Class No. 629 pulling the westbound *Perth Express*, 1938.

either to Victor Harbor or Port Elliot. Later on, the steam trains went to the big wool stores of Adelaide where the fleeces were sold at auction. It was steam locomotion that was transporting vital hinterland production, notably wool and later grain to the ports.

Along with the 500 Class there was the 620 Class, again designed by Fred Shea. All were built at Islington Workshops using a 4–6–2 Pacific-type wheel configuration. Ten of this class were built between 1936 and 1938, again with an eye to the vital new Adelaide-to-Port Pirie broad-gauge link, which connected with the standard-gauge Transcontinental from Kalgoorlie at Port Pirie.

In 1935 Webb had returned to the United States, stung by the prolonged criticism of his exorbitant expenditure and the exposure of the fact he did not have to pay income tax. However, his mantra of better and bigger equipment was established, and not much dinted by the Great Depression (although many of his administrative reforms were reversed). The next big step unfolded on the steam locomotive front was the development of a new 520 Class, building on the 500 Class and the 620 Class. With a distinctive curved streamline nose, these 200-tonne 4–8–4 workhorses soon bore the brunt of increased Second World War traffic. Twelve were built by SAR's Islington Workshops and, as many have observed, they made a powerful sight tackling the long grade up through the Adelaide Hills. Locomotive 523 is one of only two remaining on display, named *Essington Lewis* and residing in all its glory at the National Railway Museum. Locomotive 520 is out of service and now owned by and located with SteamRanger.

Sir Essington Lewis was a great Australian who was born at Burra Burra, South Australia, in 1881 and educated in Adelaide. He stumbled onto a career in mining and metal processing, and joined BHP in 1904. He worked his way up the company ranks to become its long-serving and innovative managing director before becoming chairman in 1950. During the Second World War he was made Director of Munitions and later Director of Aircraft Production, in each case getting the job done and commanding great respect. Certainly, he deserved to have the giant 523 named after him. It hauled many tonnes of vital wartime freight, but also gave sterling service in peacetime until it was overhauled then eventually retired in the 1950s – a victim of the process of dieselisation that unfolded in all states.

In 1975 SAR was sold to the Commonwealth, and all railways outside of the Adelaide metropolitan system in South Australia became part of Australian National. By this stage, it had been 15 years since any steam locomotives ran in regular service in South Australia. Later, in 1996, further reforms were introduced, with Genesee and Wyoming taking over the old SAR component, except for the key passenger trains, which went to Great Southern Rail (initially owned by Serco EG) which operates *The Ghan*, the *Indian Pacific* and the *Overland*).

⌃ BHP's Essington Lewis, 1943. During the Second World War he oversaw vital munitions and aircraft production.

⌃ SAR locomotive
No. 508, c. 1970–75.
The Adelaide Hills caused
firemen lots of very hard
work keeping the coal up
to the fire.

ARTC took over the basic track network with headquarters at Adelaide and owning and operating the east-west Transcontinental (Melbourne–Adelaide–Perth) and, through leases, many key tracks in New South Wales, including the huge Hunter Valley coal trains to the world's largest coal export port, Newcastle.

Steam today in South Australia is a rare sight, but the rail heritage operations show great potential, such as the heritage Pichi Richi Railway that runs in the Flinders Ranges. This aspect of South Australian steam will stand the test of time and will be dealt with in more detail in a later chapter.

NATIONAL RAILWAY MUSEUM

The National Railway Museum (NRM) at Port Adelaide, is Australia's largest railway museum. It has more than 100 large display items relating to four different railway gauges – five if we count the nearby Semaphore and Fort Glanville Tourist Railway it operates. Initially, the NRM was located at Mile End near the Adelaide CBD. Collecting began in 1964, and in 1988 the museum moved to superb premises at Port Adelaide where most of its valuable items are stored under cover.

Two federal government grants gave great impetus: $2 million from the Bicentennial funding of 1988 and another $1 million from the Federation Centenary funding in 1999, which allowed a Commonwealth Railways Pavilion to be built, named after Ronald E. Fluck, the museum founder. Over the years good leadership, helped by a dedicated skeleton staff and many volunteers, has given this museum real gravitas and substance.

Today Bob Sampson leads the NRM; he knows the designation of every train on the move in the state on any given day, and photographs many of them. He is helped by many, including a leading tram museum expert, John Radcliffe. (This is a nice crossover given that the Glenelg tram originally started as the Glenelg Railway Company many decades ago.)

NRM is the only true multi-gauge rail museum of any consequence in the world and houses the 'Tea and Sugar', the old resupply train that stopped and started its way across the Nullarbor, complete with a mobile butcher shop on wheels. It is well worth a visit just to see this train, and to experience how things were done not so

⌃ Ex-CR NM Class No. NM34, ex-BHP locomotive No. 4 and Ex-CR G Class No. G1 on display at the magnificent National Railway Museum, Port Adelaide – the best multi-gauge rail museum in the world.

many years ago to help isolated stations across the Nullarbor.

The naming of the museum as the 'National' Rail Museum was debated for years and for months New South Wales blocked its nationwide corporate registration. This resistance, which took some arm-twisting to overcome, was a keen reminder of the interstate conflict over railways that has emerged too often in Australia's history.

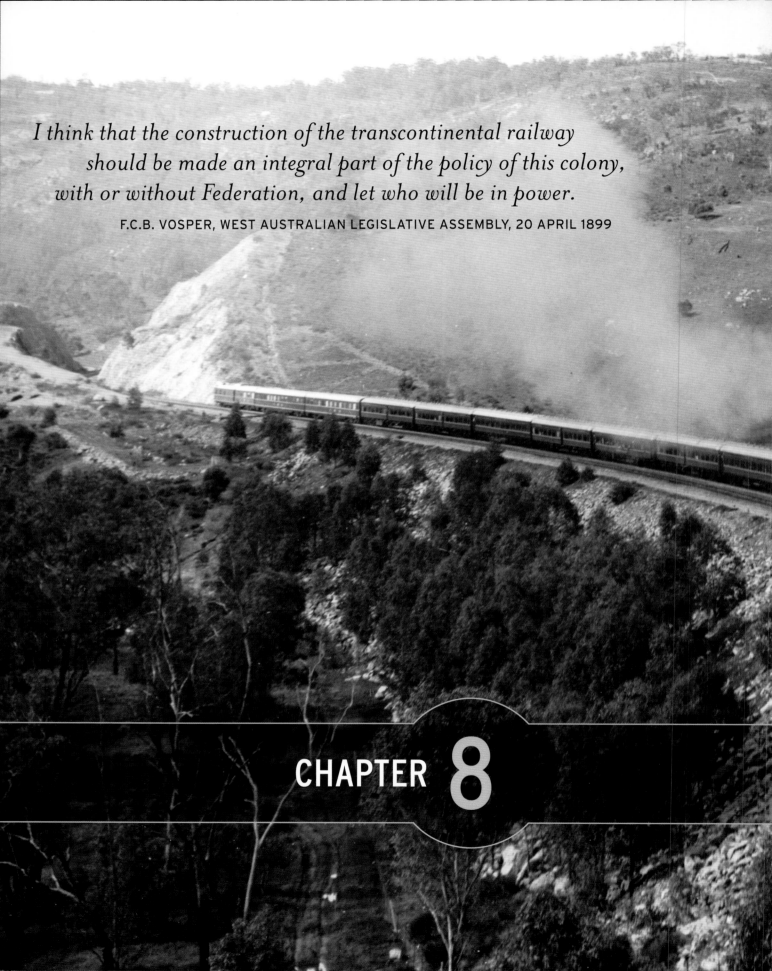

*I think that the construction of the transcontinental railway
should be made an integral part of the policy of this colony,
with or without Federation, and let who will be in power.*

F.C.B. VOSPER, WEST AUSTRALIAN LEGISLATIVE ASSEMBLY, 20 APRIL 1899

CHAPTER 8

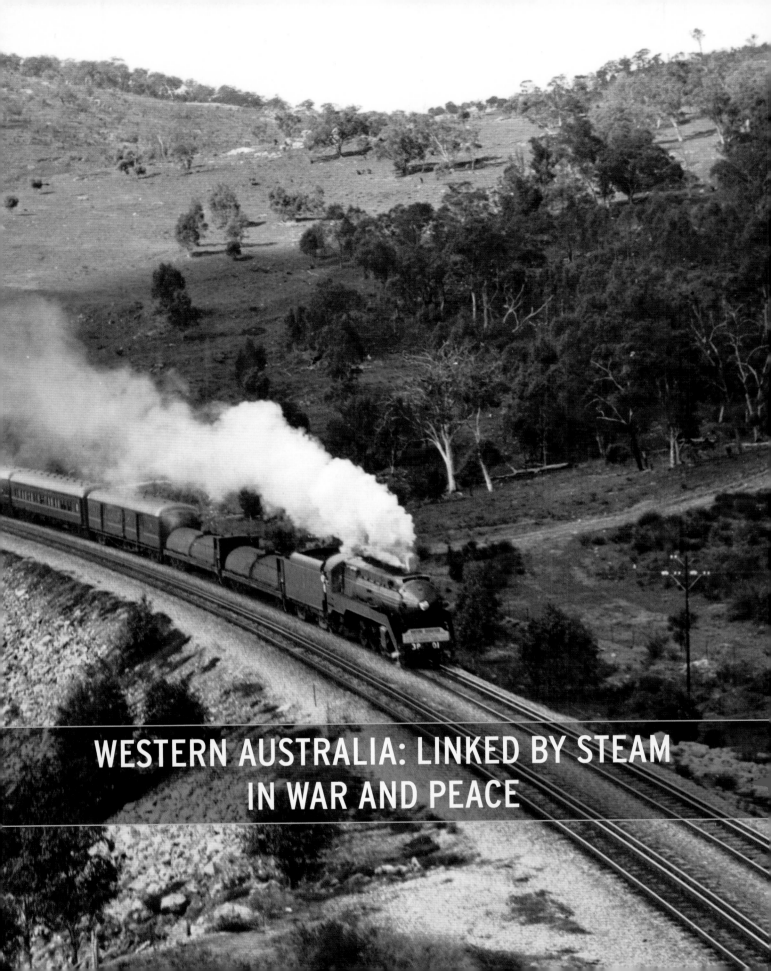

WESTERN AUSTRALIA: LINKED BY STEAM IN WAR AND PEACE

Four hundred years ago, in October 1616, a brave Dutch sailor and his crew brushed up against the western coast of *Terra Australis*, the great unknown southern land. To record his visit, Dirk Hartog, commander of the good ship *Eendracht*, left a pewter plate nailed to an oak post at what became known as Cape Inscription on Shark Island (now known as Dirk Hartog Island). Hartog called the new land *Eendrachtsland* (Land of Eendracht) after his ship, whose name meant 'unity'. It would be another 200 years before any white settlement took place, with a party sent west by ship from Sydney to King George's Sound (as Albany was then known), mainly to ensure the French did not plant a colony along the isolated Western Australian coast.

The Swan River colony was established in 1829, and three years later the Legislative Council was established – it became an informally elected body in 1867. A constitution was granted in 1890 and proclaimed – the colony was truly up and away. It had a strong premier in former surveyor and explorer Sir John Forrest, who fully supported the role rail could play in the colony. The key 'proclamation' documents were carried by the governor on a steam train from Albany to Perth!

Prodded by the combination of gold discovery, wheat-farming potential and wool production, and the prosperity of the timber industry, railway development in Western Australia ran ahead of the creation of a constitution, The embryonic railways of Western Australia on Anglo Cape narrow gauge started out in 1871 with the *Ballaarat* steam locomotive, conveying timber on a short line running inland from Lockville near Busselton to Yoganup. *Ballaarat* was the first narrow-gauge steam locomotive built in Australia, and was named for the Victorian town (spelled thus at that time) in which it was built. It still exists today. A few years later, in 1879, the first government-built railway was constructed from Geraldton to the mines at Northhampton, and in 1881 another ran from Fremantle to Perth

and Guildford. In 1894 a private enterprise railway (floated on the London Stock Exchange) opened that ran right through from near Perth to near Geraldton; it was known as the Midland Railway, but was outpaced by a parallel Government line to the east. The First World War and tough seasons did not help and the line and its assets were allowed to run down with the Western Australian Government Railways (WAGR) taking over in the 1960s.

In the last decade before Federation, there was a good deal of rail network expansion, the privately constructed Great Southern Railway was completed from Albany via York and Northam, then over the Darling Range and into Perth. The Geraldton network expanded and a direct line from Perth to Bunbury opened, traversing easy terrain to the south of Perth.

In 1896 the beginnings of an east–west network emerged with the construction of a railway inland from Perth to Coolgardie and on to nearby Kalgoorlie. This was part of the big burst of expansion by key engineer CY O'Connor in the last decade of the nineteenth century and soon the narrow-gauge main line made it over the Darling Range and into Northam, and later to Merredin and Kalgoorlie. The route tended to follow old coach routes, where settlements were already established, rather than examine the gentle Avon Valley that cuts through the Darling Range. This was to come later, in the 1960s.

In the formative years of the WAGR, steam locomotion was the only method of haulage for both the entire public network and also the various private company lines. Soon there was a steam train service from Perth to Kalgoorlie, boosting interest in rail transport.

Many Ballarat and Bendigo miners had followed the gold quest west towards the Coolgardie and Kalgoorlie area where initially gold finds were in abundance. It was a long journey between Ballarat and Kalgoorlie before 1901 or indeed before 1917. First, a train journey from Ballarat to Melbourne, then by ship from Melbourne to Perth, then initially by Cobb and Co. coach but later by steam train from Perth to Northam and on to Kalgoorlie.

Some of the early miners heading to the Goldfields landed at Albany, then travelled by train to York before turning east for the lonely long walk along 'Hunt's Track' to the goldfields. They eventually reached Coolgardie and Kalgoorlie, where they started digging for gold.

⌃ Western Australia's first locomotive, *The West Australian*, 4 April 1940. Sadly, too many first locomotives were scrapped and not preserved.

⌄ 'Meet the Westland', c. 1950. Promotional material was not a high priority for the railways, which enjoyed a monopoly before the era of the modern motor car.

MEET THE "*Westland*"

WESTERN AUSTRALIAN GOVERNMENT RAILWAYS

⌃ Locomotives Nos A21 and W901 on exhibition, Perth Station, 1951. Rail exhibitions were a low priority, but sometimes featured at annual capital city events such as the Royal Show.

» Locomotive No. G233 hauling empty passenger cars from Perth Terminal, 1970. Carriages had to be cleaned at depots, but soot from steam locomotives made it a hard task.

» Locomotives No. 300 Class E and No. 174 Class RA pulling the *Kalgoorlie Express* on the first stage of the long journey eastwards from Perth, 1930s. Until 1970, all had to change at Kalgoorlie.

It was the strong desire of Kalgoorlie citizens to have Transcontinental steam trains direct from Port Augusta and the east that drove the huge push to get the Federation campaign back on the rails around the turn of the century. Kalgoorlie and the Eastern Goldfields were furious that Perth and Western Australia were dragging the chain on holding a Federation referendum, so much so that they threatened by petition to break away from Western Australia, create the new state of Auralia and join the emerging nation.

For a while it looked like we might have ended up with a Commonwealth made up of just those states east of the Nullarbor. In the late 1890s a series of referenda were held on the issue of Federation and the draft constitution. New South Wales, Victoria, South Australia and Tasmania all voted yes in 1898 – but a specific quota had been required in New South Wales and this was not reached. And so in 1899 another vote was held on an amended draft constitution. This time Queensland also voted, and a simple majority was all that was needed in all these colonies. All voted yes, with South Australia, Tasmania and Victoria delivering thumping majorities in support.

Western Australia had declined to have a referendum in 1898 (or 1899) when the other states voted for Federation. When Perth finally made the decision to proceed with a Western Australian referendum, in 1900, the result was another clear majority in favour of Federation: 44,800 for, and 19,691 against.

Many historians ascribe this outcome to the high level of support from the Kalgoorlie region. The citizens of Kalgoorlie, led by John Kirwan, the fiery local editor of the *Kalgoorlie Miner*, had called on Premier Sir John Forrest to act. Led by Kirwan, local miners set up the Eastern Goldfields Reform League and drew up a huge petition to leave Western Australia and create the state of Auralia.

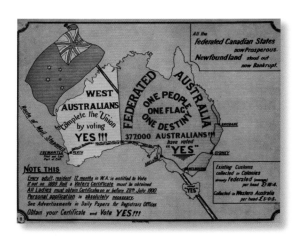

It could even be said that the desire for a transcontinental steam train service was the factor that got Federation over the line. Unfortunately, the voters had to wait another 16 years for the actual east–west railway to be built and for steam trains to start running direct to the east from Kalgoorlie. The connection was completed at Ooldea on 17 October 1917. (This development will be discussed further in chapter 10 on the history of the Commonwealth Railways.)

Meanwhile, the narrow-gauge WAGR system pushed out into the wheat belt and goldfields of the southern one-third of Western Australia. There was a burst of expansion just ahead of Federation, with the network being anchored to the key ports of Albany, Bunbury, Fremantle, Geraldton and later Esperance. It took decades, but eventually a broad classification of the wheat lines was adopted:

RAILWAY MAP of WESTERN AUSTRALIA

1897.

Scale of Miles

MILES 100   75   50   25   0   25   50   75   100 MILES

ENLARGED PLAN OF PART OF EASTERN RAILWAY

INDIAN OCEAN

OCEAN

REFERENCE
Government Railways   constructed   shewn thus
"   "   under construction   "
"   "   proposed   "
Private   "   constructed   "
Stations with distances in miles & chains   Moora 119.28 ○
Height above sea level
Refreshment Stations   Ref.

— NOTE —
Distances North of Walkaway are from Geraldton and
Distances South of Walkaway are from Fremantle measured to
centre of Platforms.

Prepared and published under the authority of
the Hon. F. H. Piesse, Commissioner for Railways
Western Australia. July 1897.

Longitude East of Greenwich

1897

CY O'Connor:
ENGINEER FOR RAIL AND WATER

Charles Yelverton O'Connor was a deep thinker. Born in Ireland in 1842, he migrated to New Zealand at age 21, where he worked as an engineer before accepting the chief engineer role in Western Australia, based in Perth in 1891.

The father of eight children, he became infamous for his suicide on 10 March 1902, on the Perth beach now named after him. (The Perth suburb of O'Connor is also named after him.) O'Connor's two biggest projects came to underpin the economic growth of Western Australia but only after initial controversy and many criticisms of his endeavours.

First, he designed and built the vital Fremantle Harbour at the mouth of the Swan River, complete with rail connection. Second, he designed and built the long pipeline from near Perth to Kalgoorlie. The project, commissioned in 1896, was finally completed in 1903. At the opening ceremony, the VIPs were assembled, patiently waiting for the water to arrive, but it took its own time coming through all the pumping stations and only arrived at the Kalgoorlie Reservoir the next day. The story goes this is why O'Connor rode along the beach and then into the water near Robb's Jetty, and shot himself.

But this aspect of the story is a complete furphy. It was in fact a bitter attack by *Sunday Times* editor Frederick Bowler on the scheme – including an accusation of corruption – a year earlier that led to O'Connor taking his own life

⌃ Statue commemorating Charles Yelverton O'Connor in Fremantle. This great man accomplished so much, but was driven to take his own life by fierce media attacks.

well before the water was even due to be pumped to Kalgoorlie. Subsequent investigations revealed no corrupt practices by O'Connor. It was a tragic waste of a life for someone who at just 59 still had much to contribute to the state's infrastructure.

It has also been claimed that the Noongar Aboriginal people were very upset with O'Connor removing a reef near the entry to Fremantle Harbour and that they 'sang' or 'willed' his early death as a punishment.

It is fitting that there is today a seat in the House of Representatives named O'Connor – it has generally been held by colourful MPs who have to cover a huge chunk of the state to get around their electorate – just as CY O'Connor did all those years ago.

Tier I, Tier II and Tier III, with the last-named always in a battle for survival. (Tier I railways were mostly part of the main-line network and along the east–west main line included dual gauge; for example, Northam to Fremantle. Tier II were key regional lines, often with a through linkage at both ends; for example, back to the main line (a kind of anabranch). Tier III were dead-end light rail branch lines that typically ended up in somewhat isolated locations where there were small reception centres for grain.)

It was in Geraldton and not Perth that the first railway was built in Western Australia, and in 1876 two steam locomotives arrived from Kitson manufacturers in England to start hauling minerals from the hinterland to the port of Geraldton. They were Anglo Cape narrow gauge with a 2–6–0 wheel configuration.

Once again it was the hand of Robert Stephenson and Co. that saw the first tank engines arrive to operate the WAGR's Perth–Guildford line. These were later designated C Class with a wheel configuration of 0–6–0. They gave worthwhile early service. Subsequently, tenders were added to enable them to go longer between coaling stops. One of these engines was called *Katie*; fortuitously, it has been preserved to this day – far too much has been scrapped over the years. It still looks good in the shade at the Western Australian Rail Transport Museum at Bassendean on the Midland line near Perth.

It has to be said that early on Stephenson's company showed flexibility in being able to build locomotives of various gauges and ship them around the world. Prior to 1872 there was not even the telegraph connection between Britain and Australia to help facilitate this trade. This meant that contracts were signed and posted off, travelling in heavy leather mail bags on ships from Australia through the Suez Canal (after it opened in 1869) to the port of Brindisi, in the boot of Italy. They were then loaded on to the fast mail trains travelling across Europe to Calais, then onto another ferry and finally by boat train from Dover to London, Victoria Station. Often, when a deposit was required, in the absence of today's electronic transfers, it was made from funds held at the various colonial offices in London; indeed, final payments were also made from this source, having been approved from afar.

It was the WAGR G Class that was to become one of the most numerous

⌄ Fitting a G Type locomotive at the Yarloop Workshop, c. 1905. Steam locomotives were complex beasts, especially when it came to maintenance.

≫ 'Welcome to Western Australia', c. 1950. In the days before television, most rail promotion took the form of pamphlets.

≫ Thursday Islanders securing the last sections of rail linking the standard-gauge railways, Kalgoorlie, 1968. This completed the much-delayed task of east-west standardisation.

Western Australian steam locomotives, initially as a 2–6–0 and later as a 4–6–0 to help track more smoothly around the tight curves of the WAGR narrow-gauge network. In all, 73 G Class locomotives were built and went into service with the WAGR. Again, it was Kalgoorlie that came to the fore.

As mentioned, there was the need to build rail from Perth to Kalgoorlie to meet huge freight and passenger demand generated by the Eastern Goldfields. This was a key factor in the ordering of so many G Class steam locomotives. Incredibly, the G Class was still in business as late as 1972. These locomotives had a sturdiness about them and they could perform a wide variety of tasks. But, as always, dieselisation eventually won out.

Many of these trains hauled troop trains to Albany and to Perth during the First World War. In November–December 1914, some 41,000 Australian and New Zealand troops sailed from Albany, the main port of departure for the first two convoys; a large proportion of these men were never to see home again. For many of those enlisting from Western Australia, it was the steam trains that had brought them to Albany. Not the least of the trains' roles was hauling coal along a crossover route from the coalmines in the Collie area to Albany; coal to resupply the steam-driven warships and converted merchant ships that formed the AIF convoys. They also brought in the food and other supplies needed to ensure the men and women in the convoy left harbour with enough to sustain them on the long voyage that lay ahead of them.

It was the G Class that had come to the fore, although the very steep grades of 1 in 30 over the Darling Range, just east of Perth, necessitated the use of a strong mountain-climbing steam locomotive – especially from 1917 onwards, when all east–west traffic was using this narrow-gauge line as far as Kalgoorlie, where it was a case of 'All change' for the standard-gauge Transcontinental. This 'break of gauge' was only eliminated in 1970.

The old problem of too many different designs of locomotives was to apply to the WAGR, as it did with every other colonial rail system in Australia. It was as if every chief mechanical engineer felt like he could have his own little fling and add another class or two to the fray. Overall, control and caution was thrown to the wind, and railway budgets were blown wide open.

Arguably, just four classes of steam locomotive were all that was needed for a system such as the WAGR, and after each four or five decades, another four classes of more modern locomotives. But this was not to be, and indeed some individuals were especially creative in developing unique locomotives for the WAGR.

Overall, there were two factors affecting the early days of the WAGR: first, the fact that for decades Albany was by far the most important port of the colony (until eventually the harbour was fully developed at Fremantle in the mouth of

FAIRLIE DOUBLE-ENDER

There were just two of these steam 'birds of a feather'. Resembling nothing so much as Doctor Dolittle's fictional double-headed creature, the 'pushmi-pullyu', which, Janus-like, faced both fore and aft, the Fairlie double-ender had two boilers and a two-way operational capacity, they had a wheel configuration of 2-4-4-2 and weighed in at some 34 tonnes. Each with a distinct number, E7 and E20 arrived into service in 1881 and, after a delay in assembly of the second Fairlie, 1885.

The main cabin in the centre faced both ways, with two boilers of smallish size, one on either side of the driver's cabin. They were certainly flexible, especially for shunting duties.

However, they were not to last long, and by Federation in 1901 they had vanished from the scene. E20 was withdrawn from service in 1891, and E7 just four years later. Poor old E20 was cut in half, with one half used as a Fremantle Workshops engine and the other made into a locomotive with tender for the Fremantle Jetty. E7 was despatched to work on the Canning jarrah timber network. The E Class was a rarity, now lost in the sands of time, but one of these engines would doubtless be a star attraction were it still in a rail museum today.

≫ The magnificent E Class Fairlie No. 2 – better known as E7 – seen here with Geraldton Workshops staff, c. 1880s.

» The huge WAGR Standard Gauge Rail Project (1962–72) being carried out through the Avon Valley; this was a feat of engineering in the west akin to the Snowy Mountains Scheme.

the Swan River, relatively close to the Perth CBD); and second, the Darling Range had to be conquered immediately east of Perth to gain access to the vital hinterland.

Private enterprise developed the so-called Great Southern Railway, connecting from Albany through to Beverley, where all changed for the WAGR trains proceeding on into Perth. This link opened in 1889 and it meant most mail from London, and from Sydney and Melbourne, came via Albany, where it was placed in special mail sorting vans and despatched to Perth.

The steam haulage reduced the Albany–Perth (or vice versa) journey from days to around 17 hours — provided, of course, that the connection with the government trains was efficient. Still this was much faster than having to travel four or five days by coach.

The long slow periods of many weeks' journey on mail ships drove the need to clip a few days off at either end. Of course, it helped that Albany has a well-placed railway station and railway yards alongside the deep port in the very protected King George Sound. Today this is a beautiful sight to behold from the new National Anzac Centre, a natural deep protected harbour, renowned as the place where the troops convoys docked and departed.

Helped along by some land grants, Great Southern Railway boomed for its first few years, although it was not helped by its long approach into Perth, which was anything but direct, nor by steep grades to be conquered. Rarely in any state were the rail networks laid out according to the best commercial criteria or the best terrain — indeed, anything but — and this was yet again the case in Western Australia.

≈ Official opening of the Great Southern Railway, 1889. VIPs always were on hand for the big openings.

In the 1890s deviations were examined with an aim to reducing grades through the Darling Range, and later implemented by O'Connor, but the big leap forward only came in 1966, when dual gauge was built on a superb new alignment down the Avon Valley from Northam to Perth — in good time for the first Sydney–Perth *Indian Pacific* service in 1970. Long sweeping curves with gentle grades finally became the order of the day.

As WAGR rail historian Rob Clark and many others have highlighted, if only the Avon valley had been selected first up as a way around the Darling Range, WAGR would have steamed ahead and achieved a great deal more before road trucks became fiercely competitive after the Second World War and those lobbying for them achieved a rollback of legislation protecting rail freight transport.

However, during the golden decades of WAGR — the big harvest years of the 1970s, 1980s and 1990s after dieselisation greatly improved operations — many steam locomotive classes were still being developed, and again far too many. Officially, there were 51 different classes ordered and operated by the WAGR, albeit in some cases there were only minor variations between classes, such as conversion from tank engine to locomotive and tender.

≫ The Standard Gauge Rail Project should have happened five decades earlier, but better late than never.

WESTERN AUSTRALIA

standard gauge rail project

Eventually, the drumbeat of the Second World War, and the onset of dieselisation not long afterwards, saw steam gradually exit Western Australia. But not before it had one last throw of the dice. During the war there had been an attempt to standardise and harmonise locomotives across Australia on grounds of efficiency and to meet the huge extra wartime demand. The Australian Standard Garratt (ASG) was developed on the basis that it would operate on all the Anglo Cape narrow-gauge systems: those of Queensland, Western Australia, Tasmania, and South Australia on at least part of its network. This project was under the overall control of Sir Harold Clapp, with WAGR personnel to help. As a result, WAGR's chief mechanical engineer, Frederick Mills, was given the task of designing this compromise beast: in the process having to balance the demands of particular systems with Queensland, he argued for a 'light' type of Garratt locomotive. Mills battled on despite much criticism, and during the darkest days of the Second World War worked from cramped quarters in Melbourne's Flinders Street Station building.

Against all odds, by November 1943 the ASG was out and about, operating in Western Australia, Queensland and Tasmania and greatly lifting haulage capacity on those systems. Just in time, there was the new ASG, glistening with its high-profile setting for the first section and possessing a performance that was under the pump to deliver in the difficult mid–Second World War years. As prominent rail historian David Burke has pointed out, the ASG had a flying start in service, but there were many minor gremlins and wrinkles that needed attention. Given that the ASGs were being produced in four different workshops – WAGR's Midland Railway Workshops, VR's Newport Workshops, SAR's Islington Railway Workshops and Clyde Engineering, Sydney – there were always going to be teething problems.

After the war, the ASG became the only steam locomotive to be made the subject of a specific Royal Commission. At the Western Australian Royal Commission into the Australian Standard Garratt Locomotive (1945–46), even Harold Young of the NSWGR was asked to give evidence; he stated that the faults with the ASG were mainly ones of detail and the that the locomotive was fundamentally 'quite all right'.

However, in 1946 an all-out strike against the ASG by Western Australian train crews forced a set of final modifications to be made. These were quickly implemented and the ASG enjoyed a decade or more of good service with the WAGR. In hindsight, it can be said that generally the ASG stacked up well, given that this beast had been produced in four separate locations in the middle of a war.

It is one of those great contradictions in rail locomotive evolution that just as the steam phase was drawing to an end worldwide, the WAGR ordered its smartest-looking and best-performing main line steam locomotive ever. This was the V Class. In a sense it went head-to-head with WAGR's first awkward early diesel locomotives, which arrived in 1953. This is seriously crazy as, by 1954, the new

⌃ Locomotive builder's plate, 1930. WAGR was up there with the best of world railway acronyms, from LNER to NSWGR.

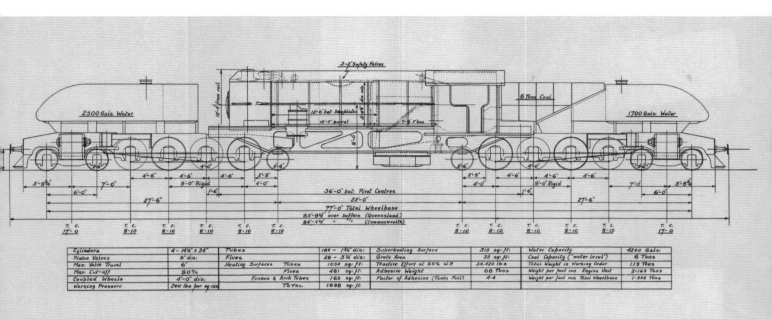

Cylinders	4 - 14¼" x 24"	Tubes		184 - 1¾" dia:	Superheating Surface	315 sq: ft:	Water Capacity	4200 Gals:
Piston Valves	8" dia:	Flues		28 - 5¼" dia:	Grate Area	35 sq: ft:	Coal Capacity ("water level")	6 Tons
Max: Valve Travel	6"	Heating Surfaces	Tubes	1054 sq: ft:	Tractive Effort at 85% W.P.	34,420 lbs	Total Weight in Working Order	119 Tons
Max: Cut-off	80%		Flues	481 sq: ft:	Adhesive Weight	68 Tons	Weight per foot run Engine Unit	2·163 Tons
Coupled Wheels	4'-0" dia:	Firebox & Arch Tubes		163 sq: ft:	Factor of Adhesion (Tanks Full)	4·4	Weight per foot run Total Wheelbase	1·545 Tons
Working Pressure	200 lbs per sq:in:		Total	1698 sq: ft:				

⩘ A diagram from the *Operating Manual: Australian Standard Garratt Locomotive for 3' 6" Gauge Railways*, 1943. This locomotive was one of the engineering projects driven by the Second World War.

⩗ ASG locomotive No. G26, 1943. Much criticised at first, the ASG was ultimately a success.

diesel and diesel-electric locomotives were well past being new start-ups and something to be wary of, they had proven their outstanding performance vis-a-vis steam. For the crews, diesels were so much easier to work. Not only did the diesel-electric locomotive take more than an hour or two off any run in excess of 200 miles (320 kilometres), it allowed rapid turn-arounds and afforded greater reliability than steam.

Nevertheless, WAGR headquarters in Perth made the decision to order from Robert Stephenson and Hawthorns Ltd of Darlington, County Durham, 24 non-articulated 2–8–2 locomotives with smart white wheel trimmings. So there was to be one last expensive engagement with steam locomotion by the WAGR.

⩔ These two trains passing each other is a rare scene, as there was not much double track outside of Perth.

In 1955 and 1956 all 24 magnificent V Class flexible-freight locomotives arrived at Fremantle and entered WAGR service. They clanked down the main line to Albany, and from Perth to Bunbury and Collie, as if their place in the sun was guaranteed for years to come. Both the W Class and the V Class were designed to burn the difficult Collie coal efficiently.

But before long the diesel and diesel-electric trains would sweep across all Australian rail systems. In New South Wales this process had started in 1951, and by 1954 the royal train with Queen Elizabeth II on board was hauled not by steam but by two diesel-electric locomotives.

Was it habit, a fear of oil shortages, or just a very bad mindset that indirectly put the modernisation of rail in so much jeopardy, persevering with steam so late in the piece? Leon Oberg and other rail historians would contend that it was for a combination of reasons, but most notably the desire not to put all of one's eggs in one very new basket. And yet, once diesel-electric locomotives proved they were practical and could deliver, the days of steam were clearly numbered.

But it cannot be denied that the magnificent WAGR V Class was a superb way to sign off on steam. Most were condemned around 1971, although four were initially preserved for posterity — not necessarily operational posterity, however, as disinterest and decay soon set in. There is one gleaming V Class at rest at Bassendean's Western Australian Rail Transport Museum — just one, as a reminder of what greatness was, once upon a time.

WAGR was as bad as all other systems in having too many types of steam locomotives, which greatly added to costs and loss of productivity, but despite numerous challenges in many ways WAGR deserves a salute for its steam endeavours: whether it was the locally designed and built S Class delivering 30,685 lbs of tractive effort for an overall locomotive weight of 119 tonnes or the ASG, ultimately adjusted and fixed, or the imported V Class, late on parade, but better late than never.

All of these steam locomotives delivered a huge impetus to the development of the southern one-third of the state, both during the two world wars and in times of peace and prosperity. Further north, the opening-up of massive iron ore deposits in the Pilbara region from 1960 onwards was achieved by giant modern diesel-electric locomotives.

Today, in an unusual development, an attempt has been made for a new heritage steam rail operation at Minnivale near Goomalling in the Dowerin Shire, inland from Perth. It could see one S Class back in action, namely S549. May the project succeed and help boost tourism in the wheat belt. It is to be known as the Wheatbelt Heritage Rail, and there will be more on it in chapter 11.

SEE WESTERN AUSTRALIA FIRST

ROUND RAILWAY TOURS

Magnificent Ocean, River, and Hill Scenery.
Marvellous Caves.
Wonderful Forests.

Further particulars obtainable and bookings arranged at

GOVERNMENT TOURIST BUREAU
62 Barrack Street, PERTH.

Telephones B 4376 and B 6174.
Telegraphic Address : "Tourist, Perth."
Branch Offices :
Victoria Quay, Fremantle. Telephone FM 412.
Kalgoorlie Railway Station. Telephone Kalgoorlie 90.

⌃ *Railway Map of Western Australia, 1929. Maps of this era are valuable, as many a branch line has vanished since.*

CHAPTER 9

I think myself very fortunate in having the pleasure ... of inaugurating the commencement of the first railway in Tasmania.

HRH THE DUKE OF EDINBURGH, LAUNCESTON, 15 JANUARY 1868

DS3

TASMANIAN RAIL: A SAGA OF LOST OPPORTUNITY

Tasmania is Australia's smallest state, and it had the nation's smallest railway network. Yet it was Tasmania which possessed the first two operational Garratt steam locomotives in the entire world. The Garratt system was the great idea of English mechanical engineer Herbert William Garratt (1864–1913). It was made possible by the skill of the Manchester-based firm of Beyer, Peacock & Co., which built the prototypes K1 and K2 at the end of the first decade of the twentieth century; as we shall see, these were later imported into Tasmania.

Tasmania is also the place where diesel-electric traction was introduced to Australian main lines with the arrival in 1950 of the first of what would eventually be 32 X Class locomotives from the English Electric Company Limited. An example of the class leader, the X1, is now preserved at the Tasmanian Transport Museum in the Hobart suburb of Glenorchy.

With the exception of the West Coast Wilderness Railway, a reconstruction of the original Mount Lyell Mining and Railway Company which still operates between Queenstown and Strahan, there has been no regular steam locomotive haulage in Tasmania for at least half a century. However, the spirit associated with steam is still present around the 'Apple Isle' today.

The annual SteamFest at Sheffield in the island's north is a great weekend of steam train, steam roller and steam tractor activity, with huge crowds soaking up the action, colour and movement, and enjoying the historical exhibits and much more. Over the years, SteamFest has not had an easy time of it, as early on

⌃ SteamFest events such as that at Sheffield have grown in many parts of Australia.

local council officers have made huge tactical errors, preventing various opportunities for logical expansion and product improvement to make it a year-round activity, which would be very feasible in this region of gourmet outlets and Stellenbosch-like vistas southwards towards Mount Roland and the Western Tiers. Nevertheless, later on, some effective local leadership helped reclaim the situation and the work of countless dedicated volunteers has guaranteed the future of SteamFest and so maintain the spirit of steam in the northern part of the island, not far from the Devonport ferry terminal and airport.

Railways had started a little later in Tasmania than on the mainland. Albeit it was back in 1832 that an 8-kilometre convict-hauled 'railway' using wooden log rails started operation near Port Arthur, in the island's south-east. Intended for use by officials and VIPs travelling from Hobart to the penal outpost there, it shortened the journey considerably by crossing a small isthmus.

The Tasmanian Government Railways (TGR) was set up in 1872 and operated under that title until 1978. The TGR had taken over from various early false starts, including a broad-gauge private company that operated between Launceston and Deloraine. This line was in fact initially opened in 1871; it was built in broad gauge but in 1888 the whole line was converted to the TGR state-wide main gauge (3 ft 6 in [1,067 mm]). It was quickly resolved that Anglo Cape narrow gauge would be used for the main line in Tasmania, and after a few years of dual-gauge operation, through Western Junction, near Launceston. This sensible decision was fully implemented across the state, except for some short logging and mining lines. Over the less than 100 years that steam reigned supreme, before diesel locomotives took over, there were no fewer than 27 different classes of TGR steam locomotives in operation.

Among the 27 classes of steam locomotives, the usual unnecessary diversity of design applied, with everything from small 4–4–0 Hunslets imported in 1873 to complex Beyer, Peacock Garratts balancing on the narrow-gauge main lines. Even with the Garratt locomotives, it was found necessary to have two types. The world's first Garratt was built by Beyer, Peacock in 1909 for TGR's narrow-gauge North East Dundas Tramway, which had opened in 1896. Just two of the original class, K1 and K2, were built and shipped from Britain to Tasmania, where they were set to work hauling ore from the local mines and mine workers on the change of shift. It was a steep 2 ft narrow-gauge track with tight curves, tailor-made for the distinctive Garratt design.

⌄ Hunslet locomotive No. 1 at Rouse's Camp, the terminus of the Emu Bay Railway Company, 1880. The Hunslet was also important on narrow-gauge operations on the Western Front during the First World War.

RHYNDASTON TUNNEL

Opened in 1876, this 955-metre-long tunnel was built 72 kilometres north of Hobart, on the crucial line from Hobart to Western Junction. It has a steep 1-in-46 grade, and steam train crews travelling in the uphill direction had to be careful they were not blinded, and even asphyxiated, by the heavy layers of smoke that gathered within the narrow confines of the tunnel. It took several minutes to climb through the tunnel, and the engine crew had to work hard to overcome the steep grade.

In some ways, the tunnel fits an unusual pattern whereby the chief surveyor or the chief engineer was of the view that every main line should have at least one tunnel. To this day, and a little like the lonely rail tunnel built between Queanbeyan and Cooma in New South Wales, some modern-day surveyors and engineers hold it could have been easily avoided, especially with better route planning at the outset.

The Rhyndaston Tunnel was widened in 1964–65 and remains in use for freight trains to this day. The only other rail tunnels of note in Tasmania were those on the Sorell line (which has some superb stone work), the North Eastern or Launceston-to-Scottsdale key branch line, and the Emu Bay railway. For a few years, the Sorell tunnel was converted to a restaurant, but today it is mainly used to store archives of the University of Tasmania.

Today, the section from the original junction at Zeehan to Williamsford includes a great walking track that goes past the magnificent Montezuma Falls. Just imagine watching a Garratt steam under the spray of the falls in winter with some light snow falling. It would have been a sight to behold as it hauled miners and empty wagons to the diggings to collect more ore.

Small Tasmania led the world in importing two K Class steam locomotives of Garratt design. Unfortunately, the distinctive nature of the K Garratt, with its sets of pistons facing each other and one set under the driver's cabin, made for very hot work in summer. K1 and K2 were dropped from North East Dundas service in 1929; both were shipped back to Britain, and K1 to the National Railway Museum at York; it was later restored by Ffestiniog. In 2007 the mighty and durable K1 was certified for operation on the Welsh

≫ K1, the world's first Garratt steam locomotive, built for the North East Dundas Tramway in Tasmania in 1909, can now be found steaming away in Wales.

≫ One of the superb vistas along the narrow-gauge system on the west coast of Tasmania: the Montezuma Falls and North East Dundas Tramway, c. 1890.

THE GARRATT
LOCOMOTIVE

Born in London in 1860, Herbert William Garratt grew up in Britain but joined the Argentinian Central Railway in 1889. Later he worked as a railway engineer in Cuba and Peru, even in Lagos, Nigeria, before returning to Britain to push his radical design of an articulated locomotive.

The Garratt locomotive design, for which he received a full patent in June 1909, became famous worldwide. It generally consisted of a first section with a large water tank and a set of pistons, a central section containing the boiler, and a third section that held coal or oil, another water tank and a further set of pistons. In its articulated form, the system had two main advantages. First, the boiler could be quite large in size, as there were no frames, pistons or wheels to restrict its size. Second, on sharp curves the central boiler part would slew inside the centre line of the railway, thereby keeping the weight slung low and to the inside of a curve.

Highlands Railway, where it can be found today when in service. Sadly, K2 was scrapped, although the valuable boiler was saved and used for local industrial purposes.

In later years, the TGR used larger Garratt locomotives for the network's main lines; the usual Garratt articulated pattern applied (2–6–2 + 2–6–2 and 4–4–2 + 2–4–4). In service, the Garratt performed very well in Tasmania, where many sharp main-line curves exist. Even the Australian Standard Garratt (ASG) locomotives introduced during the Second World War shifted a great deal of freight, as we saw. Tasmania and Western Australia favoured the ASGs; however, Queensland hated this design imposed from the south. Today, there is just one surviving ASG, No. 33, built at Newport in Melbourne and sent to Queensland, where it was rejected. Instead it was bought by a Geelong quarry company that operated a short 3 ft 6 in line, and happily it has ended up with the tourist Bellarine Railway (more on this later).

It really was somewhat absurd that the TGR management could not be stricter in its approach. It could have developed just four stayers: the tank engine for shunting and suburban operation; the light axle weight for branch-line and some main-line operation (for example, from Railton on the main line to Roland/Staverton via Sheffield); the heavy freight locomotive for main-line operation; and the express locomotive for speedy service on the main line.

There were some standout classes of locomotive in use, and two have been preserved as operational examples at the Tasmanian Transport Museum at Glenorchy; some track is now available that allows them run up the Derwent Valley. Even for the 2 ft (610 mm) mining network operations around Zeehan and Williamsford on the west coast, TGR permitted four different classes to be developed, which meant extensive spare parts inventories had to be obtained and stored.

If we step back and view the TGR in the second last financial year before the First World War, namely 1912/13, it is interesting to discover there was a net profit made after a good farm season and increased mining activity on the West Coast. This occurred despite the high cost of steam operations.

TGR enjoyed a solid gain of more than 10 per cent in gross revenue to reach £312,786; working expenses totalled a mere £221,172, leaving a net profit of £91,614. This was up £29,228 on the previous full trading year, a 30 per cent improvement during the halcyon last months of peace – all of it steam-hauled. This profit was achieved despite the plethora of steam locomotive types or classes in use in Tasmania since the inception of the TGR. In any event, some 53 locomotives were put through the TGR workshops for major maintenance that year and major main-line track upgrading was proceeding apace across Tasmania.

However, as was typical over many decades, the upgrading of main railway lines across the nation was almost inevitably done on existing bad alignments. There were two exceptions. NSWGR's southern main line upgrade (to get better grades) actually lengthened the main line considerably; conversely QR's upgrade of the northern main line took large chunks containing many curves out of the length of the main line, both near Maryborough and elsewhere.

Unfortunately, Tasmania, with a near optimum 200-kilometre rail distance between its two biggest cities, Hobart and Launceston, and relatively easy terrain in between, could never get near a two-hour express passenger service or a three-hour freight service on this vital route.

Looking through the prism of the last decade of steam operation in Tasmania, it was the case of some good, a lot of operational bad and also a great deal which was simply ugly for the vanishing passenger and freight clientele of TGR. (I am indebted to Jim Stokes for his detailed examination of this sunset period of the TGR in a recent issue of the *Australian Railway History* magazine where he highlights how dieselisation arrived with a bang with the introduction from Britain of 32 versatile diesel-electric 660-horsepower Bo-Bo locomotives; their arrival marked the beginning of the end of the steam haulage.) By the balance sheet date of 30 June 1960, the TGR still had more than 50 steam locomotives operating. This included some very old C Class locomotives: five on shunting duties and another five with the better boilers which means they were allowed out to undertake main line and suburban haulage.

⩔ A steam locomotive at Queenstown in 1961, by which time the big switch from steam to diesel was almost complete.

A VERY LIMITED SERVICE

In 1954, about 15 years after the pathbreaking *Spirit of Progress* had been developed by the Victorian Railways, the *Tasman Limited* was launched as an express passenger train running between Burnie and Hobart, with a side connection from Western Junction to Launceston.

The *Tasman Limited* ran daily (except Sundays) in each direction, and so there were two train sets, one of which can be seen today in a park at Margate, south of Hobart – a little as if it had overshot Hobart terminal and its four platforms and come to rest in a park. It took almost all the daylight hours to complete the journey, so a buffet car was necessary, staffed by TGR personnel in smart uniforms who were nicknamed the 'Tasmanettes'.

After 1955, the train's relatively modern Launceston-built carriages were mainly hauled by two X Class diesels, depending on the load

⩔ Another era, but luggage could be booked on the *Tasman Limited*.

(services with few passengers apparently required just one engine). However, the *Tasman Limited* found it hard to compete with coach road transport that could cover the key 200-kilometre Hobart-to-Launceston section, and it was withdrawn from service in 1978. Perhaps it could have survived had it been upgraded to a gourmet tourist train, in the form of a Queensland Rail-style tilt train, operating as a two-hour service between Launceston and Hobart a couple of days a week.

Unfortunately, rail in Tasmania was never given the opportunity to modernise and compete effectively, and so the community lost the chance to have smart rail passenger services. There had been too many false steps, and all too often a lack of available capital works funds for upgrading the service.

The TGR Pacific Class steam locomotives (that is, those with a 4–6–2 configuration), notably the M Class, were still around in the 1960s, but gradually they faced withdrawal with the arrival of more diesel-electric trains, including an English Electric built at Launceston to what was for then a large size of 800 horsepower.

But by 1971 it was almost all over for steam locomotive haulage in Tasmania. In fact, in February of that year TGR conducted a Festival of Steam for the centenary of Tasmanian railways; a handful of steam locomotives were out and about, including the repainted red CCS23 (it and about half a dozen others had been preserved).

« Trial run for locomotive No. CCS.23, originally built 1902 and restored for the centenary celebrations, c. 1970. Steam in Tasmania has been allowed to largely disappear; on the tourism score, this is a great pity.

⩔ Ships, cars and trucks and an Emu Bay Railway Y Class steam locomotive crowd the pier – it's all happening on the Apple Island.

⌃ TGR C Class locomotive with passenger and goods train
bound for Hobart, c. 1910. There is a certain quaintness about
steam locomotion in Tasmania.

« The Australian Standard Garratt in action was always a sight to behold: Emu Bay Railway's ASG locomotive No. G20A crossing the Pieman River, on Tasmania's west coast, 1963.

⩔ TGR locomotive No. R3 with a passenger train leaving Launceston, bound for Hobart, 1945. The war was over, but little was ever done to improve train times between Launceston and Hobart.

The current leadership of TasRail should now consider lifting an absurd ban on the use of main lines for passenger train traffic — in situations where crews are certified and licensed and locomotives and rolling stock are cleared for operation. This should certainly be done for the 150th anniversary of TGR/TasRail in 2021.

In many ways, the TGR centenary was a last hurrah, which is a great pity as a regular island festival of steam trains, gourmet local food and wines plus concerts with fine music would surely have proved a giant success. 'Steam Tasmania, Taste Tasmania' has a ring about it.

During the Second World War, as we have seen in other states, the TGR had gone with the ASG and had several of these excellent units operating until 1957. But by 1966 all had been cut up for scrap, never to be sighted again steaming away with all 28 wheels in revolution.

The Mount Lyell rack and pinion or Abt railway originally set up in 1897 remained in action until 1963. It operated over a very scenic route from Strahan to Queenstown. Four of its distinct steam locomotives were preserved and a Federal Cabinet decision in the late 1990s put $26 million dollars from the Bicentennial Fund into its restoration. (Today it operates out of Queenstown as the West Coast Wilderness Railway.) Those of us present at the Federal Cabinet table that day who were 'economic drys' shuddered, but I recall keeping quiet as I could see this decision in support of heritage rail was going to get up — and never was I going to block the allocation of Commonwealth funds for rail; more

⩗ Mount Lyell Abt No. 5 arriving at Queenstown, c. 1955. The Abt involved using a rack and pinion between rails to ensure grip on steep grades.

importantly, I later strongly supported a Federal grant of one-third of the cost of the world's newest Transcontinental railway (from Adelaide to Darwin).

It has not been an entirely trouble-free restoration, but it does mean that, technically speaking, steam locomotive haulage continues today — against considerable odds — in five locations in Tasmania: the Don River Railway at Devonport; the Tasmanian Transport Museum at Glenorchy; the West Coast Wilderness Railway; the Redwater Creek Steam Heritage Society, which runs SteamFest at Sheffield each year; and the Wee Georgie Wood Railway at Tullah.

Over the decades one set of coal mines on the St Mary's line near Fingal has kept railways going in Tasmania, giving TGR another bulk commodity to haul in addition to cement. The intermodal containers shipped from Hobart to Devonport for transfer to and from the port of Melbourne have also helped.

TGR was taken over by Australian National in 1978, and then in 2004 by Pacific National; today the railways in Tasmania are owned and operated by TasRail, a Tasmanian Government unit which is gradually improving rail in that state, but with almost a blind eye to the rich potential of heritage and tourism rail on the island. It is curious that in 2016 a wrangle broke out in Tasmania as to the best way forward once the last freight train had run from Hobart to Bridgewater through the northern suburbs and a new intermodal hub had opened north of the Derwent River. This closed railway corridor was perfectly tailored for both a metro light rail commuter service and steam heritage trains operating from Hobart to the wildly successful MONA (Museum of Old and New Art). Instead, chunks of the vital rail corridor near its southern (or CBD) end have now been lifted, plus some signals have been removed. To say the least, a grand opportunity has been missed. Cities around the world of about the same size would love to possess an existing vacant corridor running through the main spine of suburbs to the CBD.

All things considered, it is a reasonable observation that Tasmania has huge potential to run heritage gourmet tourist steam trains along its under-used main lines, to exploit the superb vistas afforded by locations such as the Western Tiers, to name just one. This potential is every bit as good as any on the

⌃ Aerial view of the railway line running beside the Gordon River, 1970s. The rugged Tasmanian terrain did not help rail construction.

Emu Bay Railway Beyer-Garratt articulated locomotive No. 13 with a goods train at Burnie, 1949. Many mines around Tasmania and the mainland depended heavily on their rail connections to ports.

mainland. The only question is, can Tasmania be bold enough to get its act together to make it happen?

Nothing can take away from Tasmania the fact that the Garratt-type locomotive, built in Great Britain, was first operated there, ahead of all other rail networks and rail operations in the world. Alas, as mentioned previously, today you have to go to Wales to see Garratt No. 1.

It is a great pity that this is all part of a pattern of lost opportunity with steam, and it is too often the case, in all too many places. Still possibilities exist, including with reopening the magnificent Scottsdale line. The obvious nomenclature for the project is easy to find: Scottsdale lies north-east of Launceston, so 'Launceston North Eastern Railway', or LNER, readily suggests itself. It could be a sister railway, a little 'down under' relation to that other famous LNER, the London and North Eastern Railway.

Certainly, rail heritage operations in Tasmania can match the pulling power of rail heritage drawcards in places like Wales, where the Ffestiniog and others are now world renowned and attract many international tourists. But it is reasonable to ask whether Tasmania has the boldness to make this happen, or whether it will lose all rail traffic over the next two decades.

∧ On tracks in hilly areas sand was used to help the steam locomotives move forward.

» TGR A Class locomotive with Hobart-to-Launceston passenger train at Colebrook, c. 1930. Never did the TGR reach average speeds of 100 kph on this key main line.

*[The Transcontinental Railway] will bring about
a community of interest which scarcely exists at present
between West Australia and the southern and eastern States.*

LORD DENMAN, GOVERNOR-GENERAL OF AUSTRALIA

CHAPTER 10

COMMONWEALTH RAILWAYS:
EAST TO WEST AND WAY UP NORTH

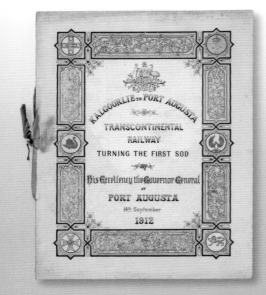

At just 76 kilometres in length, the shortest transcontinental railway in the world is the one that runs across the Isthmus of Panama that separates the Atlantic and Pacific oceans. It also just happened to be the first transcontinental railway in the world. The Panama Transcontinental was built across the isthmus in 1850–55, and operated initially in Czar broad gauge (5 ft), but in 2000 the Panama Canal Railway, under new American owners, switched to Stephenson standard gauge. Even before the construction of the enormous super locks which opened in 2016, the Panama railway boomed with container traffic, and since these new locks became operational it has continued to provide a daily commuter train and freight services.

The newest transcontinental railway in the world is that from Adelaide to Darwin, and the straightest is the one that runs east–west across the Nullarbor Plain. The Adelaide–Darwin railway opened in 2004, and enjoyed an initial freight surge with intermodal traffic and mined ore. Today it is owned by the US-based Genesee & Wyoming and is subject to 'boom and bust' mining cycles, but it remains profitable and has great potential, especially if one day it obtains a link to Mount Isa in Queensland, as has been long sought.

As for the great connector that runs across the Nullarbor, it was originally built from Kalgoorlie to Port Augusta, a distance of 1,692 kilometres. One section near Ooldea is the longest section of dead straight railway in the world: just short of 480 kilometres without a curve. The Australian Transcontinental Railway was completed at Ooldea, 684 kilometres from Port Augusta, at 1.45 pm on 17 October 1917, in the darkest days of the First World War. Steam-hauled passenger and freight trains started running on it a few days later. Today Ooldea is a basic

⌄ One world record never likely to be beaten: nigh on 300 miles (480 kilometres) without a curve on the Trans-Australian Railway, c. 1917.

passing loop with a few remnant buildings of a bygone era, plus a statue in honour of Daisy Bates, saluting her work among Indigenous people. Bates was briefly the wife of the legendary 'Breaker' Morant, who was court-martialled and executed during the Boer War.

Against the odds, but in accordance with the promise given by parliamentarians at the time of Federation, this vital rail link proved very useful from its inception right up to the present, when rail freight is booming. In recent years, more than 80 per cent of all freight to and from Perth goes by rail, mainly on efficient double-stacked container trains. Today the track is owned and maintained by the Australian Rail Track Corporation (ARTC), a Federal Government quango.

However, in the early days, only steam locomotive haulage was available in the outback and huge steam locomotive workshops with good design units already existed in New South Wales, South Australia and Victoria, but only New South Wales used standard gauge.

To administer the Transcontinental Railway, the Commonwealth Railways (CR) was set up under the *Commonwealth Railways Act 1917*. This Act was the key to having one administration that covered two states (South Australia and Western Australia) and later the Northern Territory. It provided the legal architecture for the CR, and this in turn allowed operations to commence quickly as soon as construction was completed on 17 October 1917. Wisely, it was decided initially that to operate the Kalgoorlie–Port Augusta railway it made sense simply to buy from the NSWGR rather than waste time and resources on developing a new set of steam locomotive classes from scratch.

△ Flynn of the Inland, the founder of the Royal Flying Doctor Service, was a great outback photographer, as witnessed by this shot of a CR G Class locomotive on the Trans-Australian Railway.

And for once common sense prevailed and the leadership team at CR, whose headquarters were at Port Augusta, saved millions of pounds and delivered against considerable odds by proceeding with the purchase of existing steam locomotive types from the relatively nearby New South Wales. This meant the first six locomotives were from NSWGR's Q Class, small 4–4–0 converted tank engines that were used mainly for the construction phase and later for shunting work in the big yards at Parkeston near Kalgoorlie, at Port Augusta and (after 1937) at Port Pirie. Then CR wisely turned to the tried and true C32 Class, which it renamed G Class. The locomotive G1, based on the C32 Class, led the way as the main-line CR's first operational locomotive. Thankfully, G1 in all its glory now has pride of place at the National Railway Museum in Port Adelaide.

In all, 26 G Class 4–6–0 steam locomotives were made for the CR, by three very widely dispersed manufacturers: Baldwin Locomotive Works, Philadelphia (USA); Clyde Engineering, Sydney; and the Toowoomba Foundry. Just how the standard-gauge G Class travelled from Toowoomba to join the Commonwealth Railways is not clear, as there was no standard gauge in Queensland at the time and no standard gauge connection between Broken Hill and Port Augusta.

The G Class locomotives were designed to haul freight trains, but they were also used on passenger trains. The first of these was known as the Great Western Express (much later renamed the Trans-Australian Railway); in 1970, when 'same gauge' operations became available from Sydney all the way to Perth, it gained a new name: the *Indian Pacific*.

≫ Port Augusta Station, 1917. Owing to wartime restrictions, it was not very ornate.

Prime ministers soon found it convenient to use this east–west rail route. In August 1919 a triumphant Billy Hughes returned from the Versailles Peace Conference; the 'Little Digger', as he was more or less affectionately known, arrived in Perth, then travelled by a WAGR narrow-gauge train to Kalgoorlie for a huge reception. He then boarded the regular CR east–west train for the journey through Port Augusta to the east. Crowds turned out at various whistle stops and larger centres — even at 5 am at Port Augusta. Hughes was dubbed the 'Conquering Caesar' in the headlines and this epic six-day journey, involving five separate trains, laid the basis for an election victory a few weeks later.

An essential ingredient to the success of the CR was its strong and stable leadership. The CR commissioners were giants in their time and conferring great stability: Norris G Bell (1917–29); GA Gahan (1929–48); PJ Hannaberry (1948–60); Keith Smith (1960–75). This kind of stability ensured that not only were unique solutions successfully devised for this incredible railway, operating way beyond any population centres in severe desert country, but also those in the leadership, together with the dedicated workforce, were able to produce years of profit and internally financed upgrades. Furthermore, they had the good sense to preserve key icons; hence the 'Tea and Sugar' has lived to tell its extraordinary tale, along with locomotives G1 and *Robert Gordon Menzies* — the name chosen for the first ever CR diesel-electric locomotive (numbered GM1).

The CR not only operated the east–west route from 1917 until 1975, when Australian National took over, but it also operated the North Australia Railway from Darwin through Adelaide River and Pine Creek to Birdum. This line,

THE 'TEA AND SUGAR' TRAIN

In those very remote locations where gangers and other track maintenance teams lived, in the days before the advent of the big deep-freeze units, the 'Tea and Sugar' resupply train would come along every fortnight or so. Today this train can be found in all its white-painted glory in the National Railway Museum (NRM) at Port Adelaide.

The 'Tea and Sugar' had shops on board, plus a pay carriage with a big money safe, but most elaborate of all was the butcher's carriage, with much provision made for keeping the willing flies away from the fresh meat on sale. This train loaded at Port Augusta with supplies and headed slowly west, pulling up at all sidings where CR staff resided; then, on reaching Kalgoorlie, it reloaded with fresh supplies and reversed, heading back eastwards with the vital mail bags.

Over its 58 years, from 1917 to 1975, when it was revamped and rebranded as Australian National, the CR had just four commissioners. All four were devotees of the 'Tea and Sugar' until it was finally withdrawn (the last ever service ran on 30 August 1996); fortunately, this iconic train is held under cover in careful preservation mode at the NRM.

≪ Checking purchases beside the 'Tea and Sugar' train on the Trans-Australian Railway that delivered vital provisions to outback residents, 1968.

» The butcher's car from the 'Tea and Sugar' train is now on display at the National Railway Museum at Port Adelaide, complete with a large leg of beef hanging from hooks in the coolroom.

which had started out as the Palmerston and Pine Creek Railway in 1889, was allocated to CR in 1918.

The rail links to Central Australia became part of the CR, via Marree, and later, after the CR had become AN, via Tarcoola. In turn, a narrow-gauge operation from Port Augusta to Marree (via Quorn) that went through the beautiful Pichi Richi Pass was later replaced by a heavy-duty standard-gauge link designed to carry coal from the Leigh Creek mine to a big power station at the top of the Gulf near Port Augusta. In addition, the CR had one branch line of significance, that from Whyalla to Port Augusta. This opened in standard gauge in 1972 and was in full use again in 2016, carrying new steel rails rolled in Whyalla towards Tarcoola as part of an upgrade project for today's east–west railway.

Common sense applied with the CR in that it had less diversity of steam locomotive classes than did the various state systems. The four main types of early steam locomotives for the CR reflected well-tested designs from, most notably, the NSWGR system and its P Class: G Class: 4–6–0 (quantity: 26); K Class: 2–8–0 (quantity: 8); GA Class (upgrading 7 of the G Class with superheating); KA Class (upgrading 6 of the KA Class with superheating).

⌃ A rail crossing in central Australia, c. 1929. The empty centre of this great continent was greatly helped by the arrival of rail.

Faced with the Second World War, CR headquarters did permit a few 'out of sorts' steam locomotives to creep in, some of which were ordered from Canada and the United States. These were classified CN and CA respectively. They helped meet the huge demand for locomotives created by the need to move war freight which peaked in 1943.

Crews working on the CN and CA complained about the 'priming' difficulty, whereby water – instead of just steam – would find its way into the pistons. After a while the CN and CA locomotives were kept close to depots, mainly operating between Port Augusta and Port Pirie. Overall, the CR developed just eight types of steam locomotives, excluding the imports from North America. This was a much better and more disciplined approach than that adopted by the state rail networks.

In 1944, at the height of the Second World War, the CR required no less than 104,098 tonnes of coal, three times more than in 1939. Additional coaling stations were added along the route (peak at eight); Pimba in South Australia was the most easterly of these, and Zanthus in Western Australia the most westerly. The logistics were a nightmare, and military traffic had priority, with just one very crowded civilian train permitted per week. Even prisoners of war were raked in to help the maintenance and operation of the Trans-Australian Railway; notably, some Germans were used along the main track, fortunately with no hint of any sabotage activities.

By and large, simplicity and a lack of costly diversity was to the fore with the CR steam locomotives; there were just eight classes of steam locomotive plus two adjusted classes (GA and KA). Even the legendary railway historian AE Durrant of South Africa gave the CR full marks for its disciplined approach to types of steam locomotives. When dieselisation came along, the CR adopted a similarly simple approach.

In 1951 the CR ordered the GM Class diesel-electric; as previously mentioned, the first one, GM1, was named *Robert Gordon Menzies* after the prime minister of the day. In 2016 GM1 made it to Goulburn for a superb 'streamliner' display; it is now stored in Perth.

≫ Soldier standing on a station platform beside a locomotive, Northern Territory, c. 1942. Australian railways played a big supporting role in two world wars.

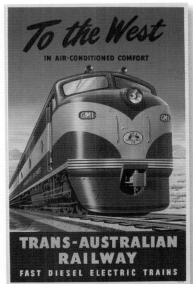

≪ Marree railhead, c. 1940–57. Today Marree is a rail ghost town, but it still boasts a good pub.

≫ 'To the West' – advertising the Trans-Australian Railway, c. 1951. Bold colours dominated the original diesel-electric 'Trans'.

By 1954 dieselisation had been rolled out on both the narrow- and standard-gauge networks operated by CR. Not only did dieselisation massively lower operating costs across the Nullarbor, it also allowed for higher average speeds, which meant a significant speeding up of services. Indeed, dieselisation for the Trans-Australian route operated by CR was to constitute a huge productivity boost just as it began to face competition from long-distance road transport and coastal shipping. The east–west Transcontinental actually became very competitive, in part as a result of these versatile strong locomotives and a steady program of track upgrading, but also because Commissioner Keith Smith was progressive enough to ensure that better ballast, concrete sleepers and heavier rail were installed.

One little-known fact is that, for once in this country's history, the rail route between two major centres (Kalgoorlie and Port Augusta) was significantly shorter than the road route: 1,692 kilometres versus 1,898 kilometres. Furthermore, the east–west Eyre Highway was not completely sealed until the 1970s. And so, for a change, the odds favoured rail.

The CR steam locomotives were always known for their enormous stamina, with extra-large tenders to carry more water and coal. Typically, the westbound trains in winter found themselves heading into strong headwinds and using more fuel to get to Kalgoorlie compared with travelling eastbound.

As a true interstate railway body, the CR made a huge contribution to the economic fabric of Australia in the first half of the twentieth century. Throughout this period there was steam locomotion only, and this showed that steam could perform both over short and long – indeed very long – distances.

To those who had to shovel the coal across the Nullarbor goes a special salute. They are a hardy, brave, all-male cohort of dedicated men; these CR firemen made the whole operation possible in the years before dieselisation. In summer, they shovelled tonnes and tonnes of coal, in boiling temperatures and against huge odds. In winter, there were frosts and frozen puddles to contend with.

Way up north, from 1889 to 1918, there was the Palmerston Division of the South Australian Railways (SAR) operating in Anglo Cape narrow gauge from the Port of Darwin down to Katherine and a little further south to Birdum. In 1918 the CR took over this unit, which largely serviced the isolated population of the 'Top End' and the sprawling cattle industry. As a modest network, it still managed to gather some seven types or classes of steam locomotive, all of which started with the designator 'N', for various operations down the track from Darwin.

≫ A driver's-eye view of the line ahead: drivers needed great skill just to stay awake while crossing the Nullarbor.

≫ During the Second World War the railway station and yard at Palmerston (later Darwin), seen here in 1890, were heavily strafed and bombed by the Japanese forces.

The North Australian Railway of the CR has the dubious honour of being the only Australian railway bombed by the Japanese during the Second World War. It played a vital role in military movements, including at Adelaide River, where a huge ammunition and explosives depot was developed, with many bunkers, all serviced by narrow-gauge rail sidings.

Snake Gully, as the RAAF Depot at Adelaide River was known, was closed decades ago, but to this day it has many concrete bunkers and may yet see a heritage train operation, over the small 10-kilometre track network between the Adelaide River Station and the Railway Museum. The RAAF Depot's last commanding officer was Bob Halverson, who went on to be Speaker of the Federal Parliament, and later Ambassador to Ireland and the Holy See. He always maintained Snake Gully was aptly named.

Today *The Ghan* luxury train glides past Adelaide River using part of the old track bed of No. 3 loop, but it has been upgraded with heavy ballast and heavy-duty standard-gauge steel track and concrete sleepers — a far cry from the old narrow-gauge steam train operations. One lonely old steam locomotive is stored under cover at Pine Creek, an 1877 Beyer, Peacock NF Class locomotive; it is designated as operational and is officially meant to be able to steam, but I doubt it is about to accelerate out of Pine Creek Railway Station and Museum anytime soon.

⌃ Celebrating the 10th anniversary of *The Ghan* running straight through to Darwin.

A double-headed train carrying coal from the Flinders Ranges to Port Augusta, 1968. Both this coal mine and the big power station it fed have ceased to operate.

« CR locomotive No. NM35 at Stuart Railway Station, Northern Territory, c. 1929. Fortunately, this narrow-gauge operation was never extended from Katherine to Alice Springs, eventually allowing standard-gauge development, which opened in 2004.

˅ The superb Heavitree Gap was a rail engineer's dream. Here an NM Class locomotive with cattle train is en route through the MacDonnell Ranges to Port Augusta, 1950s.

GRAND OLD GHAN ADVENTURE, 1966

It was my first big trip away from home. Aged 19, I was setting off with two mates, Max Day and Graham Schirmer, both from Lockhart, New South Wales, to catch the 'Old Ghan' from Marree to Alice Springs; the idea had been to put the car on board for the 24-hour journey and then go camping in the Northern Territory. However, on this trip I picked up my National Service call-up notice at the Darwin GPO, and so a few months later entered the army.

We arrived at Marree mid-afternoon on a winter's day and, after handing over the car for loading onto the narrow-gauge flat car, headed off to the Marree Hotel to await the standard-gauge train from Port Pirie and Port Augusta.

The standard-gauge track had arrived in Marree in 1957, as an extension from the Leigh Creek brown coal mine a few kilometres to the south; it replaced the old narrow-gauge one that had been steam-operated via the Pichi Richi Pass and Quorn and Hawker.

After way too many beers, I went looking for some remnant steam locomotives but found only one; it was looking the worse for wear and by now it is probably buried in the shifting sands of the nearby desert. I understand there are some old narrow-gauge diesel locomotives – and one carriage – still there today, fading

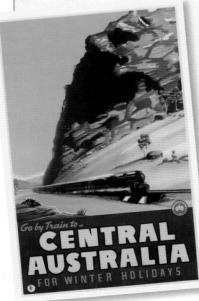

« 'Go by train' – promotional posters, such as this one from the 1950s, often reflected the art norms of the era.

away near the famous Marree Pub, which remains open for business.

After it got dark, I suddenly noticed a huge searchlight to the south and an old fettler said, 'Here she comes, but it will be another 25 minutes before arrival.' Exactly 25 minutes later, the train with all the connecting passengers pulled into the 'break of gauge' platform, and people began swapping over to the narrow-gauge Old Ghan.

I still recall, as if it was yesterday, a huge leg of beef being transferred from one dining car to the other, but soon enough the whistle blew and we departed, northbound into the night at the grand speed of about 24 kph – on a good stretch. The reason for this was not only the lightly ballasted track (about to be bypassed by the new track from Tarcoola direct to Alice Springs), but also our nice sleeper carriages and dining car were of standard gauge, so very wide for the narrow-gauge track, but safe if operated at slow speeds.

CR management had wisely decided to use surplus east-west rolling stock for the Old Ghan and earn a few dollars more in the process; furthermore, I happily recall the carriages were air-conditioned. For this region, CR management had restricted steam locomotion on the Old Ghan section to just four classes: NM, NB, NMA and NMB. Alas, I was a decade or so late on the scene, so missed seeing the steam in action.

About 24 hours later, we arrived at Alice Springs, in the middle of the night and somewhat legless. With assistance from Max and Graham I managed to make it to a hotel; the car was due to be unloaded the next morning. Although sad to have missed steam locomotion on this line, I was pleased to have done the Old Ghan before it was withdrawn and this section of track was bypassed forever.

At one stage in the early years, there had been plans to link up with the narrow gauge from Alice Springs to Birdum, there being a gap along the north–south corridor through two-thirds of the Northern Territory, but the Great Depression ended that notion — and in any event it would have been a case not just of 'wrong gauge' but also of 'wrong corridor' given that it was subject to a great deal of flooding. The gap was finally closed only in 2004, when the Alice Springs-to-Darwin section was built.

In many ways, the CR and its steam operations from 1917 to 1957 (or thereabouts) were first-class: not too many types of locomotives, and all of them with large size tenders to cope with the big distances across the Nullarbor.

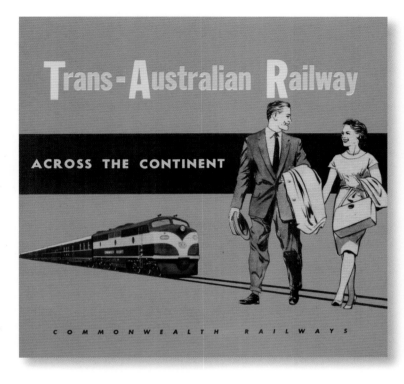

⌃ 'Trans-Australian Railway: Across the Continent', c. 1960. Promotion by pamphlet dominated then, but not now.

These large tenders, with many tonnes of coal on board, were in great demand, especially heading west to Kalgoorlie into the strong winter westerlies.

The CR's operation of the Trans-Australian route was so good over the decades that it raises the question whether long-distance rail in Australia should have been a Commonwealth function from the outset. CR is an exemplar, with its strong stable leadership, few classes of steam locomotives (and even fewer classes of diesel-electric locomotives), profitable years of operation and the huge contribution it made to the core fabric and well-being of the nation.

It remains flexible in adapting to needs of the twenty-first century: across the Nullarbor, for the first few weeks of each year, thousands of chocolate Easter eggs are loaded on pallets then gently — and coolly — conveyed from Altona near Melbourne to Perth by SCT intermodal trains. The ARTC now maintains this standard-gauge main line from Melbourne to Adelaide, then on to Crystal Brook and Port Augusta, and finally across to Perth. Several large freight operators compete for the available freight business and then pay the ARTC for the track access for their trains — a competition-driven template that works well with all kinds of freight: from motor vehicles to Easter eggs and even cut flowers in season. The east–west transcontinental rail route has certainly come a long way since G1 steamed out of Port Augusta on that first run west on 22 October 1917. The centenary of this departure was celebrated by large crowds at Port Augusta on the weekend of 21–22 October 2017.

If you've got … the money, and you've got the people who are willing to do it, then I don't see any reason why [the steam trains] shouldn't be out on the tracks all the time.

STEAM TRAIN FIREMAN ASHLEY FITTON, ABC NEWS, 5 JUNE 2015

CHAPTER 11

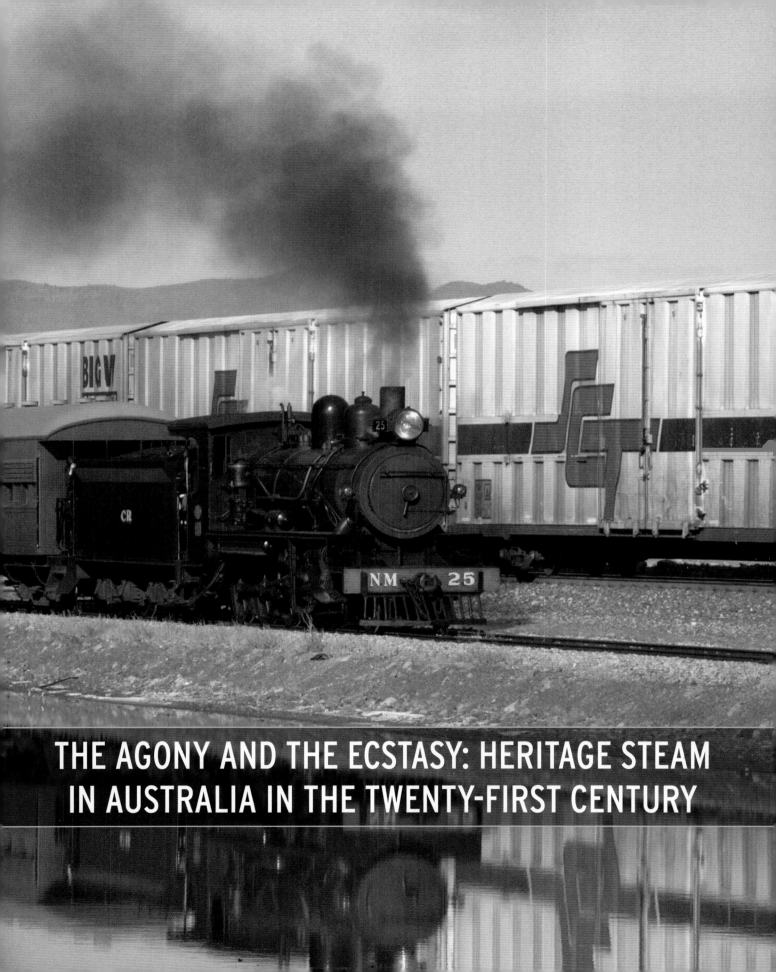

THE AGONY AND THE ECSTASY: HERITAGE STEAM IN AUSTRALIA IN THE TWENTY-FIRST CENTURY

There are some crown jewels in the grand Australian rail heritage scheme of things; for example, the *Puffing Billy* in the Dandenong Ranges, the Zig Zag Railway in the Blue Mountains (when it is operational), the Pichi Richi based at Quorn in the Flinders Ranges and the SteamRanger Heritage Railway in the Adelaide Hills. And then there are all the rest. The rail heritage movement has also worked some notable miracles, such as recreating the magnificent Garratt 6029 in Canberra and the Bellarine Railway at Queenscliff, Victoria, which has recreated the only Australian Standard Garratt locomotive still in existence.

It is a great pity, however, that some units with terrific potential have not been operating for years: the Tumut-to-Batlow Railway, for example, had tremendous potential but the project was derailed by heavy insurance premiums and sadly collapsed. To be fair, in this and so many other cases, it was not always the management or the volunteers that were at fault.

Apart from various operational rail heritage units, Australia has a set of rail museums that match even the best of Britain and the United States; National Railway Museum (NRM) at Port Adelaide, springs especially to mind. It has the best multi-gauge range of locomotives and rolling stock in the world — a big statement but true nonetheless, as I can attest having visited most key museums worldwide, with the exception only of Nuremberg in Germany.

Let us start with some gloom before we switch over to considering those aspects of rail heritage that are blooming and booming across Australia. In many ways, there is a need to capture and record every heritage steam operation for posterity as they are all, to varying degrees, under serious threat.

Indeed, there are several existential threats to rail heritage steam operations around the world and particularly in Australia. The biggest is the ability to attract the rising younger generation to learn about steam locomotive operations and, in particular, how to drive these grand old engines. The second biggest threat is the difficulties associated with obtaining the necessary

quantities of quality coal – not to mention the problem of obtaining community support and the relevant approvals for the use of this coal in heritage steam locomotives. The drumbeats of 'extreme green' political warriors are being readied to veto steam locomotive operation simply because it is fired by coal.

Wattrain (World Alliance of Tourist Trams & Trains), the world's supreme rail heritage body, which was set up in Great Britain in 2010, is examining this fuel issue in an effort to get ahead of the game before any veto actions come into play. The good news is that alternatives exist and that in this the United States leads the way. Steaming to the edge of the Grand Canyon on the Grand Canyon Railway has been available again since 2008; it has involved collecting and screening all the liquid cooking oils from the fast food restaurants in the region, then using this 'waste vegetable oil' as fuel to power locomotive 4960, which sets off about once a month. So it is a case of 'eat more chips' near Las Vegas and the Grand Canyon if you want to send more steam trains scuttling back and forth to the brink of the vast canyon at a stunning lookout site.

⌃ Milwaukee Zoo train, 2009. Many steam tourist trains operate on narrow gauge in the United States.

⌃⌃ Arizona Centennial Steam Locomotive being serviced, Grand Canyon, 2012. Steam train tourism abounds in the United States.

More recently, US magazine *Trains* has brought news of a new alternative to coal for heritage steam locomotives that is being trialled on the Milwaukee County Zoo train in Wisconsin. The new fuel is called 'torrefied biomass' and it comprises thin compressed and toasted carbon pellets made from the wood of yellow pine trees.

Trials in June 2016 saw massive boiler heat generating plenty of steam for the Bronte gauge 15-inch railroad and these trials are expected to extend to Stephenson standard-gauge locomotives in the near future. It is the act of toasting the pellets in an oxygen-free oven that confers coal-like performance of this fully sustainable fuel.

Meanwhile, coal is not going to cease to be used overnight. Its production worldwide is not going to end by 2020, or even 2040, but if the rail heritage movement can get out in front of the threat to it, then all the better.

Currently, the *Puffing Billy* near Melbourne is Australia's leading rail heritage operation, with five NAs (that is, Narrow Gauge A Class) and two Garratts (although one of these is still undergoing restoration). *Puffing Billy* leads in

⌃ Wangaratta Railway
Station, c. 1908. In its
heyday this was a busy
rail junction.

⌄ Railway bridge at
Walhalla, 1920s.
Fortunately, this railway
way east of Melbourne
still operates as a tourist
operation today.

most aspects, including having the largest annual patronage as international tourists flock to it daily. Currently, all its steam locomotive power comes from coal, but wise heads are starting to think about getting ahead of the game and turning to 'torrefied biomass pellets', the environmentally sustainable toasted wood pellets. Just maybe, the *Puffing Billy* will lead the Southern Hemisphere down this path. We shall see, but the drumbeat of change in this area of endeavour will certainly grow louder and louder.

With *Puffing Billy* it was a case of 'if at first you don't get started, then try and try again'. In fact, Victoria developed four small add-on narrow-gauge networks, all connecting and feeding into the main Victorian Railways (VR) broad-gauge system. After initially giving consideration to a 2 ft (610 mm) gauge, all four were eventually built in 2 ft 6 in gauge (762 mm), to ensure more capacity and stability. First of all, there is the Moe–Walhalla line via Erica; this has resumed operation today from the Thompson River terminal to Walhalla — a very pretty section of track with discussion taking place on a vital further extension back towards Erica to a new parkway station to be called Monash.

Next, in the north-east of the state, there is the Wangaratta–Whitfield (King Valley) tramway or railway, which carried milk and other products daily on a north–south axis single track in the 1920s. Today remnants of it can still be sighted just south of Wangaratta Station. The line never made a profit — sadly, this was the case with all the VR narrow-gauge lines.

Trestle bridges are a feature of the *Puffing Billy* railway.

The Beech Forest ('Beechy') network, located to the west of Geelong, was designed for timber haulage out of the Otways. In its heyday — from 1902 to 1962, although it really boomed between the world wars — it was a very busy system with an extension, or its own branch line, but all feeding into the main line at Colac. Today it has been converted to a very successful set of bike trails.

Finally, there is the *Puffing Billy*; as the system closest to Melbourne, it has potential access to a market of more than 4 million people. However, it was nearly lost forever when it was officially closed around the same time the electrified broad-gauge suburban system was extended from Upper Ferntree Gully through Upwey to Belgrave. It was rescued just in the nick of time. (The existing narrow-gauge track operated mainly as a means of conveying various seasonal fruits and vegetables such as potatoes to the Melbourne produce markets.) A hardy bunch of volunteers saddled up: the first job was to remove a large landslip before operations resumed, from Belgrave to Emerald. In 1998 an extension was opened to Gembrook, and so *Puffing Billy* in all its glory is able to operate today all the way to the original terminus on the edge of the beautiful Dandenongs. Unfortunately, Gembrook, though blessed with this tourist asset, has done little to capitalise on regular steam tourist trains. Meanwhile, on most weekends, Belgrave and the modern *Puffing Billy* rail museum at Menzies Creek are a hive of activity.

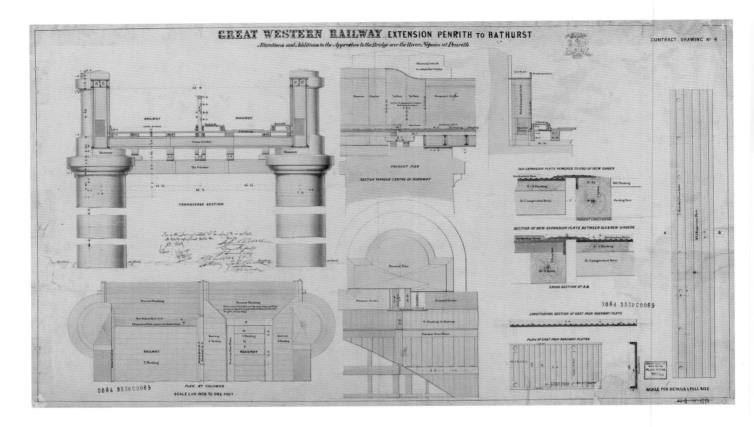

0084 35BRC0069

⌃ Yes, there were two GWRs: Brunel's in Britain and also one operating west of Sydney in the mid-nineteenth century.

Plans are afoot to revamp an old Tait electric train set and run it out of Flinders Street around 9 o'clock each morning up to Belgrave as the great *Puffing Billy* connector — a splendid idea that should have been done years ago. *Puffing Billy* has a reputation for handling international tourists well; diplomatic meetings have even been conducted in its one large enclosed passenger carriage. It has a future but needs to quickly resolve its locomotive haulage capacity issues.

Several hundred thousand people visit and use the *Puffing Billy* every year, as well as the nearby Menzies Creek museum, but it needs to be wary of walking away from its base hub at Belgrave, with its direct connection to Metro trains to Melbourne CBD and space for further development. As with all rail heritage units, *Puffing Billy*, now 50 years on from its establishment, probably needs to look to renewing its leadership and revamping its structure.

In 2013 the great Zig Zag Railway, west of Sydney, came under direct attack from a huge fire started by an Australian Army live firing exercise on its firing range in a tinder-dry section of the Blue Mountains. The damage was enormous, wiping out equipment and workshops, and rendering locomotives inoperable. The army might as well have fired its ammunition direct at the Zig Zag on that hot windy fateful day. Subsequent investigations found the army guilty on all counts — or at least that small portion of the army directly involved — and it and the

Department of Defence have had to pay up to put things right. Only in 2016 has the Zig Zag managed to operate a work train from the bottom points to the top points, and it still has a way to go before it can swing back into full-scale operation.

The Zig Zag could be one of the real stars of Australian rail heritage, but it will need unified dynamic leadership to bring this about — and some good marketing. Located about two and a half hours west of the more than 5 million people in the Sydney Basin hub, and accessible by direct platform at the bottom points to the Sydney–Lithgow inter-urban trains, it should be relatively simple to build to 300,000 patrons a year, once all the track and buildings are repaired and it is ready to resume full-scale operations (which it is hoped will happen in 2019).

One snag that is unfortunately not reversible is the decision taken about 40 years ago to switch the Zig Zag to Anglo Cape gauge and bring in Queensland steam locomotives to operate its passenger train services. The Zig Zag was originally built as part of John Whitton's mighty standard-gauge Western main line from Sydney to Bathurst, thence on to Dubbo and Bourke to the north-west and Parkes and Broken Hill to the west. For purists this remains an issue, but when the Zig Zag was starting out as a rail heritage operation it was said that no NSWGR steam locomotive equipment was available. Nevertheless, the sandstone bridges and the vistas from the Zig Zag remain sensational, and if properly promoted, it should again become a big drawcard.

⌄ Zig Zag Railway, Blue Mountains, 1878. There are so many angles that portray the engineering efforts of the Zig Zag.

South Australia must be rated the state that possesses three crown jewels of rail heritage, owing to some farsighted dedication and good leadership (even if two small operations have fallen by the wayside over recent decades). Operated by the NRM at Port Adelaide is the Port Glanville steam train, which runs along the beach about 30 minutes from the Adelaide CBD; on weekends in spring and summer it draws very big crowds.

Both the Pichi Richi and the SteamRanger deserve specific praise as being reliable operators based in South Australia; they meet the demand of a sometimes fickle market and are to be found steaming away at least once or twice a month, especially in autumn and spring. SteamRanger is also busy in summer.

In many ways, the Pichi Richi Railway is the most historic railway in the country. In years gone past, it was both the east–west link (from 1917 to 1937) and, at Quorn, the link to Marree and Alice Springs. Prime ministers, senators and even opera singers (such as Dame Nellie Melba) all passed through Quorn. After huge efforts, the Pichi Richi was extended to operate as a heritage railway all the way from Port Augusta to Quorn; it gains height after Woolshed Flats as it moves up through the colourful Pichi Richi Pass towards the summit and then down a gentle grade into the large Quorn terminus yard.

For many years, despite being battered by drought followed by huge storms and floods, the Pichi Richi has shown great resilience; it just gets up and goes again. In 2016 a massive tornado-like storm ripped through the region, but just south of the Pichi Richi Pass, as it happened. The railway's distance from Adelaide does not help — it is a four- to five-hour car drive — but those running the railway have been clever at building up a strong weekend clientele.

For years I have argued that the westbound *Indian Pacific* should offer passengers the option of alighting at Peterborough in the mid-north of South Australia for a visit to the revamped rail museum there; this could be followed by a coach trip to Quorn and then a steam train down to Port Augusta, where the *Indian Pacific* could be rejoined after it has been into Adelaide and back. Maybe one day this option will be developed; it would surely be attractive to repeat *Indian Pacific* travellers looking for a journey with an attractive difference.

⌄ This crowded station may be that at Quorn, South Australia, c. 1880. Today Quorn is the headquarters of the great Pichi Richi Railway.

The Pichi Richi Railway Preservation Society (PRRPS) currently has three key steam locomotives in operation, plus the 'Coffee Pot' (a delightful small narrow-gauge steam powered rail motor owned by the PRRPS), and many more have been preserved. The table below details how diverse the PRRPS's collection is, but like many rail heritage units the danger is that it owns too many old locomotives that are unlikely ever to be used again.

Over the years, the Pichi Richi Railway has been well served by its leadership, but it must plan carefully for the future and plan for the transition to a younger generation of leaders and volunteers. It would also help if the Pichi Richi were to compile a list of the famous travellers who, over the decades, went by train through the Pichi

⌃ Pichi Richi Railway locomotive No. W22 awaits its departure from the railway station at Quorn, 2017. General Douglas MacArthur changed trains here during the Second World War.

CLASS	NUMBER	FORMER OPERATOR	WHEEL CONFIGURATION	CONDITION	COMMENTS
W	916	WAGR	4-8-2	Operational	Rebuilt as W22
W	931	WAGR	4-8-2	In storage	
W	933	WAGR	4-8-2	In storage	
W	934			Undergoing mechanical overhaul	
W	22			In storage	ex Silverton Railway
T	186	SAR	4-8-0	In storage	
YX	141	SAR	2-6-0	Undergoing long-term restoration	
WX	18	SAR	2-6-0	In storage	Disassembled
BHP	3	BHP	2-6-2T	In storage	Tank locomotive
NM	25	CR	4-8-0	Operational	
NB	30	CR	C	Operational	Diesel hydraulic locomotive
NSU	51	CR	A1A–A1A	In storage	
NSU	52	CR	A1A–A1A	Operational	
NSU	54	CR	A1A–A1A	In storage	
NT	76	CR	Co-Co	Operational	
DE	10	BHP	Bo-Bo	In storage	
SMC	1	SAR/CR	2-2-0WT	Operational	Steam motor coach No. 1 ('Coffee Pot')
RC	106	SAR		Operational	Diesel railcar

TABLE 2: LOCOMOTIVES IN PRRPS COLLECTION

Richi Pass; for example, Dame Nellie Melba, Billy Hughes and General Douglas MacArthur, who came through Quorn from Alice Springs and Hawker, travelling onto Terowie and Adelaide. (It was at Terowie on 20 March 1942 that MacArthur uttered his famous promise: 'I came out of Bataan but I shall return.' Of course, while the general did keep his promise to return to the Philippines, he never returned to Terowie, and sadly no trains of any gauge run there today.)

On a balmy summer's day the pleasant sound of a passenger steam locomotive can be heard plying between Goolwa, Port Elliot and Victor Harbor. This rail heritage unit draws good customer support and good revenue each year; in particular, during the holiday weeks of January, but at other times as well. It features the Cockle Train, which operates on broad gauge, and offers one of the best rail experiences available in Australia. It has some of the most stunning coastal scenery to enjoy. Full marks go to its operators for maintaining this crown jewel that helps anchor the tourism region south of McLaren Vale and Mount Barker. If only the renowned South Australian landscape painter Hans Heysen had spent more time there, as opposed to nearby Hahndorf, we might have had a plentiful supply of glorious steam locomotive oil paintings in this country.

⌃ Terowie Railway Station, 1994. The 'break of gauge' here really should have been just to the north, at Peterborough.

Back in Adelaide, the NRM at Port Adelaide is the world's best multi-gauge museum, with its iconic collections of Irish broad, Stephenson standard and Anglo Cape narrow-gauge rail locomotives and carriages. The collection includes GI, the CR's first steam locomotive, the one that knitted Australia together. Some have even suggested that GI could should have been called Federation, given its vital role. I would settle for having a stamp that featured the mighty GI, which could be issued on each occasion of a significant anniversary of the east–west link. However, the NRM needs to expand its tiny fulltime professional staff. It requires a bigger operational budget, and surely one day this will happen. Perhaps donations by bequest should be sought, with substantial bequests to be recognised by naming the various loops or siding tracks after the donor.

Overall, Victoria can claim the most successful set of rail heritage operations, with the Bellarine Railway operating a variety of services (such as the well-known the Blues Train) between Queenscliff and Drysdale. This runs to exactly 16 kilometres — the distance judged by experts as the optimum length for rail heritage operations. There are others, such as the Victorian Goldfields Railways and the Walhalla Goldfields Railway — and, of course, the famous Puffing Billy. To some extent the success of Puffing Billy disguises the less-than-successful attempts to finally provide for a giant well-housed Victorian Railway Museum that would feature the huge Irish broad-gauge equipment that is still around, including *Heavy Harry*, which has been preserved but is not operational. Williamstown is the current location for the existing museum, maintained by a dedicated bunch of volunteers who were devastated by a spate of deliberate arson attacks a few years ago. Some consideration has been given to a total relocation, with a good report to this end prepared by John Hearsch Consulting Pty Ltd in 2015.

The Victorian Goldfields Railway has eight steam locomotives with just three operational at last count, this points to the problem of rail heritage organisations taking on too much preservation and the need sometimes to do less but do it well.

Between Drysdale and Queenscliff on the Bellarine Peninsula there is a steam train rail heritage operation of renown, known as the Bellarine Railway. Today after converting the old Irish broad-gauge branch line to Anglo Cape narrow gauge, it operates most weekends and has had great success with music-themed trains catering to lovers of jazz and blues. Well located for the huge crowds in

» Many historic signal boxes have been preserved, such as this one at the ARHS Railway Museum, North Williamstown.

WHY CASTLEMAINE MAKES SENSE AS THE SITE FOR A RAIL MUSEUM

Much can be made of a name for promotional purposes. Take, for example, the Victoria and Albert Museum ('the V&A') in London, or the Museum of Old and New Art (MONA) in Hobart. With reasonably fast hourly services to and from Melbourne, Castlemaine on the Bendigo main line is tailor-made to be the location for what might be called the 'Great Victoria and Castlemaine Railway Museum'. It has plenty of space on the 'down' or western side of the existing heritage Castlemaine Railway Station, with a grand signal box in good shape and an elongated area running a kilometre towards a turntable.

The bonus here is that, most weekends, patrons could steam away on the Maldon steam express; called the Victorian Goldfields Railways, it is an interesting operation with good vistas of central Victoria. Still there are always local tangles, and sometimes a lack of boldness holding back good ideas.

When the award-winning film *The Dressmaker* was launched in 2015, it featured a section of the Maldon line. All the Victorian Goldfields Railway had to do was brand its main train service for the next dozen weekends 'The Dressmaker Express', and include a lunch stop, with optional coaching in dressmaking or talks by the author (who grew up in the country near Jerilderie and later moved to Melbourne), and a bonanza would have been created.

So someone should go create a proper rail museum at Castlemaine, and watch the tourists come – perhaps some even from as far away as the United States, following in the footsteps of Mark Twain, who changed trains at Castlemaine – after a long wait in the heat – in 1895.

summer that descend on the peninsula, the Bellarine Railway is a good example of creating a useful tourist asset. It has steam locomotives from interstate, including Western Australia and is currently rebuilding Australia's only remaining ASG.

It is a great pity that elsewhere in Victoria there is an example of outright state vandalism: the Port of Echuca branch rail was disconnected—for no good reason —in 2000 and this has prevented weekend tourism trains from running from Melbourne right to the main wharf at Echuca on the Murray River. Flooding on the Murray is predictable a fortnight ahead at Echuca, so special trains could be run up from Melbourne to witness the rare super floods on the mighty river. This is still an opportunity that could—and should—be taken up as soon as possible.

The sad truth is that steam rail heritage is something of a mixed bag right across the nation. In 1952 the Australian Railway Historical Society (ARHS) emerged from the Australasian Railway and Locomotive Historical Society Railway

Rail enthusiasts at Picton Station, south of Sydney, in 1946. Picton once had three platforms, but today is a 'no nonsense' two-platform station.

The Workshops Rail Museum, North Ipswich, 2016. This jewel of Ipswich is well worth visiting.

Circle organisation, which had been established in 1933. The need for legal entities in each state, to ensure appropriate accreditation to operate trains under the ARHS banner and to limit liability for key managers, eventually became apparent; in this, the New South Wales branch of the ARHS led the way, and variations now exist across the land. In Western Australia it is known as Rail Heritage WA; in Canberra it is the ARHS ACT (currently under administration). Under these umbrella organisations, separate units have emerged, some happily and some in conflict with their neighbours or parent organisations. In most states, there are key anchor museums; notably the North Ipswich Workshops Rail Museum near Brisbane, NSW Rail Museum at Thirlmere near Picton, the National Railway Museum in Port Adelaide, the Tasmanian Transport Museum at Glenorchy in Hobart and the Western Australian Rail Transport Museum at Bassendean. Then there was the Canberra Railway Museum, now closed, which had some terrific operational units, including the mighty Garratt, restored against impossible odds but now privately owned and housed at the NSW Rail Museum in Thirlmere. In Victoria, there is the Australian Railway Historical Society Museum at Williamstown, but deep thinking and planning is currently taking place as to where and when a revamp should be pursued. Sadly, previous Bicentennial and Centennial funding opportunities to undertake a major refurbishment of the museum were allowed to slip by, notwithstanding having some heavy hitters as local state MPs at the time.

Much that has been preserved is carefully stored in these museums, under cover and in some cases in good operational order. The NSW Rail Museum operates a steam train passenger service every Sunday from March to December, as well as main-line tours and special charters. These charter trains include a set of *Southern Aurora* cars, generally diesel-hauled, and with its access to main-line

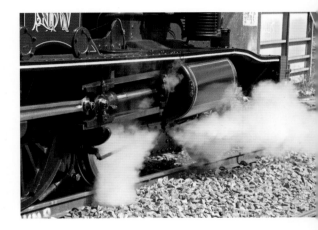

⌄ Huge crowds always attend Steamfest at Maitland in the Hunter Valley.

routes, it has had some success. (St James Rail does this, as was the case during the centenary of Anzac when the train arrived at Yarrawonga to a warm greeting from around 2,000 people.) Likewise, at Glenorchy and Ipswich, steam passenger trains operate on key weekends, but access to main-line track can be — and often is — a problem.

Somewhat counterbalancing the absence of a fully operational Zig Zag, New South Wales has both the vibrant NSW Rail Museum near Picton and the annual Maitland Steamfest, which draws huge crowds and often sees four steam trains abreast flying down the quadruple track from Maitland to Broadmeadow. The museum has recently come under new management, following a restructure in 2016; Peter Lowry was the inaugural NSW Chairman of Transport Heritage NSW (a post currently held by Rob Mason) and Andrew Moritz, the highly capable former head of the North Ipswich Workshops Rail Museum in Queensland, continues as its CEO.

Location can often be a headache: two hours driving from the Sydney CBD or two hours steaming from Sydney Central to the south-west is a hurdle Thirlmere must overcome. One solution would be to develop regular steam locomotive–hauled passenger trains direct to the museum, on day trips departing Sydney Central at (say) 9 am on Saturdays and Sundays. There is certainly a big inventory to see at Thirlmere, and it is well laid out with good parking, but perhaps the local town and region could do more to plug into a marketing master plan for the site.

⌃ The Main Exhibition Building at the NSW Rail Museum, Thirlmere, 2016. Thirlmere is getting there despite its somewhat inconvenient location.

To my way of thinking, the Lachlan Valley Railway has terrific potential; it is based primarily at Cowra, but also, through force of circumstance, at Cootamundra Depot since the Blayney–Cowra–Young–Harden connector between the Western main line and the Southern main line is locked out of service at present.

» *Tilly*, Tenterfield
Railway, during winter
in 2016, but not Siberia
– northern New
South Wales.

Across New South Wales, there are many large and small rail heritage projects. At Paterson, in the Hunter Valley, there is an outstanding collection of rail motors, notably the CPH rail motor that used to rattle down many a branch line for decades across the NSWGR system. Of course, one of the old CPH fleet should already have been modernised with a new engine, air-conditioning and main line high-speed bogies to allow VIPs to travel efficiently to certain events, especially on the outer fringes of Sydney but also into the regions as well.

Entrepreneur Ross Jackson of Albury is busy restoring a DEB set of four attractive Tuscan Red rail motor power and trailer carriages. (These were diesel multiple units built by NSWGR in the 1950s.) It will be available for hire; for example, from Albury to the Melbourne Cup or to The Rock mountain for a climb and picnic lunch.

Proposed Cowra Woodstock Chardonnay Express

As luck would have it, there is an optimal length of existing track in good condition in the grass along a corridor north-east of Cowra with no major bridge requirements and just one key level crossing. It is part of the Cowra–Blayney regional line, but it could easily be operated as far as Woodstock. It lies at a good driving distance from two key markets: Sydney and Canberra.

Now the name 'Woodstock' conjures up certain images for the baby boomer generation, so to arrive there after departing the Cowra Heritage Station an hour or so earlier, having consumed some medal-winning local chardonnay, seems to have great potential. A gourmet lunch could be served at Woodstock before a gentle run back to Cowra later in the afternoon. As the heritage market grows for this product, perhaps a low-cost triangle could be installed at Woodstock by the Lachlan Valley Railway to allow the steam locomotive in use to be turned.

⌃ Hopefully, this station will anchor the
Cowra-Woodstock tourist train.

Anyway, an application has been submitted to the efficient John Holland, who has the relevant lease on these New South Wales lines at present, so – fingers crossed – perhaps something will come of it in the form of a sub-lease to operate a new venture.

Up at Tenterfield, in northern New South Wales, there is an incredible rail collection, located in the town's railway yard, which was meant to be where the narrow-gauge Queensland network would meet the standard-gauge NSWGR one. In the event, this happened at Wallangarra, but there is no reason why a rail trike could not be restored and a superb operation made to happen within two years; it could travel southwards down the first few kilometres of this historic main line to a local feature called 'The Bluff'.

⌃ Rail motor CPH6 and diesel railcar 607 at Cootamundra, New South Wales, 1983. Cootamundra remains a rail motor hub to this day.

Sadly, however, in New South Wales, some rail heritage units are in disrepair or have either vanished or very nearly vanished: for example, at Armidale and Glenreagh. One wonders if the massive Dorrigo Project, which has been collecting, over more than four decades, various rail icons from the old NSWGR system (operations along this line ceased in 1972), has had an impact or not.

Dorrigo sits on the top of an escarpment inland from Coffs Harbour, in a high-rainfall zone at the end of a branch line that was handed over in working condition complete with two magnificent tunnels; there is a huge collection of steam locomotives — this is the biggest single collection in Australia, in fact. There are no fewer than 44 mainly NSWGR steam locomotives stored here, and also some 26 diesel locomotives, four steam cranes and four electric locomotives. The site is operating under the title of Dorrigo Steam Railway and Museum Limited, spearheaded by Keith Jones. They have been receiving some preservation treatment, but most are currently sitting outside in the weather slowly rusting away. The Dorrigo Rail Museum is still not yet open to the public. Some vistas of the extensive site can be viewed online, but it is legitimate to ask when the museum will be opened to the public, and when even limited operations will be offered down the stunningly beautiful Dorrigo–Glenreagh branch line.

CLASS/NUMBER	WHEEL ARRANGEMENT	MANUFACTURER and DATE	YEARS of OPERATION
1. 'JUNO'	0-4-0ST	Andrew Barclay, Sons & Co. Ltd, 1923	1923–
2. 'Bristol Bomber'	0-6-0ST	Avonside Engine Co. – Bristol (UK), 1922	1922–
3	0-6-0ST	Kitson & Co. – Leeds (UK), 1878	1878–
3	0-6-0T	Andrew Barclay, Sons & Co, Ltd, 1911	1911–
4	0-4-0T	H. K. Porter, Pittsburgh (USA),	1915–
5	0-6-0T	Andrew Barclay, Sons & Co, Ltd, 1916	1916–
'CORBY'	0-4-0ST	Peckett & Sons Ltd – Bristol (UK), 1943	1943–
'MARIAN'	0-4-0ST	Andrew Barclay, Sons & Co, Ltd, 1948	1948–
'BADGER'	0-6-0ST	Australian Iron & Steel (Port Kembla), 1943	1943–
14 (S.M.R.)	0-8-2T	Avonside Engine Co. – Bristol (UK), 1909	1909–
20 (ROD 1984)	2-8-0	North British Locomotive Co. – Glasgow, 1918	1918–
24 (ROD 2003)	2-8-0	Great Central Railway – Gorton (UK), 1918	1918–
27 (S.M.R. No. 2)	0-4-0ST	Avonside Engine Co. – Bristol (UK), 1900	1900–
	0-4-0	Appleby Ltd – Leicester (UK),	–
17 SMR 10 Class	2-8-2T	Beyer, Peacock & Co. Ltd, 1913	1913
20 SMR 10 Class	2-8-2T	Beyer, Peacock & Co. Ltd, 1920	1920–
23 SMR 10 Class	2-8-2T	Beyer, Peacock & Co. Ltd, 1920	1920–
26 SMR 10 Class	2-8-2T	Beyer, Peacock & Co. Ltd, 1922	1922–
27 SMR 10 Class	2-8-2T	Beyer, Peacock & Co. Ltd, 1923	1923–
28 SMR 10 Class	2-8-2T	Beyer, Peacock & Co. Ltd, 1923	1923–
31 SMR 10 Class	2-8-2T	Beyer, Peacock & Co. Ltd, 1925	1925–
1050	T–T–D–D–T	Craven Brothers Ltd (UK), 1911	1911–
1052	0-4-0T	R. & W. Hawthorn Leslie (UK)	1914–
1061	0-4-0	Alfred Harman & Co. (Port Melbourne), 1918	1918–
1067	0-4-0T	R. & W. Hawthorn Leslie (UK), 1924	1924–
1068	0-4-0T	R. & W. Hawthorn Leslie (UK), 1923	1923–
1070	0-4-0	Henry J. Coles – Derby (UK), 1928	1928–
1075 (P1129)	0-4-0	Grafton Crane Co. (UK) 1923	1923–
1081	T–D–D–T	Industrial Brownhoist (USA), 1943	1943–
1904	0-6-0	Beyer, Peacock & Co. Ltd, 1877	1877–
1923	0-6-0	Beyer, Peacock & Co. Ltd, 1879	1879–
2408	2-6-0	Dubs & Co. – Glasgow (UK), 1891	1891–
2414	2-6-0	Dubs & Co. – Glasgow (UK), 1891	1891–
2535	2-6-0	Beyer, Peacock & Co. Ltd, 1883	1883–
3028 Saturated	4-6-0	Beyer, Peacock & Co. Ltd, 1904	1904–
3046	4-6-4T	Beyer, Peacock & Co. Ltd, 1908	1908–
3090 Superheated	4-6-0	N.S.W. Government Railways, 1912	1912–
3813	4-6-2	N.S.W.G.R. Cardiff Workshops, 1946	1946–
5069 Saturated	2-8-0	Beyer, Peacock & Co. Ltd, 1903	1903–
5132 Superheated	2-8-0	Beyer, Peacock & Co. Ltd, 1908	1908–
5353	2-8-0	N.S.W. Government Railways, 1913	1913–
5920	2-8-2	Baldwin – Lima – Hamilton (USA), 1953	1953–
6039	4-8-4 + 4-8-4	Beyer, Peacock & Co. Ltd, 1956	1956–
6042	4-8-4 + 4-8-4	Beyer, Peacock & Co. Ltd, 1956	1956–
BHP No. 3	2-6-2T	Beyer, Peacock & Co. Ltd, 1890	1890–
NB30	C	Vulcan Iron Works, Wilkes Barre, Pennsylvania (USA), 1916	1916–72
NJ	[not given]	Clyde Engineering	1971–
NM	4-8-0		1925–
NSU51	A1A–A1A	Birmingham Carriage and Wagon Company (UK), 1954	1954–80
NSU52	A1A–A1A	Birmingham Carriage and Wagon Company (UK), 1954	1954–81
NSU54	A1A–A1A	Birmingham Carriage and Wagon Company (UK), 1954	1954–80
NT76	Co-Co	Tulloch Ltd – Rhodes (N.S.W), 1965	1968–89?
SMC – NJAB1 'COFFEE POT'	2-2-0WT	Kitson & Co. (engine unit), 1905	1906–32
T	4-8-0	Islington Workshops – Gawler (Qld)	1903–70
W (later Wx)	2-6-0	Beyer, Peacock & Co. Ltd, 1878?	1878–59
Y (later Yx)	2-6-0	Beyer, Peacock & Co. Ltd	1904–58

TABLE 3: LIST OF LOCOMOTIVE STOCK AT
DORRIGO STEAM RAILWAY AND MUSEUM LIMITED

THE DORRIGO SAGA

State Members of Parliament in the area around Dorrigo in northern New South Wales have beavered away to try to get some timelines and solutions in place with regard to the stalled Dorrigo Project. When the Dorrigo branch line ceased to operate, there was a strong belief that a tourist train operation would work brilliantly up the escarpment through two short tunnels to a smart museum at the terminus.

Glenreagh, at the bottom on the main line, eventually obtained a set of permissions to operate such a line, but it struggled against impossible odds – for example, the difficulties experienced in gaining access to the congested single-track Sydney–Brisbane main line at

Glenreagh, further track damage resulting from lack of use since 1972, and the need to re-certify the two tunnels en route. The original promise was for an operational service from the Dorrigo end down the great descent, but seemingly not before some 40 or more steam locomotives had been purchased and stored at Dorrigo.

It is a case of right ideas but wrong applications, and this has resulted in the loss – at least for the time being – of what was a fully operational branch line. It may well be a long time before we will see the magnificent vista of a steam locomotive hauling heritage carriages up to Dorrigo. But it is a clearly a year-round market of great potential.

« Dorrigo Steam Railway and Museum, 2012. With enormous tourist potential, located so close to the World Heritage National Park, this site, with its wonderful scenery, has much to offer. although the high annual rainfall creates challenges for preserving heritage railway stock.

▲ Trains at Kuranda,
Queensland, 2010.
The Kuranda service
remains very popular
with tourists.

Queensland has a couple of very good operators, including DownsSteam Tourist Railway and Museum based at Toowoomba, Southern Downs Steam Railway at Warwick and the Rosewood Railway Museum near Ipswich. Sadly, the Mary Valley Heritage Railway with a superb ghost-like heritage terminus at Gympie is currently out of service for various reasons. On another scale is the famous Cairns–Kuranda scenic rail line with its several operators (patrons can choose either to go up or come back via bus, train or the Skyrail cableway). Kuranda Railway Station and surrounds is a tourist hub with a great village atmosphere, offering a variation from the crowded highly urbanised coast, but unfortunately with no steam train operations to be enjoyed.

In Tasmania, the Don River Railway should be allowed more flexible main-line access so that it can provide an expanded service; for example, Devonport–Deloraine regular services or a 'Tassie Steam Safari' connecting with the daily *Spirit of Tasmania* ferry service from Melbourne. Ida Bay Railway is Australia's most southern rail heritage operation, but is a rather lonely two-hour drive south of Hobart. It certainly needs a revamp to build into the future, and the Tasmanian Transport Museum does have some resources and operational steam locomotive units.

Tasmania as an island with so much to offer should further develop its autumn festival genre to create a huge 'Tassie Tango in Steam and Fine Wines and Gourmet Food', plus of course the fine classical music the Tasmanian Symphony Orchestra offers. Simply call it the 'Tassie Tango Festival' or even 'Steam Tasmania, Taste Tasmania'.

Indeed, every state has much to offer, but too often there are natural disasters and other problems that prevent the realisation of maximum potential. In Western Australia the Hotham Valley Railway has been seriously affected by deadly large bushfires over recent decades. Meanwhile, after operating for a while as a gourmet train, the preserved *Robert Gordon Menzies* GM1 diesel now seems to be missing in action, along with a set of heritage standard-gauge carriages. Also in Western Australia, the Wheatbelt Heritage Rail is about to unfold from a base at Minnivale in the middle of the dynamic Dowerin Shire, but it will need good marketing to draw patrons from the big Perth market located a two-hour drive away.

The Northern Territory has two small heritage units, at Pine Creek and Adelaide River, both with good potential, but often officialdom throws up bizarre hurdles precluding realisation of full potential.

In surveying the steam heritage scene across Australia, it has to be said it is a case of so near and yet so far. Almost all units need revamped marketing plans

⌄ The Don River Railway in Devonport is still in operation today as a tourist railway.

linked to services that will create expanded broad interest. Britain now has over 100 steam rail heritage operations making regular profits and employing more and more young professional staff as they build for the future. A few years ago, at Sheringham, a seaside town in the county of Norfolk, 10,000 people turned up, as did the BBC, just to witness the opening of a level crossing by a steam locomotive travelling all of 50 metres. This small act signalled the reconnection of the North

Norfolk Railway (known as the 'Poppy Line') with the broader British rail network. Can Australia match this dynamic steam endeavour? Admittedly, Britain is the birthplace of steam locomotives and has a population base nearly three times that of Australia. Nevertheless, even if on a smaller scale, I feel strongly that Australia can build a set of products that will draw serious tourist dollars on a regular basis. Here is a list of ten of the best, all with steam locomotive operations on a good day (apart from those of the seven large rail museums, which each have their own niche):

Best static display: Steamtown Heritage Rail Centre, Peterborough, SA

Best authentic rail operation: Victorian Goldfields Railway, Castlemaine–Maldon, VIC

Most historic link: Pichi Richi Railway, Quorn, SA

Best coastal heritage railway: SteamRanger Heritage Railway, SA

Best sugar cane rail heritage: Bally Hooley Steam Railway, Port Douglas, QLD

Only Abt heritage railway: West Coast Wilderness Railway, Queenstown to Strahan, TAS

Only interstate rail heritage: Southern Downs Steam Railway, Warwick, QLD

Best vista railway: Zig Zag Railway, Blue Mountains, NSW (when operational)

Railway with greatest potential: Don River Railway, TAS (but also the Puffing Billy, VIC).

On the major rail museum front, each state has its main centre, but in some cases there is a spillover to other locations (for example, in New South Wales, the Museum of Applied Arts and Sciences has two steam locomotives that would be regarded as crown jewels in any body's collection):

Queensland: Workshops Rail Museum, North Ipswich

New South Wales: NSW Rail Museum, Thirlmere

Victoria: Australian Railway Historical Society Museum, Williamstown

South Australia: National Railway Museum, Port Adelaide

Western Australia: Rail Transport Museum, Bassendean

Tasmania: Tasmanian Transport Museum, Glenorchy

Australian Capital Territory: Canberra Railway Museum (now closed).

⩔ Great Australian Railway Journeys, 2010. Some iconic trains and railways featured on a series of stamps issued by Australia Post.

The many and varied steam locomotives that make up the story of 'Steam Australia' have done so much over the decades to open up the hinterland, to connect the capitals and to boost the dynamic economic and social development of Australia. Flowing on from this, steam train rail heritage in Australia sprung into existence, albeit in a haphazard way. Of course, steam heritage is not automatically guaranteed a place in the sun, even when it comes to maintaining the vital steam icons of the past. It will need farsighted leadership, some governmental assistance — mainly to remove obstacles — and some good fortune. But from Leneva, near Wodonga, where steam engine buffs gather each Easter Saturday right across to the mighty Bennett Brook Railway in Perth, there is so much to see and enjoy.

≫ Pacific locomotive M4 at Coles Beach on the Don River Railway in Tasmania.

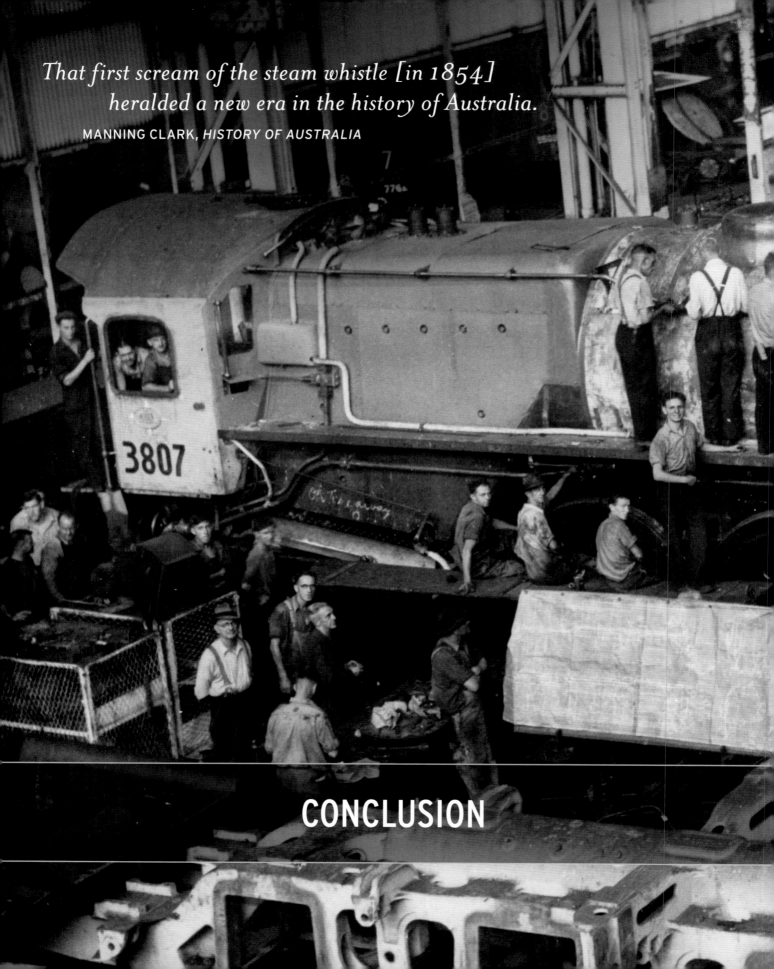

That first scream of the steam whistle [in 1854] heralded a new era in the history of Australia.

MANNING CLARK, *HISTORY OF AUSTRALIA*

3807

CONCLUSION

STEAM WILL LIVE ON

On reflection, it has to be said that from the first ever 'Hobson's Choice' to the famous polished wood 'Coffee Pot' steam rail motor of the Pichi Richi Railway and the giant Garratt 6029, the grand steam locomotives of Australia have come a long way over the decades. And of course they still have much to offer: there will doubtless be some great Australian steam locomotives operating well into the future.

For a century, from 1850 to 1950, steam locomotive haulage totally dominated Australia's various rail systems. Grand locomotives pulled express passenger trains and their slower brethren, and freight trains both fast and slow. They even hauled the 'all stops' mixed trains that combined a single passenger carriage with several freight wagons. During that period rail networks expanded from a few short routes in the big capital cities to huge networks reaching every corner of each state. In network operational length, Government rail networks reached their zenith in about 1913, just ahead of the First World War.

The biggest expansion of rail since 1950 was in the Pilbara region of Western Australia, where diesel-electric engines hauled trainloads of iron ore from the mines to the coast: around 30,000 tonnes of iron ore per train, each travelling a distance on average of about 200 kilometres. By way of example, the newest and heaviest axle load in the Pilbara, the Fortescue Railway, operates on average 14 trains daily from the mines down to Port Hedland.

As was the case elsewhere in the world, it was steam locomotives that gave momentum to the economy. But they also gave much-needed connectivity and even cohesion as isolated country towns became less so; unlike the old Cobb and Co. horse-drawn coach days when it might take a few days to reach the big smoke, now it could be accomplished in a matter of hours.

MILESTONES IN AUSTRALIAN HISTORY

Today: IT'S THE *SPEEDY* AIRMAIL THAT CONQUERS DISTANCE AND SAVES TIME.

⌃ Another breakthrough highlighted: for mail delivery, trains and Cobb and Co coaches eventually gave way to air.

For a few decades between the world wars, before the modern road truck took over, there were even special late Saturday night trains from Sydney Central, racing the Sunday morning newspapers out to the bigger nearby regional centres. Competition was fierce between the three main Sunday newspapers: *The Sunday Telegraph*, *The Sunday Mirror* (now defunct) and *The Sun-Herald*.

For most of the twentieth century, Victoria had no Sunday papers, but there were the big Saturday evening newspapers *The Herald* and *The Sporting Globe* for all the race results. For a while, rail was used to rush these papers out early on Saturday evening after all football results were in print and the VFL ladder positions calculated.

Special steam trains used to run annually to big local events; for example, from Mansfield to Seymour for the annual Seymour Show, necessitating a reverse by the train at Tallarook because of the lack of a triangle junction.

When Her Majesty Queen Elizabeth II made her first visit to Australia in 1954, she travelled many sections of that long journey by special Royal Train, but they were mainly diesel-hauled. However, earlier Royal Trains, notably those running between the world wars, were all steam-hauled.

The Queen's visit to the Riverina did generate what proved to be the last school excursion steam-hauled passenger train on the route from Oaklands through Urana, Boree Creek and Lockhart, then to the main line and Wagga Wagga. Since then, this one surviving Riverina branch line has been truncated, extending now just 56 kilometres to Boree Creek from the Sydney–Melbourne main line at The Rock. There is still the odd steam train venture out as far as Boree Creek: one in 1988 for the Bicentenary drew huge crowds, and another due to operate in 2018, but scheduled not in summer so as not to start any fires along the way. Yet again, the power of steam locomotives to be big drawcards was amply demonstrated.

The two big issues affecting steam locomotion remain much the same as they were at the beginning of the nineteenth century, when the Stephensons first started out. The first related to the problems with coal, which was frankly dirty, then as now. Burning it in locomotives meant loads of soot-stained walls and bridges at big railway stations, not to mention the environmental carbon footprint issues very much to the fore nowadays. Toasted wood chips, or variations of the same, are on the menu of solutions under consideration. The second took in all aspects relating to safety, all OH&S issues, especially all boiler maintenance issues.

≫ A Victorian railway station newspaper stand around the time of a failed attempt to kill the King in Hyde Park, London, in 1936. Newspapers and commuter railways remain in harness today.

≫ The Royal Train at Thornleigh, in suburban Sydney, 1954. This train is now superbly displayed at Thirlmere.

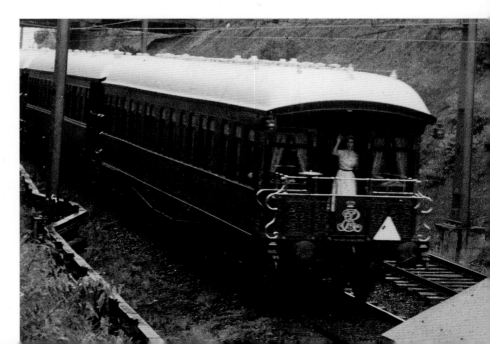

LOCAL STATE MPS AND THEIR STATIONS

Good state members of parliament always worked the railway stations and depots in their electorates as these were hubs of activity where they could mix with rail staff and with voters alike. It has always been important that state governments be seen to be the level of government responsible for making the railways work, and for answering the need for greater expansion of services. Often this has led to some colourful exchanges, with country MPs sometimes complaining bitterly about steam locomotives starting fires in summer time that quickly got out of control and did much damage. Some classes of steam locomotive had bad reputations for throwing hot coal particles into the air, so there was always a demand for weed-spraying to be undertaken early and often in spring each year, to keep the grass under control and the fire risk down.

Other complaints were more colourful; for example, Max Ruddock MP objecting to the big overnight trains from Brisbane, the North Coast and the North West, that descended through suburban Ryde in Sydney spewing black smoke on commuters, but worst still, owing to the 'straight through' toilets, leaving foul smelling business behind as long-distance passengers rose from their bunks to complete their morning ablutions. This problem was only fixed with the elimination of the 'straight through' from 1960 onwards, but remains a problem in some parts of the world to this day. Clouds of white limestone powder, laced with various additives, are sometimes deployed to help maintain health standards.

Then there was the case of Peter Anderson MP, whose electorate covered the Blue Mountains. His objection was to the big newspapers' distribution managers arbitrarily deciding to allocate early country editions to the Blue Mountains. As a result, the last stumps scores on a big Test cricket day could not be included.

Now both Ruddock (Liberal) and Anderson (Labor) went on to fill key front bench ministerial positions in New South Wales – their staunch advocacy while backbenchers of specific improvements on rail-related matters clearly did not harm their political careers.

» An engine driver instructs an apprentice on locomotive No. 1919, Eveleigh Railway Workshops, 1968. In their heyday, railways were great incubators of talent, and they remain so today.

Boilers are the very core of all steam locomotives. Poorly maintained or badly operated boilers can cause boiler explosions resulting in instantaneous death. This is a real but avoidable hazard. This is why regular boiler inspections, internal and external, with proper certification provided is really essential. The work of the Argentine steam locomotive engineer Livio Dante Porta remains vital here. His innovations regarding water treatment greatly lessened scaling in the pipes that carry water and the boilers, and his innovations regarding exhaust greatly improved efficiencies around burning fuel. However, there is nothing insurmountable with the onward operation of the steam locomotive in the twenty-first century.

Even though the great age of steam in Australia has passed, we are fortunate because we can follow its history thanks in large measure to the work of those enthusiastic collectors who have taken pains to amass collections of rail-related photographs and other material down the years. As a result of the work of John Buckland and a few others, including Nick Anchen (one of the successful new generation of rail book authors) and Jim Stokes (a key National Library of Australia volunteer who has done such splendid work sorting the huge Buckland Collection), there exists a huge historical photographic record of the operation of the steam locomotive worldwide over the previous two centuries. This has been the case in every country that the steam locomotive plied its trade, perhaps with just one exception, the USSR, which had its secretive decades under Lenin and Stalin and their successors. Still the magnificent recreated scenes featuring steam locomotives operating across snowlands and steppes in films such as *Doctor Zhivago* remain available to fill in some of the gaps.

In some ways, this book has sought to fill in some gaps itself and stimulate renewed interest in all aspects of the grand story of Steam Australia and reveal how this mode of haulage did so much to help so many over ten vital decades of great transformation in Australia's history.

Apart from the great national endeavours, many regional centres, notably in Queensland, New South Wales, Victoria and South Australia, developed huge foundries and steam locomotive factories and workshops. At Bendigo,

» Looking good after a brush up: a D57 Class steam locomotive in Sydney's Clyde Engineering workshop, 1930s.

GREAT STEAM TRAIN MOVIES

Classic Hollywood films often featured steam locomotives in action; for example, *Doctor Zhivago* (1965), set in Russia, and *North West Frontier* (1959), in India. The film versions of Tolstoy's *Anna Karenina* also famously featured a steam train at its tragic climactic moment. The year 1959 also saw the release of Alfred Hitchcock's classic thriller *North by Northwest* in which the *20th Century Limited* featured crucially. Sadly, its steam-driven engine had been replaced in 1948 by a new diesel-electric one, so a change to feature a world-famous train running with steam was missed.

More recently, *The Railway Man* (2013), a great British-Australian film about a prisoner of war, also dealt with his past links to steam rail; despite its somewhat dark and sombre subject matter, it also featured the huge curved LNER viaduct at Berwick, on the Scottish border north of Newcastle upon Tyne.

It is to be hoped that film directors and producers continue to film scenes employing dashing steam locomotives. Doing so helps to remind the public not only of what once was such a common aspect of everyday life, but also it helps to boost rail heritage revenue through the large fees paid to use classic steam trains.

Maryborough and many more places, people toiled to work through the complex calculations needed to produce smooth-running reciprocal motion steam locomotives of renown. Workers toiled away at lathes before proudly seeing their creations steam out onto the network ready for action. This aspect of the rich tapestry of history relating to steam locomotion should never be forgotten — indeed its key anniversaries should be regularly and joyously celebrated.

Steam locomotion in Australia is here to stay. It has done so much over past years, and on an admittedly smaller scale it can continue to add greatly to regional tourist endeavours in future years. In short, it has the potential to entertain and excite whole generations of people, but it can also provide viable albeit limited haulage in the future. Long may this continue to be the case!

In closing, I salute steam locomotion, and all that it has achieved for this nation. Perhaps we should leave the final word to a British steam railway enthusiast, the Reverend Wilbert Vere Awdry, creator of the 'Thomas the Tank Engine' series of books, who once compared the Church of England to British Railways:

Both had their heyday in the mid-19th century; both own a great deal of Gothic-style architecture which is expensive to maintain; both are regularly assailed by critics; and both are firmly convinced that they are the best means of getting man to his ultimate destination.

THE FABULOUS BUCKLAND COLLECTION

Steam Australia: The Locomotives That Galvanised the Nation was inspired by the Buckland Collection held at the National Library of Australia.

John Leonard Buckland (1915–1989) was born in Camperdown, Western Victoria. He began his career working on a coastal steamer and later became a cadet journalist for Victorian Railways in their public relations department. After serving in the RAAF and the Australian Army in the Second World War, he returned to journalism, working for a transport publisher and later for the Trade Publicity Branch of the Department of Trade. The last five years of his career were spent working with the Conservation Foundation. His retirement was spent as a 'full-time railway enthusiast'. Throughout his fascinating career, Buckland developed an astounding collection of photographs and documents on Australian railways. In both his working and his personal lives, he travelled Australia inspecting and photographing railway operations and steam locomotives. He was an inquisitive character, with his camera always at the ready.

In 1979 Buckland lent a great number of negatives to the National Library of Australia for copying, and later bequeathed his entire collection, which the Library received from his executors in 1989.

The collection includes a vast range of photographs, papers, maps, diagrams, memorabilia and books relating to railways. With approximately 25,000 photographs, and 6,200 nitrate negatives, it is one of the largest collections on Australian railways in public ownership. It predominantly covers the period 1930–80, comprising photographs of railway lines, goods yards, steam and diesel locomotives, bridges, accidents, coal lines, passengers and more. Many photographs were taken by Buckland, and others were sent to him by friends and acquaintances. Beyond photographs, the collection includes 257 folders and 34 boxes of related papers.

The National Library of Australia, with assistance from the Australian Railway Historical Society, has undergone an extensive process of cataloguing this collection, which is also being digitised. Currently, 5,082 documents have been digitised.

» SAR locomotives Nos Rx207 and Rx224 with a special passenger train bound for Victor Harbor, South Australia, 1984. There is a case for more special trains even today.

ACKNOWLEDGEMENTS

At the outset I would like to thank my mother-in-law, Mary Brewer, who kindly did the pre-edit on each chapter and greatly helped improve the syntax of the manuscript. Also my thanks go to my family members putting up with the spread of books and papers created by a big book undertaking.

Overall, I received and appreciated great guidance from Nick Anchen (Melbourne), David Burke (Kiama), John Fullerton (ARTC), Professor Philip Laird (Wollongong), Chris Le Marshal (Melbourne), Andrew Moritz (Ipswich and now Thirlmere), Leon Oberg (Goulburn) and Phillipa Rogers (Perth).

State-by-state I received great assistance from:

Queensland: Robert Amos, Paula Boatfield, Greg Hallam

New South Wales: Jennifer Edmonds, Ross Jackson, Ross Verdich, the Sloane family

Victoria: Bernie Greene, Peter Ralph

South Australia: John Evans, John Radcliffe, Robert Sampson

Western Australia: Jeff Austin, Geoffrey Highan, Peter Hopper, Brian Williams

Tasmania: Ben Johnston, Chris Martin

From the National Library of Australia team, I thank Susan Hall for her helpful leadership and guidance throughout, Mary Pollard on the research front and Jim Stokes with the photographic sort plus the editor, Robert Nichols, Jemma Posch for image research, and Kerry Blackburn for reading the manuscript. It was a huge effort by all involved.

Finally, I salute John Buckland (1915–1989), born at Camperdown in Victoria. He embarked on several careers, but also had a passion for superb rail photography and then donated his enormous collection to the National Library of Australia; these are the source for the majority of the photographs used in this book.

» The author at the Tenterfield Railway in northern New South Wales, 2016. Unexpected great rail collections can be found at many country locations.

LOCOMOTIVE WHEEL ARRANGEMENTS

EXTRACT: Tim Fischer, *Trains Unlimited in the 21st Century*, ABC Books/Harper Collins, Sydney, 2011

The following table of steam locomotive and diesel/diesel-electric/electric locomotive wheel arrangements has been devised to highlight key category names of interest, especially where ocean names have been used.

The table has been developed from independent research, assisted by the definitive book *Locomotives* by Brian Reed, Temple Press Ltd, 1958, London. Red ○ symbols indicate wheels and axles that are powered directly.

STEAM	
Class	Wheel arrangement
Adriatic	o OOO oo
Atlantic	oo OO o
Baltic	oo OOO oo
Columbia	oo OO o
Decapod	o OOOОО
Javanico	OOOOOO o
Mikado	o OOOO o
Mogul	o OOO
Mountain	oo OOOO o
Pacific	oo OOO o
Prairie	o OOO o
Santa Fe	o OOOOO o

DIESEL/DIESEL-ELECTRIC/ELECTRIC	
Descriptor	Layout
Co Co	OOO OOO
Bo Bo	OO OO
Ao Ao	O O
A1A A1A	OOO OOO *

*middle axle not powered.

LIST OF ILLUSTRATIONS

All images are from National Library of Australia Collections, except where otherwise noted. Page numbers in this book are given in bold type, as are positions on a page, indicated as follows: **t** = top, **b** = bottom, **c** = centre, **r** = right, **l** = left, **f** = front, **ba** = back. To view catalogue information and full National Library of Australia images online, enter into your browser **nla.gov.au/** followed by the item's catalogue identifier (e.g. nla.gov.au /nla.cat-vn6342168).

Items from the Buckland Collection are denoted BC.

Front cover: see **p76-77**
Back Cover: see **p90-91**
Title Pages: see **p93(b)**

Introduction

p1 *Steam Locomotive Crossing over a Bascule Bridge on Shea's Creek, Tempe, New South Wales, 1930s,* nla.cat-vn6342168, courtesy Fairfax Syndication, www.fairfaxsyndication.com; **p2** John McMillan, *South West Mail Train in Cootamundra Station, New South Wales, 1939,* BC, nla.cat-vn4542723; **p4** James Waltham Curtis, *The Harvest of 1880— The Goulburn Valley, 1880,* State Library Victoria, IAN16/02/80/24; **p5** Frank Hurley, *Steam Locomotive Number 7 on an Elevated Railway Track near Three Towers, B.H.P. Steelworks, Newcastle, New South Wales, between 1910 and 1962,* nla.cat-vn1640604; **p6** *Albury Station, New South Wales, c.1890,* BC, nla.cat-vn4544020; **p7** Pusterla Bros., *Albury Railway Station Decorated for the Duke of Cornwall's Visit, c.1905,* State Library New South Wales, *At Work and Play—O*, 2011*; **p8** David T. Morgan, *The Caritas Express, 2011,* courtesy Tim Fischer; **p9** John Kramer, *Locomotive 4472 with Train … Coffs Harbour, New South Wales, 1989,* BC, nla.cat-vn7504946, courtesy John Kramer.

Chapter 1
The Arrival of Steam Locomotion on Rail

p10-11 John Buckland, *Locomotive 6029 Hauling Australian Railway Historical Society Train Southbound on Wagga Viaduct, 1980,* BC, nla.cat-vn4540495; **p12** S.T. Gill, *The City Terminus of the M. & H.B. Railway Compy, 1854,* nla.cat-vn1797515; **p13** Joe deSousa, *Joseph Cugnot's 1770 Fardier à Vapeur, Musée des Arts et Métiers, Paris, 2015,* commons.wikimedia.org/wiki/File:Joseph_Cugnot%27s_1770_Fardier_à_Vapeur,_Musée_des_arts_et_métiers,_Paris_2015.jpg; **p14(t)** 'Drawing of the Double-acting Engine Laid before Parliament, 1775', *James Watt: Craftsman and Engineer by H.W. Dickinson, 1935,* nla.cat-vn2493472; **p14(b)** Thomas Griffiths (artist) and Thomson (engraver), *James Watt Esq., 1820s,* nla.cat-vn2711082; **p15(tl)** John Lucas, *George Stephenson, c.1847,* Institution of Mechanical Engineers, archives.imeche.org/archive/railways/stephenson/593808-1847-1848-george-stephenson; **p15(tr)** 'The No. 1 Engine at Darlington', *The Story of the Life of George Stephenson, Railway Engineer by Samuel Smiles, 1859,* nla.cat-vn1748679; **p15(bl)** W.J. Welch, 'Trevithick's London Railway and Locomotive of 1808', *Life of Richard Trevithick, with an Account of His Inventions by Francis Trevithick, 1872,* nla.cat-

vn2625263; **p15(br)** John Linnell, *Richard Trevithick, 1816,* commons.wikimedia.org/wiki/File:Richard_Trevithick_portrait.jpg; **p17(t)** 'The "Rocket"', *The Story of the Life of George Stephenson, Railway Engineer by Samuel Smiles, 1859,* nla.cat-vn1748679; **p17(b)** T. Bury (artist) and S.G. Hughes (printmaker), *Taking in Water at Parkside, 1831,* commons.wikimedia.org/wiki/File:Coloured_View_on_the_Liverpool_and_Manchester_Railway,_1831.jpg; **p18-19** Isaac Shaw (artist) and S.G. Hughes (printmaker), *Travelling on the Liverpool and Manchester Railway, 1831,* Yale Center for British Art, B1993.30.129; **p20(l)** E.A. Tilly, *Henri Giffard, French Balloonist, c.1885,* Library of Congress Prints and Photographs Online Catalog, LC-DIG-ppmsca-02239; **p20(r)** Henry de La Vaulx, *Le premier projet de ballon dirigeable à vapeur de Henri Giffard, 1851,* New York Public Library Digital Collections, b13792024; **p21** Tony Hisgett, *North Star, 2011,* www.flickr.com/photos/hisgett/5734080524, reproduced under CC BY 2.0: creativecommons.org/licenses/by/2.0; **p22-23** J.M.W. Turner, *Rain, Steam and Speed–The Great Western Railway, 1844,* commons.wikimedia.org/wiki/File:Rain,_Steam_and_Speed_-_The_Great_Western_Railway.jpg; **p24** *Steam Locomotive No. 1N at Wangaratta, Victoria, 1900s,* BC, nla.cat-vn2478577; **p25** 'Scotch Express (London and North Eastern Railway)', *The Picture Book of Trains, 1940s,* nla.cat-vn4926160; **p26** 'The "Flying Scotsman" Leaving King's Cross', *The Picture Book of Trains, 1940s,* nla.cat-vn4926160; **p28** Samuel Charles Brees, *View of North Church Tunnel, London & Birmingham Railway, 1837,* State Library Victoria, H83.50/7; **p29** 'Approaching the Sierra Nevada', *Illustrated Memoirs of R.W. Jesper's Travels in England, Australia, North America and Other Countries by R.W. Jesper, 1831-1887,* nla.cat-vn5883069; **p30-31** *Night Scene at a Junction, c.1885,* Library of Congress Prints & Photographs Online Catalog, LC-DIG-pga-00842; **p32-33** John Buckland, *Southbound Spirit of Progress Passing Kilmore East Hauled by 3 Cylinder Locomotive S301 Sir Thomas Mitchell, Victoria, 1939,* BC, nla.cat-vn4468541; **p34** *WAGR "W" Valve Gear, c.1954,* BC, nla.cat-vn3565337; **p35** 'Railway Information', 1950s, Railways (New South Wales) Ephemera Material, nla.cat-vn1072284; **p36** Andrew J. Russell, *Military Railroad Operations in Northern Virginia: African American Laborers Working on Rail, c.1862,* Library of Congress Prints and Photographs Online Catalog, LC-DIG-ppmsca-10400; **p37(t)** *There's Room for You, Jump Aboard, c.1915,* nla.cat-vn756075; **p37(b)** Herbert H. Fishwick, *German Krupp SK L/40 28 cm Railway Gun Known as the Amiens Gun on a Railway Siding, Canberra, 1927,* nla.cat-vn6342883, courtesy Fairfax Syndication, www.fairfaxsyndication.com.

Chapter 2
The Agony of 'Break of Gauge'

p38-39 *Victorian Railways DDE-class Locomotive Decorated with Flags and with a Train of Volunteers for the Australian Imperial Force, Victoria, 1914,* BC, nla.cat-vn7504566; **p40** David Brossard, *Losing the Steam Locomotive: at Coonoor Station along the Nilgiri Mountain Railway, 2014,* www.flickr.com/photos/string_bass_dave/15441235925, reproduced under CC BY-SA 2.0: creativecommons.org/licenses/by-sa/2.0;

p41 Tim Fischer, *Great Australian Railway Gauges, Past and Present, 2003,* courtesy Tim Fischer; **p42** *Locomotive P458 and Train at Wollongong, New South Wales, 1900,* BC, nla.cat-vn4543945; **p43(t)** Map in *Linking up of the Railway Systems of Australia by George A. Lefroy, 1911,* nla.cat-vn2367097; **p44(b)** 'Geelong to Melbourne', *Illustrated Memoirs of R.W. Jesper's Travels in England, Australia, North America and Other Countries by R.W. Jesper, 1831-1887,* nla.cat-vn5883069; **p44** Edward Stewart Maclean, *Steam Locomotive on a 3 Foot 6 Inch Track Gauge, Adelaide, 1927,* nla.cat-vn7466403; **p45** Étoile du Nord (North Star), 1927, commons.wikimedia.org/wiki/File:Étoile_du_Nord,_1927_Ontwerper_onbekend.jpg; **p46** George E. Peacock (artist) and John Allan (lithographer), *First Australian Railway, 1850,* nla.cat-vn2666277; **p47** John Buckland, *Locomotive 2517 at Dual Gauge Turntable, Oaklands, c.1929,* BC, nla.cat-vn4540635; **p48(t)** *The First Locomotive Manufactured at the Government Railway Workshops, Adelaide, 1875,* nla.cat-vn1123236; **p48(b)** *Sleeps Hill Railway Viaduct, South Australia, between 1859 and 1898,* nla.cat-vn2648374; **p49** *Queensland Railways: Tours in the Mackay District, c.1912,* nla.cat-vn705377; **p50(t)** *Interior of Railway Workshops, Ipswich, Queensland, 1911,* courtesy Picture Ipswich, Ipswich City Council; **p50(b)** 'Perth Central Railway Station is in the Heart of the City', 1940s, Railways (Western Australia) Ephemera Material, nla.cat-vn1072300; **p51** Bill Brindle, *A Mobile Crane Lifts the Body of a 70 Ton Ore Carrier on to Its Bogies on the New Railway Built by Mount Goldsworthy Mining Associates, Western Australia, 1960s,* nla.cat-vn4588761, Australian News and Information Bureau; **p52** W.R.B. Johnson, *Tasmanian Government Railways Locomotive B7 at Fitzgerald with a Passenger Train from Hobart, Tasmania, 1937,* BC, nla.cat-vn4593051; **p53** *Ore Shoots, Mt Bischoff Tin Mine, c.1885,* nla.cat-vn199925.

Chapter 3
Gold, Coal, Wool and Wheat

p54-55 *Coal Stage with Four Wheel Hopper Wagons on Top and 30, 32 and Standard Goods Class Locomotives Coaling, Newcastle, New South Wales, 1930s,* BC, nla.cat-vn4544637; **p56(t)** Nicholas Caire, *View of the Railway Tunnel through The Big Hill, 1875,* nla.cat-vn2250405; **p56-57(b)** *Darling Harbour, New South Wales, between 1885 and 1903,* nla.cat-vn1555065; **p57(t)** Victorian Railways, *450 Tons of Gold, c.1901,* State Library Victoria, H92.301/326; **p58(t)** *Murray River Paddle Steamers, c.1880,* nla.cat-vn2117740; **p58(b)** Julius Albert von Rochlitz, *The Geelong-Melbourne Railway Polka, c.1866,* nla.cat-vn884391; **p59** Sandra McEwan, *Signs at Stanthorpe Museum, 2016,* courtesy Sandra McEwan; **p60(t)** Robert Marsh Westmacott, *Newcastle, the Coal Mines of New South Wales, 1832,* nla.cat-vn3013940; **p60(b)** Australian News and Information Bureau, *Coal Bridge at Newcastle Steel Works Lifts Coal Trucks off Their Frames and Conveys Coal to Dump, 1930s,* BC, nla.cat-vn4543725; **p61** Charles Dickson Gregory, *Sophia Jane, Australia's First Steamer, c.1920,* State Library Victoria, H13781; **p62(t)** *A Mile of Wheat Stacks, Victoria, between 1920 and 1925,* nla.cat-vn2313565; **p62(b)** Wolfgang Sievers, *Hamersley Iron's Train*

Carrying Iron Ore from Mt Tom Price in the Pilbara to Port of Dampier in Western Australia, 1974, nla. cat-vn843613; **p63** Charles H. Kerry, Coal Wagons at Wollongong Harbour, New South Wales, 1880s, nla. cat-vn5547892; **p64** Frank Hurley, Duplicate Coal Discharge Terminal for Briquette Factory, Yallourn, Victoria, 1947, nla.cat-vn118490; **p65** Arrival of Sir John Monash Stepping out of a Train Carriage, Sydney, 1929, nla.cat-vn6303745, courtesy Fairfax Syndication, www.fairfaxsyndication.com; **p66** Arthur Cratchley & Associates, Coal for Export to Japan is Loaded into Railway Wagons for Shipment at Port Kembla by This Loading Conveyor at Coalcliff Colliery, c.1970, BC, nla.cat-vn4543718; **p67** Jim Fitzpatrick, Transcontinental Railway across the Nullarbor Plain, near Forrest, Western Australia, 1954, nla.cat-vn4589365; **p68(t)** Samuel White Sweet, Port Pirie, South Australia, c.1878, nla.cat-vn2222687; **p68(b)** A. Pout, Unloading Bunkering Coal for Storage Bins from Tip Trucks to Elevators at a Harbour Terminal at Sydney, 1953, BC, nla.cat-vn4543094; **p69** Mike Brown, Loading Rail Trucks with Wheat at Henty, New South Wales, c.1965, nla.cat-vn3420010, Australian News and Information Bureau.

Chapter 4
Victoria Leads the Way

p70-71 William H. Lee, Victorian Railways Narrow Gauge Locomotive 9A with the First Train from Moe to Walhalla, Victoria, 1910, BC, nla.cat-vn7503929; **p72** S.T. Gill, Laying the Foundation Stone of the Geelong & Melbourne Railway, 1853, nla.cat-vn467132; **p73** John Buckland, Locomotive S300 'Matthew Flinders' Leads Southbound 'Spirit of Progress' out of Albury, 1939, BC, nla.cat-vn2147697; **p74(t)** Victorian Railways, Melbourne & Suburbs, 1875, nla. cat-vn3623923; **p74(b)** Albury Station, North End, with Broad Gauge Locomotive and Truck on Right, and Standard Gauge Locomotive and Train on Left, c.1920, BC, nla.cat-vn3422852; **p75** M. Daly & Co., Railway Construction, 1890, State Library Victoria, H2013.70/2; **p76-77** First Standard Gauge Spirit of Progress, Locomotives 3830 and 3813, 1962, BC, nla. cat-vn4544539; **p78** Ballarat Station with a Phoenix Built 'S' Class No. 197, and Staff on the Platform, 1885, nla.cat-vn3512124; **p79** Locomotive H220 Heavy Harry and Goods Train at Wodonga, Victoria, 1956, BC, nla.cat-vn4468590; **p80(t)** Victorian Railways Employee Testing Staff Exchanger with a Gauge, Sunshine, Victoria, c.1950, BC, nla.cat-vn7504591; **p80(b)** Victorian Railways Narrow Gauge Locomotive 3A with a Train of Potatoes ... near Wright on the Gembrook Line, Victoria, 1947, BC, nla.cat-vn7503853; **p81(t)** Victorian Railways Narrow Gauge Locomotive 3A En Route to Collect Rolling Stock Stranded at Belgrave by a Landslide, Upwey, Victoria, 1954, BC, nla.cat-vn7503916; **p81(b)** Victorian Railways Three Aspect Colour Light Signal with Rectangular Hood, Victoria, c.1950, BC, nla.cat-vn7504610; **p82** Victorian Railways, H220 in the Erecting Shop, Newport, Victoria, 1940, BC, nla.cat-vn3523839; **p83(t)** Australian News and Information Bureau, Puffing Billy in the Dandenong Ranges, Victoria, between 1948 and 1971, nla.cat-vn4591259; **p83(b)** Victorian Railways, Operation Phoenix, c.1949, nla. cat-vn2832462; **p84** Victorian Railways, The Spirit of Progress, Approaching Kilmore East, Victoria, Being Hauled by 'Sir Thomas Mitchell' (S301), 1939, BC, nla. cat-vn3523847; **p85(t)** Chief Railways Commissioner Mr Harold Clapp at a Railway Station, New South Wales, 1928, nla.cat-vn6262178, courtesy Fairfax

Syndication, www.fairfaxsyndication.com; **p85(b)** Donaldson Bros. (lyrics) & Joe Slater (composer) The Light in the Window, c.1908, nla.cat-vn4608265; **p87(t)** Victorian Railways, Spirit of Progress Menu, between 1937 and 1963, State Library Victoria, H2012.76/1a and 1b; **p87(cl)** Victorian Railways, Dining Car, Spirit of Progress, c.1945, State Library Victoria, H2010.76/20; **p87(cr)** 'Introducing the New Roomette Car', 1940s, Railways (Victoria): Ephemera Material, nla.cat-vn2594516; **p87(b)** Victorian Railways, Spirit of Progress with Steam Locomotive S302 Edward Henty, 1937, nla.cat-vn6449078; **p88(t)** Victorian Railways Demonstration of Dropping Staff from Section in Rear and Picking up Staff for Section in Advance for Setting up Former to Retrieval of Latter, Victoria, c.1950, BC, nla.cat-vn7504583; **p88(b)** Victorian Railways Signal Box Interior with Miniature Electric Lever Panel, Diagrams and Instruments, Dandenong, Victoria, c.1950, BC, nla.cat-vn7504617; **p89** John Buckland, Victorian Railways Narrow Gauge Locomotive 6A Shunting Passenger Carriages at Belgrave, Victoria, 1968, BC, nla.cat-vn7503896; **p90-91** Robert B. McMillan, Victorian Railways Narrow Gauge Beyer-Garratt Articulated Locomotive G42 Leaving Moe with a Goods Train for Erica, Victoria, 1947, BC, nla.cat-vn7503918; **p92** Victorian Railways, In the Old Erecting Shop at Newport Workshops, X.27 near Completion, 1929, BC, nla.cat-vn3523835; **p93(t)** Men and a Woman on the Railway Station Platform at Wodonga, Victoria, c.1905, State Library Victoria, H95.65/40; **p93(b)** Raymond de Berquelle, Engine Driver and Fireman, Eveleigh Railway Workshops, Sydney, 1968, nla.cat-vn2561649; **p94** Victorian Railways Signal Box Interior with Miniature Electric Levers, Diagrams and Instruments, Victoria, c.1950, BC, nla.cat-vn7504596; **p95** Victorian Railways, Map of Melbourne and Suburbs, 1934, nla.cat-vn3357457; **p96(t)** Victorian Railways, North Melbourne Engine Shed, 1890, BC, nla.cat-vn3523559; **p96(b)** N. Fletcher, Victorian Railways Centenary, 1854-1954, 1954, nla.cat-vn3416450; **p97** Bahnfrend, V/Line N Class Locomotive No. 465 'City of Ballaarat' with a V/Line Passenger Train, and a CountryLink XPT Set, at Albury Railway Station, New South Wales, 2007, commons.wikimedia.org/wiki/ File:N465_XP2010_Albury,_2007.JPG, reproduced under CC BY-SA 3.0: creativecommons.org/licenses/by-sa/3.0/deed.en.

Chapter 5
Full Steam Ahead in New South Wales

p98-99 Locomotive 3612 Hauling Passenger Train up Steep Grade, New South Wales, 1940s, BC, nla.cat-vn4544514; **p100(t)** John Buckland, Builders Plate from Locomotive No. 1, 1900s, BC, nla.cat-vn4541438; **p100(b)** Locomotive of 1855, Built by Stephenson Builders, 1860s, BC, nla.cat-vn4544423; **p101(t)** Walter G. Mason, Arrival of the First Railway Train at Parramatta from Sydney, 1855, nla.cat-vn2664185; **p101(b)** Down (Westbound) Starting Signals at Parkes Showing West End Signal Box with Boom Gated Level Crossing, New South Wales, 1948, BC, nla. cat-vn4544591; **p102** Frank Hurley, Where the Train Made Smoke for Hurley through Hawkesbury Tunnel, New South Wales, 1910, nla.cat-vn359070; **p103** Old No. 1 Train in Redfern Yard, c.1889, BC, nla.cat-vn4543834; **p104(t)** 'Railway Lines Completed or in Course of Construction', New South Wales: Principal Towns & Districts in New South Wales Possessing Railway Communications with Sydney, 1884, nla. cat-vn3313268; **p104(b)** 'The Late Mr. John Whitton',

Thirty-five Years on the New South Wales Railways: The Work of the Late Mr. John Whitton by John Rae, 1898, nla.cat-vn1793095; **p105(t)** Albert Charles Cooke (artist) and Robert Bruce (engraver), The Zig-Zag, Great Western Railway, from the Lithgow Valley, New South Wales, c.1869, nla.cat-vn1153724; **p105(b)** Opening Day of the Hawkesbury River Bridge, New South Wales, 1889, nla.cat-vn6106011; **p106(t)** John Buckland, Locomotive 5614 (Oil Burner) Hauling Westbound Freight Train down towards the 'Grand Canyon' from Zig Zag, 1955, BC, nla.cat-vn4540817; **p106(b)** John Buckland, Hand Swapping Miniature Electric Staff without Carrier, Troy Junction near Dubbo, New South Wales, 1938, BC, nla.cat-vn4541616; **p107(t)** Rear View of Vintage Train Hauled by Two Locomotives, 1960s, BC, nla.cat-vn4544545; **p107(b)** Andrew Lyell, Locomotive 3082 Hauling Train with Workmen's Accommodation Van, 1950s, BC, nla. cat-vn4542530; **p108** Hugh Llewelyn, Sydney Railway McConnell '1' Class 0-4-2 No. 1 at the Powerhouse Museum, Ultimo, Sydney, 2016, www.flickr.com/photos/camperdown/27987559481, reproduced under CC BY-SA 2.0: creativecommons.org/licenses/by-sa/2.0/; **p109** 'Funeral of Mr Eddy', The Australian Town and Country Journal (Sydney), 3 July 1897, nla. news-page5253056; **p110(t)** John Buckland, The Red Steam Locomotive 3265 Named the 'Hunter' at the Newcastle Railway Station, 1934, BC, nla. cat-vn967781; **p110-111(b)** Pioneer Locomotive P6 at the Head of the Melbourne Express, c.1892, BC, nla. cat-vn4543755; **p111(t)** Eveleigh Locomotive Depot, New South Wales State Archives & Records, Series NRS 17420; **p112** John Buckland, New South Wales Government Railways D57 Class Steam Locomotive, c.1930, BC, nla.cat-vn2196443; **p113** Overturned Train Engine of the Brisbane Limited that Crashed at Aberdeen, New South Wales, 1926, nla.cat-vn2713613; **p114-115** Cootamundra Smash, New South Wales, 1885, BC, nla.cat-vn4543807; **p116(t)** A. Dunstan, Old O 466 Class, Later Z23 Class, off Turntable at Binnaway, c.1930, BC, nla.cat-vn4541976; **p116(b)** Seven Hills Signal Box Interior, New South Wales, 1947, BC, nla.cat-vn4544597; **p117** John Buckland, Bracket Signal at South End of Old Hawkesbury River Bridge, 1935, BC, nla.cat-vn4541615; **p118** C38 Loco, Lowering Boiler into Frame, New South Wales, 1945, BC, nla.cat-vn3419888; **p119** 'Train Yourself to Relax in Comfort', 1940s, Railways (New South Wales): Ephemera Material, nla.cat-vn1072284; **p120** Western Endeavour Train... Western Australia, 1970, BC, nla.cat-vn3421116; **p121** Lindsay Lucas, Lachlan Valley Railway Volunteers Prepare 3237 and 5917 to Work a Special Train from Cowra to Sydney, while 'Rosie' (5367) Contemplates Her Future, 2009, www.flickr.com/photos/catchpoints412/5180468417, courtesy Lindsay Lucas; **p123(t)** Steve Burrows, ARHS ACT's Colossal Beyer Garratt 6029 Stands Ready on Platform 1 at Sydney Terminal with the Thirlmere Flyer, 2016, www. flickr.com/photos/122537078@N08/24897159093, courtesy Steve Burrows; **p123(b)** 2 x 60 Class Garratt Locomotives at Junee Roundhouse, New South Wales, 1950s-1960s, BC, nla.cat-vn4543996.

Chapter 6
Queensland Rail

p124-125 Locomotive B15C 237 on Stoney Creek Viaduct, Cairns Railway, Queensland, between 1936 and 1939, BC, nla.cat-vn3420098; **p126** Reckitt and Mills, Locomotive on Viaduct, River Estate, c.1875, nla.cat-vn636171; **p128(t)** Frank Hurley, Sugar Cane Fields, with Light Railway Lines on Left Side of Image,

No. 1 at Rouse's Camp, the Terminus of the Emu Bay Railway Company, 1880, Tasmanian Archive and Heritage Office, PH7-1-1; **p188** *K1, the World's First Garratt Steam Locomotive, Built for the North East Dundas Tramway in Tasmania*, 1909, commons. wikimedia.org/wiki/File:K1_works_photograph. jpg; **p189** John W. Beattie, *The Montezuma Falls and North East Dundas Railway, Tasmania*, c.1890, nla.cat-vn4668800; **p191** Michael Terry, *Steam Locomotive on the Tracks, Queenstown, Tasmania*, 1961, nla.cat-vn6980501; **p192** Luggage labels, Railways (Tasmania): Ephemera Material, nla.cat-vn1072291; **p193(t)** *Trial Run–Steam Locomotive CCS.23, Built 1902 and Restored for Centenary Celebrations, Climbs Relbia Bank during a Test Run*, c.1970, Railways (Tasmania): Ephemera Material, nla. cat-vn1072291; **p193(b)** Frank Hurley, *S Class Steam Locomotive, Ships Momba, Cape Corso, Cars, Trucks and Jones Pier, Burnie, Tasmania*, between 1910 and 1962, nla.cat-vn120139; **p194(t)** Wilbur Vigus, *Emu Bay Railway's Australian Standard Garratt Locomotive G20A Crossing the Pieman River with the Northbound Westcoaster Passenger and Motor Vehicle Transport Train, Tasmania*, 1963, BC, nla. cat-vn7504058; **p194(b)** *Tasmanian Government Railways C Class Locomotive with a Passenger and Goods Train Bound for Hobart at Apsley, Tasmania*, c.1910, BC, nla.cat-vn7504935; **p195** John Buckland, *Tasmanian Government Railways Locomotive R3 with a Passenger Train Bound for Hobart Leaving Launceston, Tasmania*, 1945, BC, nla.cat-vn7504927; **p196** Andrew R. Lyell, *Mt Lyell Abt No. 5 Arriving at Queenstown, Tasmania*, c.1955, BC, nla.cat-vn3422003; **p197** John Russell Ashton, *Aerial View of Gordon River, with Railway Line beside It, Tasmania*, 1970s, nla.cat-vn4538751; **p198** Robert Barrie McMillan, *Emu Bay Railway Beyer-Garratt Articulated Locomotive No. 13 with a Goods Train at Burnie, Tasmania*, 1949, BC, nla.cat-vn7504883; **p199(t)** John Russell Ashton, *Railway Locomotive and Shed, Tasmania*, c.1960, nla.cat-vn4538138; **p199(b)** John Grimwade, *Tasmanian Government Railways A Class Locomotive with Hobart to Launceston Passenger Train at Colebrook, Tasmania*, c.1930, BC, nla.cat-vn7504885.

Chapter 10
Commonwealth Railways

p200-201 James Pinkerton Campbell, *Federal Parliamentary Party at Brocks Creek Station*, 1912, nla. cat-vn2174000; **p201(t)** 'Kalgoorlie to Port Augusta Transcontinental Railway: Turning the First Sod', 1912, Railways: Programs and Invitations Ephemera Material , nla.cat-vn3804208; **p201(b)** *For Over 300 Miles, Line Runs without a Curve, Trans-Australian Railway*, c.1917, nla.cat-vn4366333; **p203** John Flynn, *Work Train, G Class, Commonwealth Railways, Possibly on the Western End of Construction Line for Trans-Australia Railway*, between 1912 and 1955, nla. cat-vn647715; **p204** *Port Augusta Station*, 1917, nla. cat-vn3098712; **p205(t)** Keith Fellowes, *Residents of Coonana Check Their Purchases beside the Provision Store Carriages of the Tea and Sugar Train on the Trans-Australian Railway*, 1968, nla.cat-vn4589291, Australian News and Information Bureau; **p205(b)** Keith Fellowes, *A Resident of Karonie Buys Meat in the Butcher's Car of the Tea and Sugar Train on the Trans Australian Railway*, 1960s, nla.cat-vn4589311, Australian News and Information Bureau; **p206(t)** Michael Terry, *Railway Crossing, Central Australia*, c.1929, nla.cat-vn6576880; **p206(b)** *Marree*

Railhead Showing the Narrow Gauge Goods Shed in the Background before the Advent of Standard Gauge, South Australia, between 1940 and 1957, BC, nla.cat-vn4247882; **p207(t)** *Soldier Standing on Station Platform beside Locomotive with Engine Bit in Foreground, Northern Territory*, c.1942, nla. cat-vn4347961; **p207(b)** Commonwealth Railways, *To the West in Air-conditioned Comfort: Trans-Australian Railway*, c.1951, nla.cat-vn3279447; **p208** Keith Fellowes, *Driver's Eye View of the Line as a Diesel Electric Train Begins the Long Haul across the Nullarbor Plain on the Trans Australia Railway*, 1968, nla.cat-vn4589287, Australian News and Information Bureau; **p209(t)** *Tim Fischer Standing in Front of The Ghan*, 2014, courtesy Tim Fischer; **p209(b)** *Railway Station and Yard at Palmerston, Later Renamed Darwin, Northern Territory*, 1890, BC, nla. cat-vn3513541; **p210(t)** Michael Terry, *Commonwealth Railways NM35 Locomotive at Stuart Railway Station, Northern Territory*, c.1929, nla.cat-vn6576884; **p210(b)** John Crowther, *A Double Headed Train Carries Coal from Leigh Creek in the Flinders Ranges to the Sir Thomas Playford Power Station at Port Augusta, South Australia*, 1968, nla.cat-vn4589085, Australian News and Information Bureau; **p211** *Southbound from the Alice, an NM Class 4-8-0 Traverses Heavitree Gap through the MacDonnell Ranges En Route to Port Augusta with a Cattle Train*, 1950s, BC, nla.cat-vn4247714; **p212** Commonwealth Railways, *Go by Train to Central Australia for Winter Holidays*, 1950s, nla.cat-vn5880357; **p213** 'Trans-Australian Railway: Across the Continent', c.1960, Railways–Trans Australian/Indian Pacific: Ephemera Material, nla.cat-vn1072309.

Chapter 11
The Agony and the Ecstasy

p214-215 Geoff Doecke, *Pichi Richi Railway's Narrow Gauge Steam Locomotive NM25 Heads across Lake Knockout, while an SCT Modern Freight Train Makes Its Way towards Perth*, 2016, courtesy Geoff Doecke; **p216(t)** 'All About Puffing Billy: Timetables October 1983 to September 1984', Railways (General): Ephemera Material, nla.cat-vn1072276, courtesy Puffing Billy Railway; **p216** Canfield Business Design Pty Ltd, *The Great Lithgow Zig Zag Railway 1998-99 Timetable*, nla.cat-vn409646, courtesy Zig Zag Railway; **p217(t)** Grand Canyon National Park, *Arizona Centennial Locomotive Being Serviced at Grand Canyon*, 2012, reproduced under CC BY 2.0: creativecommons.org/licenses/by/2.0/; **p217(b)** Dave, *A Small Train at Milwaukee Zoo*, 2009, commons. wikimedia.org/wiki/File:Train_at_Milwaukee_Zoo-11April2009.jpg, reproduced under CC BY 2.0: creativecommons.org/licenses/by/2.0/deed.en; **p218(t)** Wangaratta Railway Station, c.1908, State Library Victoria, H90.140/915; **p218(b)** *Railway Bridge Walhalla*, 1920s, State Library Victoria, H90.140/361; **p219** Stephen Edmonds, *Puffing Billy*, 2006, www. flickr.com/photos/popcornx/424968309, reproduced under CC BY-SA 2.0: creativecommons.org/licenses/by-sa/2.0/; **p220** *Great Western Railway Extension, Alterations and Additions to the Approaches to the Bridge over the River Nepean at Penrith, New South Wales*, 1869, nla.cat-vn4738331; **p221** Robert Wendel and Charles Troedel & Co., *Zig-Zag Railway, Blue Mountains*, 1878, nla.cat-vn2666463; **p222-223** *Stationary Steam Train in a Crowded Station, Believed to Be Quorn*, c.1880, State Library South Australia, B 57536; **p224** Bahnfrend, *Pichi Richi Railway Steam Locomotive W22 Awaits Departure*

from Quorn Railway Station, South Australia, 2017, commons.wikimedia.org/wiki/File:W22_%2B_Pichi_ Richi_Explorer_Quorn,_2017_(04).jpg, reproduced under CC BY-SA 4.0: creativecommons.org/licenses/by-sa/4.0/deed.en; **p225** Bob Miller, *Terowie Railway Station*, 1994, nla.cat-vn764603; **p226** Hugh Llewelyn, *Signal Box at the Victoria Railway Museum, North Williamstown*, 2016, www.flickr.com/photos/camperdown/28317607731, reproduced under CC BY-SA 2.0: creativecommons.org/licenses/by-sa/2.0/; **p228(t)** John Buckland, *Australian Railway and Locomotive Historical Society Tour at Picton Station, New South Wales*, 1946, BC, nla.cat-vn4540283; **p228(b)** Paul Cunningham, *The Workshops Rail Museum*, 2016, www.flickr.com/photos/paul_ cunningham/25911367670, reproduced under CC BY 2.0: creativecommons.org/licenses/by/2.0/; **p229(t)** Nomad Tales, *Steamfest, Maitland, New South Wales*, 2010, www.flickr.com/photos/pnglife/4542280499, reproduced under CC BY-SA 2.0: creativecommons. org/licenses/by-sa/2.0/; **p229(b)** Hugh Llewelyn, *The Exhibition Hall at Trainworks, New South Wales Railway Museum, Thirlmere*, 2016, www.flickr.com/ photos/camperdown/28092784136, reproduced under CC BY-SA 2.0: creativecommons.org/licenses/by-sa/2.0/; **p230** Brendon Kelson, *Disused Cowra Railway Station Building and Track, Cowra, New South Wales*, 1996, nla.cat-vn778706; **p231(t)** Peter Reid, *'Tilly', Tenterfield Railway*, courtesy Tim Fischer; **p231(b)** John Buckland, *Rail Motor CPH6 and Diesel Railcar 607 at Cootamundra, New South Wales*, 1983, BC, nla.cat-vn4540410; **p233** Mike Russell, *Dorrigo Train Museum*, 2012, www.flickr.com/photos/ nullawar/7034225657, reproduced under CC BY 2.0: creativecommons.org/licenses/by/2.0/; **p234** Graeme Churchard, *Trains at Kuranda*, 2010, www.flickr.com/ photos/graeme/5231015268, reproduced under CC BY 2.0: creativecommons.org/licenses/by/2.0/; **p235** Steven Penton, *Playing in the Signal Box, Don River Railway, Devonport, Tasmania*, 2016, www.flickr.com/ photos/136315829@N03/29463410700, reproduced under CC BY 2.0: creativecommons.org/licenses/ by/2.0/; **p236** Melinda Coombes (designer), *Heritage Rail Stamps*, 2010, © Australian Postal Corporation; **p237** Steven Penton, *Don River Railway at the Coles Beach End*, 2016, www.flickr.com/photos/136315829@ N03/29754454555, reproduced under CC BY 2.0: creativecommons.org/licenses/by/2.0/; .

Conclusion

p238-239 *Locomotive 3807 under Construction at Cardiff Workshops, First Locomotive Built There*, 1946, BC, nla.cat-vn4543766; **p240** *Milestones in Australian History*, 1959, nla.cat-vn6578033; **p241(t)** *Newspaper Stand in a Railway Station Headlining Attempt to Kill King, Victoria*, 1936, nla.cat-vn6455214; **p241(b)** C.C. Singleton, *Royal Train at Thornleigh, New South Wales*, 1954, BC, nla.cat-vn3258173; **p243** Raymond De Berquelle, *Engine Driver Instructing an Apprentice, Eveleigh Railway Workshops, Sydney*, 1968, nla.cat-vn1039750; **p244** *Steam Locomotive Inside the Clyde Engineering Workshop, New South Wales*, 1930s, nla. cat-vn6303626, courtesy Fairfax Syndication, www. fairfaxsyndication.com.

p246 A.D. Lockyer, *South Australian Railways Locomotives Rx207 and Rx224 with a Special Passenger Train Bound for Victor Harbor, South Australia*, 1984, BC, nla.cat-vn7504821; **p247** Dr Ian Unsworth, *Tim Fischer at Tenterfield Railway*, 2016, courtesy Tim Fischer.

INDEX

Page numbers in **bold** refer to illustrations.

The publishing imprint of the
National Library of Australia

Published by NLA Publishing
Canberra ACT 2600

ISBN: 9780642279293

Editor: Robert Nichols
Designer: Stan Lamond
Printed in China by Asia Pacific Offset

The National Library of Australia would like to thank the following people for their
help with this book: Jim Stokes, Jennifer Edmonds, Mary Pollard, Kerry Blackburn
and Sandy Clugston.

The tradition in New South Wales is not to name a locomotive with 'No.' in front of
it and we followed this convention for this state.

Find out more about NLA Publishing at nla.gov.au/national-library-publishing.

Front cover: see pages 76–77 for full caption
Back cover: see pages 90–91 for full caption
Previous pages: see pages 93 for full caption

A catalogue record for this
book is available from the
National Library of Australia